To Have and Have Not

To Have and Have Not

Southeast Asian Raw Materials and the Origins of the Pacific War

Jonathan Marshall

UNIVERSITY OF CALIFORNIA PRESS
BERKELEY LOS ANGELES LONDON

University of California Press
Berkeley and Los Angeles, California

University of California Press, Ltd.
London, England

© 1995 by
The Regents of the University of California

Library of Congress Cataloging-in-Publication Data

Marshall, Jonathan.
  To have and have not : southeast Asian raw materials and the origins of the Pacific War / Jonathan Marshall.
    p. cm.
  Includes bibliographical references and index.
  ISBN 0-520-08823-9
  1. World War, 1939–1945—Causes. 2. World War, 1939–1945—Pacific Area. 3. Raw materials—Asia, Southeastern. 4. Asian, Southeastern—Foreign economic relations. I. Title.
D741.M275 1995
940.53′113—dc20
                                                                                     94-13367

9 8 7 6 5 4 3 2 1

To my parents

Contents

Preface	ix
1. Raw Materials and National Power	1
2. The Rush to Stockpile	33
3. The Emerging Threat: 1940	54
4. War of Nerves: January–June 1941	95
5. Japan Moves South: July–December 1941	121
6. Roosevelt Plans for War	157
7. Defining the National Interest	173
Notes	189
Bibliography	257
Index	273

Preface

Since the 1991 Desert Storm operation against Iraq, few Americans have questioned the premise that countries, including their own, sometimes fight wars for control of "strategic" natural resources. Whatever the claims of White House spokesmen about preserving liberty in Kuwait, Washington and its allies intervened to prevent Iraqi dictator Saddam Hussein from dominating the world's richest oil-producing region, the Persian Gulf.

More than a decade earlier, a series of oil embargoes, the famous prediction in *The Limits to Growth* of imminent resource depletion, and warnings by conservatives over Soviet plots to grab the resources of southern Africa gave rise to numerous treatises on the strategic importance of vital raw materials. "Whoever controls world resources controls the world in a way that mere occupation of territory cannot match," one popular book declared in 1980. " . . . If there is another world war, the conflict will most likely be over what the industrial states have come to regard as the elements of survival. Oil, of course, but also iron, copper, uranium, cobalt, wheat, and water."[1]

A vast body of literature now exists to explain international conflict in terms of competition over material resources, including oil and strategic minerals.[2] Yet most historians have shied away from considering material influences on recent U.S. foreign policy, perhaps because of the apparent Marxist cast to that approach.[3]

This book aims to show that half a century before Desert Storm, the United States fought another, much costlier war for strategic resources. The United States' war with Japan from 1941 to 1945 was primarily a battle for control of Southeast Asia's immense mineral and vegetable wealth. The region, comprising Burma, British Malaya, French Indochina, the Netherlands East Indies, the Philippines, and Thailand, held rich supplies of rubber, tin, tungsten, and other tropical commodities essential to the economies of the advanced industrial nations. Japan sought to end Western dominance of Asia and build a self-sufficient economy by integrating these lands into its own bloc, isolating the United States and Great Britain from their primary sources of these products. Defending a status quo that favored the Western liberal powers, the United States drew the line for Japanese expansion at Southeast Asia.

U.S. economic stakes in the region had been growing for years. By 1939, the United States was importing more goods from the Far East than from any other part of the world. The region's share of total U.S. imports soared to 30 percent from only 13 percent in 1910.[4] By far the most important source of those imports was Southeast Asia. Three colonies alone—British Malaya, the Netherlands East Indies, and the Philippines—shipped more than half a billion dollars' worth of goods to the United States in 1940, accounting for roughly a fifth of all U.S. purchases abroad.[5]

Southeast Asia was an inexhaustible source of mineral and vegetable products for U.S. industry. The United States bought most of its rubber and tin from British Malaya.[6] As for the Netherlands East Indies, one contemporary observer declared that it "constitutes the richest colonial plum in the world. It produces rubber, tin, petroleum, sugar, coffee, tin, tobacco, copra, palm oil, and a host of other products, agricultural and mineral."[7] By 1939, the Dutch colony supplied more than half of the United States' needs for no fewer than fifteen distinct commodities, including nutmeg, pepper, and palm oil, besides exporting large quantities of rubber, tin, oil, and bauxite.[8]

But simple trade figures do not begin to tell the whole story of U.S. economic dependence upon Southeast Asia. With the world engulfed in war, vital industrial materials took on a strategic importance far outweighing their dollar value. Cut off from their Southeast Asian supply lines, whole industries would be unable to begin even the first stage of production and would face agonizing readjustments or total ruin. Production lines of tanks, trucks, and ships might grind to a halt. These were the real stakes, as popular economic analyst Eliot Janeway asserted at the time: "It is on the economic front that Japan's drive threatens us most dangerously: the American economy, and with it American defense, cannot be operated without rubber and tin, which at present cannot be obtained in adequate quantity except from the British and Dutch colonies in southeastern Asia. And Japan today commands the trade route connecting the west coast of the United States with the Malaysian Straits. . . . Here, ready to hand for Japan, is a safer and more powerful weapon against the United States than the folly of naval attack."[9]

And as the State Department's chief Far East expert, Stanley Hornbeck, concurred in 1940, "the United States finds itself so vitally and overwhelmingly dependent on southeastern Asia that our entire foreign policy must be adjusted to that fact. . . . It is not an exaggeration to say that the United States would be compelled, for its existence as a major industrial state, to wage war against any power or powers that might threaten to sever our trade lines with this part of the world."[10]

This explanation of the origins of U.S. involvement in the Pacific War is "radical" in its departure from the conventional historical wisdom, but it is not dogmatically unicausal. Although stressing material factors, my account of U.S. motives and interests embraces the importance of subjective factors. Perceptions of material reality are always filtered through ideological lenses. Thus, Washington's fear of losing raw materials was based on assumptions about the unwillingness of autarkic powers to sell goods freely and about the limits of the U.S. economy's ability to absorb supply shocks. Washington's sense of dependence was also conditioned by its perception that the nation's security depended on maintaining an industrial base to support a world-class navy capable of projecting power on all oceans. Its sense of threat was magnified by a history of antagonism with Japan and a belief that new aggressor nations were bent on forcefully revising the international division of resources at the expense of established powers.

Unlike some theorists, moreover, I make no claims for the universal application of a materialist model to international relations. Any single explanation is likely over the long term to run up against the reality of shifting interests, ideals, and passions that sway publics and decisionmakers. But whatever the motives behind U.S. foreign policy at other times and places, the evidence shows that in 1940 and 1941 a series of contingent circumstances elevated Southeast Asia to a position of fundamental importance to Washington. These circumstances included the United States' preoccupation with recovering from the Great Depression, its sense of economic, political, and physical insecurity in a world of rising totalitarian powers, the reliance of its mass-production economy on huge imports of raw materials, and the extraordinary geographic concentration of many of those materials in Southeast Asia.

Washington's response to these circumstances was fundamentally shaped by a worldwide resurgence of mercantilism in the 1930s. With the onset of the Depression, states increasingly treated international trade less as a mutually enriching activity than as a win-or-lose competition for limited spoils. Mercantilists stressed that from international economic advantage derives national power and the ability, in turn, to dictate the rules of the international system. Neomercantilist logic dictated that states could only preserve their independence by minimizing their dependence on unstable or hostile sources of supply, including trading blocs and cartels.[11]

Even Americans who remained faithful to liberal economic principles granted the importance of avoiding dependence on unfriendly foreign powers, but a vigorous debate emerged over the means. Isolationists maintained that the country could secure its economy solely by stockpiling precious raw materials and developing new sources of supply in the Western Hemisphere. In contrast, interventionists (whom the Roosevelt administration heeded) insisted on the need to augment such measures with defense of distant raw material "lifelines." Just as Tokyo took up arms to end Japan's dependence on the United States as a supplier of oil and other raw materials, so Washington was ready to defend its economic and political independence from a Japanese "new order" encompassing Southeast Asia.

Historians who see "ideals" motivating the United States and "interests" driving other nations have freely accepted Japan's economic interests in the region as an explanation for its policy of southward expansion. But many otherwise fine and perceptive accounts of U.S. policy ignore a wealth of evidence that policymakers in Washington were no less determined to maintain control over the region's resources for economic and strategic ends, even at the risk of war.[12]

Interpretations of what motivated President Roosevelt and his advisers include virtually every explanation but this one. Paul Schroeder, summarizing the consensus of scholars in the 1950s, declared: "In judging American policy toward Japan in 1941, it might be well to separate what is still controversial from what is not. There is no longer any real doubt that the war came about over China."[13] Many historians still agree. Wayne Cole, for example, has asserted that "the United States and Japan went to war in 1941 because they were unable or unwilling to compromise their conflicting interests in China."[14] Frederick Marks III blames Washington's confrontation with Tokyo in part on the sentimental attachment Roosevelt and other key policymakers had for China.[15]

Other historians trace the causes of war to the firmly held, if perhaps unrealistic, principles of Secretary of State Cordell Hull and his associates. Norman Graebner sees Washington defending the principles of international law and the "post-Versailles treaty structure" rather than concern for China.[16] David Reynolds argues that "the United States had no vital interests in the Far East" and that its concerns "sprang from confused moralizing rather than a hard-headed assessment of U.S. interests."[17] In a similar vein, Akira Iriye, Waldo Heinrichs, and Michael Barnhart believe the administration was driven by the general canons of Wilsonian liberalism—the principles of peaceful change, the Open Door, national sovereignty, and territorial integrity.[18]

A variant on the Wilsonian theme, emphasizing its economic content, was elaborated years ago by William Appleman Williams and his followers. They saw a constant hunger for markets, reflected in the Open Door policy enunciated by Secretary of State John Hay in 1898, as the dominating force in U.S. foreign policy in the twentieth century. Through its invasion of China, Japan violated the Open Door principle by threatening to cut the United States off from markets of immense potential.[19]

A more recent offshoot of this "Open Door" theory of U.S. policy grants the existence of an expansionist economic ideology—but not with respect to China. For Jonathan Utley, "The important factor, the factor that would transform dislike for Japan into action against Japan, was the Japanese assault on the liberal commercial world order." Yet Utley stresses that the United States "had never been prepared to pay a price to preserve China's integrity or the Open Door there." China was merely a "pawn whose inexhaustible manpower would be sacrificed to keep Japan from moving into the important region of Southeast Asia." Utley also rejects the proposition that Southeast Asian raw materials were the issue. He is thus left arguing that the administration defended an abstract principle without any specific application.[20]

Deborah Miner also views Southeast Asia as the central theater of U.S.-Japan confrontation but claims that Washington simply never bothered to analyze the nature of U.S. interests in the region. Instead, she asserts, it accepted at face value dubious British declarations of the region's importance to the European war effort. Like other historians of the period, she ignores the extensive studies produced at the time by military and civilian experts of U.S. and British dependence on "strategic materials" from Southeast Asia.[21]

One final group of diplomatic historians blames public opinion for pushing the Roosevelt administration, whose real concern was Europe, into war. Robert Dallek, a leading chronicler of Roosevelt's foreign policy, believes the president had to get tough on Japan in order to win a national consensus for mobilization against Nazi Germany.[22] Similarly, Israeli scholar Abraham Ben-Zvi describes a relatively weak and indecisive Roosevelt who was "unwilling to alienate the pro-internationalist forces whose support was essential in the struggle to contain Hitler in Europe." FDR thus ceded policy toward Japan to hard-line hawks who believed that Japan, in conjunction with Nazi Germany, threatened to "disrupt the balance of power."[23]

Despite this plethora of theories, most historians have paid surprisingly little attention to how top policymakers defined the "national interest." Instead, with few exceptions, their many excellent accounts chronicle the various diplomatic blunders, bureaucratic maneuvers, and tactical detours along the road to war.[24] In some cases, this obliviousness to larger interests has led historians to view the war as a product of avoidable factors such as "mutual misunderstanding, language difficulties and mistranslations" rather than a profound conflict over national objectives.[25]

My intent is not to belittle the importance of ideals, misunderstandings, cultural barriers, and human frailty in explaining U.S. conduct during this period. Rather, I wish to highlight previously ignored motives that finally prompted the Roosevelt administration in late 1941 to set aside its paramount goal: avoiding a two-front war of unimaginable costs and risks. The specter of such a calamity had long mandated a policy of caution even in the face of flouted principles and serious provocations. Japan had been slamming the Open Door in the United States' face for years. From China to Ethiopia to Czechoslovakia, lawless nations trampled on international law and outraged decent peoples without prompting the United States to take up arms. It took a larger threat to U.S. security and interests to bring the Roosevelt administration to the verge of war with Japan—even before Pearl Harbor.

In making this case, I do not try to supplant more detailed day-by-day accounts of the prewar negotiations. Nor do I make any original or extended effort to evaluate Japanese policy, for which a number of fine histories also exist. My focus is on decisionmaking in Washington: how policymakers defined the national interest, how they viewed Japan's threat to it, and how they weighed the prospects and perils of various means of meeting that challenge.

To this end, I have relied primarily on a wealth of published documents and unpublished material in the manuscript collections of such officials as President Roosevelt, Secretary of State Cordell Hull, Treasury Secretary Henry Morgenthau, Secretary of War Henry Stimson, and various officials of lower rank.[26] Records of the State Department, Navy, War Production Board, Council on Foreign Relations, British Foreign Office, and British War Cabinet also proved useful. Most of these sources are not novel; my reading of them is. In addition, I have reviewed a large but largely forgotten literature from the time, produced by academics, business writers, journalists, and other pundits, to gauge the extent of popular concerns over U.S. dependence on foreign supplies of strategic materials. By exploiting the untapped potential of all these sources, I hope to shed new light on the origins of this terrible war and make future historians argue the question of interests more deeply and thoughtfully.

The usual author's disclaimer—that all mistakes and misjudgments are mine alone—certainly applies to this work. But if those faults have been kept at a minimum, thanks must go to a number of careful readers. Barton Bernstein provided invaluable support, penetrating criticism, and the high example of his own scholarship. Anthony Barnett, Diane Clemens, Robert Keohane, Leonard Liggio, Ronnie Lipschutz, and Laurence Shoup also read the manuscript in earlier forms and offered useful advice. I am grateful to the Center for International Studies at Stanford University for a research grant and to archivists in Cambridge, Hyde Park, London, Stanford, and Washington for generous assistance. My wife Lorrie helped in ways too numerous to list, including distracting our playful daughters from the computer while I completed this manuscript.

1

Raw Materials and National Power

> Great as are the material resources with which our country is endowed, they are not sufficient to enable us as a nation to meet the needs of our people on the level of well-being to which we aspire. Today we supplement our own resources by imports from abroad. Some of which, like rubber, tin, manganese, though small in relative volume, are essential to the functioning of our greatest national industries. Some of the things we now purchase in other countries we can, perhaps, produce domestically, but at a much higher cost in terms of economic effort than is required for the production of exports with which we now buy these foreign products. For others, we can develop substitutes, of inferior quality and, again, at a relatively higher cost. Still others we cannot produce at all, and, if we did not import them, we would have to do without them altogether. In each case, the net result would be a decline of our national efficiency and, consequently, an inexorable lowering in the level of satisfaction of our people's wants.
>
> *Secretary of State Cordell Hull,*
> *May 28, 1939*

The United States' rapid transition from an agrarian society to an industrial powerhouse in the early twentieth century fundamentally transformed its international economic position. Once a significant exporter only of crude materials and foodstuffs such as cotton, tobacco, wheat, and meat, the United States was by 1939 predominantly a seller of finished goods such as machinery and vehicles. And where the country once primarily imported finished products from Europe, it had since become a heavy buyer of raw materials from the underdeveloped world to feed its hungry assembly lines. Thus, in the period 1901-1937, the United States' imports from Asia and Oceania jumped more than sixfold, to a level 25 percent higher than U.S. imports from Europe.[1]

Although the United States, with its strong mercantile traditions, had always engaged in world trade, the shift to a mass-production economy drew the country ever more inextricably into a web of international dependence. As early as 1926, the eminent economist Jacob Viner could write that the United States was "in some respects in a particularly vulnerable position." Although richly endowed with mineral resources, "we are nevertheless because of our very prosperity so tremendous a consumer, and we have devoted so much of our productive effort to manufacturing, that there are comparatively few raw materials of which we produce a supply adequate for our needs."[2] By 1940, the United States was consuming 60 percent of the world's rubber, 45 percent of its chromium, 40 percent of its tin, and 36 percent of its manganese, mostly or entirely purchased from foreign suppliers.[3] As a staff report for President's Commission on Foreign Economic Policy observed in 1954: "This transition of the United States from a position of relative self-sufficiency to one of increasing dependence upon foreign sources of supply constitutes one of the striking economic changes of our time. The outbreak of World War II marked the major turning point of this change. Both from the viewpoint of our long-term economic growth and the viewpoint of our national defense, the shift of the United States from the position of a net exporter of metals and minerals to that of a net importer is of overwhelming significance in shaping our foreign economic policies."[4]

This trend profoundly influenced a spirited, high-stakes debate during the 1930s over the desirability and feasibility of national economic self-sufficiency. The political victory of those who argued the need for open doors abroad "resulted in the sweeping political and economic reorientation of American foreign policy," in the words of editor Hamilton Fish Armstrong, whose journal, *Foreign Affairs*, was one of the great forums for this debate.[5]

The examples of autarkic, state-planned economies in Germany and the Soviet Union, as well as the fear of foreign entanglements that could suck the country into war, prompted numerous Americans in that troubled decade to call for economic "nationalism" and self-sufficiency. Critics on the left and the right, from historian Charles Beard to corporatist economist Lawrence Dennis, argued that high tariffs and economic planning would ensure healthy domestic demand and insulate the United States from political and economic turbulence in the rest of the world. Such notions enjoyed wide appeal; in a 1939 *Fortune* magazine survey, nearly two-thirds of the respondents believed that the United States should "try to develop its own industries to the point where it does not have to buy any products from foreign countries."[6]

Against this popular current were arrayed many corporate leaders, influential commentators such as Walter Lippmann, and the State Department, with its firm commitment to expanding international trade. Of all the arguments this coalition marshaled against the advocates of self-sufficiency, one was particularly cogent: Without export sales and unrestricted access to markets abroad, the United States could not afford the scarce and exotic materials upon which both modern industrial civilization and national power depend. In making this argument, they could draw support from recent historical experience and a host of official studies.

A Matter of Dependence

Even before World War I, when the United States still exported more raw materials than it imported, the quest for new sources of some materials helped guide U.S. foreign relations.[7] But the demands placed upon industry during World War I, as well as the temporary wartime disruption of world trade, forced government leaders and private experts to recognize the strategic value of certain natural resources. War Department planners knew that one of Germany's first moves upon entering France had been to seize iron mines to feed industries back in Germany.[8] The United States likewise suffered war-induced shortages of certain materials. When a ship laden with manganese from Brazil disappeared, the entire steel industry of the East Coast was nearly paralyzed.[9] President Wilson's secretary of commerce, William Redfield, later declared that if a German ship "had interrupted the movement of manganese and shellac from India or graphite from Ceylon and Madagascar to the western nations or the stream of tin and rubber flowing from the Malay Peninsula and Sumatra, the result would have been disastrous."[10] Germany was not the only threat; when Great Britain tried to squeeze its foe in 1914 by embargoing foreign sales of rubber, manganese, chrome, tungsten, and other materials, Secretary of State William Jennings Bryan complained that the policy "would cripple American manufacturers." The British relented only after pressuring the United States into limiting exports to Germany.[11]

Bernard Baruch's War Production Board reported that "the country was constantly threatened with a shortage in available supply of nitrogen, manganese, chrome, tungsten, dyestuffs, coal-tar derivatives, and several other essential materials." In 1919, Baruch submitted to President Wilson a report urging that the government secure adequate supplies of raw materials for future emergencies.[12] The next year, Congress amended the National Defense Act to make the assistant secretaries of the Army and the Navy responsible for planning industrial mobilization and procuring raw materials. The two departments began coordinating their plans in 1922 when they formed the joint Army and Navy Munitions Board. The board prepared lists of which vital raw materials the United States lacked and worked with other government agencies to prepare for emergencies.[13]

But, as Redfield pointed out in the mid-1920s, the United States' dependency was "not confined to times of war. It exists to-day as it did [in World War I]. There are materials which the United States must draw from the Far East for which there are no known substitutes. They are necessary to the continued working of great industries."[14] Of all the materials the United States imported from the Far East, he pointed out, none was more important than rubber. Almost the entire world's supply came from the rubber trees of Southeast Asia. During the 1920s—a time of peace—this dependence caused U.S. leaders great concern.

Herbert Hoover, secretary of commerce under Presidents Harding and Coolidge, brought the issue to the American people while crusading against a British attempt to boost Malayan rubber prices. British producers had been hit by a devastating drop in the price of rubber after World War I—from a high of more than a dollar a pound during the war to a low in 1921 of only 11 1/2 cents a pound. Even at these prices, production vastly outstripped demand. British rubber growers, who produced about 70 percent of the world's supply, pushed legislation through Parliament to restrict output and force prices back up. Under the guidance of Sir James Stevenson, a producers' committee began establishing export quotas in 1922, a year in which output of rubber exceeded consumption by 100,000 tons. To relieve this glut, the Stevenson Committee in 1924 restricted output by 55 percent. Prices hit $1.23 a pound in July 1925. Annually, this government-enforced cartel was costing the United States more than half a billion dollars.

Secretary Hoover counterattacked with little delay. He strongly encouraged U.S. rubber companies to expand their investments overseas to ensure control of rubber supplies. Firestone began a large new plantation in Liberia; other companies experimented with rubber trees in Central and South America. Hoover helped the companies coordinate their buying by setting up import pools. He encouraged stockpiling and a vast program of rubber reclamation, which by 1928 met over half of the

United States' demand. Hoover's campaign soon won allies. In 1925, the State Department began protesting officially to the British. Following hearings in 1926, the House Committee on Interstate and Foreign Commerce recommended that the United States refuse loans to British rubber interests, develop synthetics, establish rubber supplies in friendlier territory and begin a full-scale conservation campaign.[15]

In his speeches and writings, Hoover stressed the enormous cost the United States was paying to import rubber at artificially high prices. He warned the public of the strategic implications of U.S. dependence on geographically concentrated supplies of rubber, given its tremendous importance to industry. And he decried the likelihood that foreign cartels would force the U.S. government to "negotiate the terms, and thus fix the prices on behalf of the consumer." Such government intervention could prove costly to liberties as well as to the Treasury, since "our Government, which we wish to keep out of business, is forced into the worst kind of it—dealing with commodities on behalf of whole nations of consumers."[16] A Department of Commerce publication in 1926 declared that foreign controls on raw materials were a matter of "great moment to the United States" and represented a "growing menace" to "international good will."[17]

Ultimately the rubber restriction scheme failed, as cartels are prone to do. Rising use of reclaimed rubber in the United States and growing production from areas outside of British control squeezed the British growers' markets. Their share of world rubber production fell more than 8 percent between 1922 and 1928.[18] However, the shocking display of U.S. dependence on foreign rubber supplies taught the public important lessons.[19] "It was the Stevenson Restriction Act that forcibly brought to the attention of the American public our dependence on foreign sources for our supplies of so important a commodity of crude rubber," one expert wrote in the prestigious journal *Foreign Affairs* in 1924. He concluded that in the future, "We have to consider, for example, our national defense, especially as concerns the protection of our lines of transport in the remote contingency of war; again, we must consider the trend of social and political conditions in the [Far] East; thirdly, there is the question of the desirability of having our risks more widely scattered and of not being dependent upon one geographical region."[20]

Concern in the Roosevelt Administration

In 1933 the War Department published its Revised Industrial Mobilization Plan, which addressed the problem of raw material scarcity. The War Department classified twenty-six different primary products as "strategic"—meaning they were "essential to national defense, for the supply of which in war dependence must be placed in whole, or in substantial part, on sources outside the continental limits of the U.S.; and for which strict conservation and distribution control measures will be necessary."[21] Adding its voice to the chorus in 1933, the American Society of Metallurgical Engineers recommended stockpiling manganese ore, chromium ore, mercury, mica, tin, nickel, tungsten ore, cobalt, radium, rubber, and coconut shells.[22]

Further alarm was sounded by the House Foreign Affairs Committee. It launched an ambitious investigation of the tin market in 1935, as official concern mounted over the fact that foreign sources accounted for 99 percent of U.S. consumption. The committee's exhaustive report examined every workable deposit of tin, domestic and foreign. Its conclusions regarding domestic production possibilities were pessimistic, although the report advocated further development of U.S. mines. Careful conservation and recycling programs seemed to be the only practical responses to U.S. dependence.[23] Following congressional action resulting from the investigation, Secretary of State Hull issued a decree in April 1936 placing a temporary embargo on exports of scrap tin and thereafter subjecting such exports to licensing arrangements.[24]

Writing for *Foreign Affairs* in 1938, government minerals consultant Charles K. Leith revealed the surprising extent to which the age of mass production and heavy industry had made the United States reliant on overseas resources:

If all our imports were cut off, our industry would indeed return to the 'horse and buggy' days. We could build neither an automobile or a battleship. Our deficiencies are mainly in the so-called ferro-alloy group of minerals used in the steel industry, including chromite, manganese, nickel, tin and tungsten. There is also a lack of antimony, mercury, certain varieties of mica and graphite, as well as of other minerals. No one has yet found an adequate steel-making process which can dispense with manganese even though only fifteen pounds of this mineral are required in each ton of finished steel. The ramified interrelations of the use of all of these minerals are so complex in modern industry that the lack of a single one often has far reaching consequences. Most attempts to remedy our mineral deficiencies by applying new technologies to our sub-marinal deposits have thus far been unsuccessful. Intensification of these experiments would most likely lead only to the same difficulties which the autarkic nations are experiencing.[25]

In an age of aggressive dictators, moreover, it was hard to separate the needs of the economy from the needs of national defense. In 1940, as chief minerals consultant for the Advisory Commission to the Council of National Defense, Leith offered a sweeping view of the linkages between access to raw materials and national power: "With control of the sea, the United States is in a position to dominate the [world] situation. With control of the sea, it is able to go to the full limit of industrial development for modern war. But to hold control of the sea its minerals must be used, and in huge amounts.... Our mineral domain is literally world-wide.... In short, it is our field that is being invaded."[26] In another essay published in 1941, Leith pushed the same grand theme. "The huge scale of the movement of strategic minerals required by modern industry gives an unprecedented significance to the part played by control of the sea in waging modern war," he declared. "If the English-speaking peoples retain their control of the sea, they will retain control of the raw materials necessary to win the war." But loss of sea control, indeed loss of only a "single [alloy] constituent," could have "far-reaching and disastrous effects on industrial operations."[27]

Such views became official dogma within the Navy, which took every opportunity to publicize its responsibility for defending U.S. sea lanes. In a famous policy memorandum to Roosevelt, Adm. Harold Stark, the chief of naval operations, declared that "we should recognize as the foundation of adequate armed strength the possession of a profitable foreign trade, both in raw materials and finished goods. Without such a trade, our economy can scarcely support heavy armaments."[28]

This perspective was not confined to the Navy, however. In 1939, Col. H. K. Rutherford, director of the War Department's Planning Branch, told the House Committee on Military Affairs that his branch "for many years has considered the study of the raw materials needed by industry as a most important part of its activity." Rutherford noted that a total of seventeen scarce materials were of "major importance to our national welfare" and vital to the country's defense effort. "Manganese, tin, chromium, and tungsten occupy a position of highest priority because of their importance in industry and the problems involved in assuring an adequate supply in an emergency," he said. Rutherford regretted that none of these strategic materials could be developed domestically and concluded that only an intensive stockpiling program could assure the United States of adequate material supplies during a crisis.[29]

A written statement submitted to the committee by John Finch, director of the Bureau of Mines, and his assistant, James Furness, offered a similar assessment. Arguing that "the position of the United States with respect to [raw materials] is now far more acute than at any other time in its history," the two experts pleaded for an energetic national effort to conserve vital raw materials. Finch and Furness declared that preventing a supply interruption was "of primary importance in any program of industrial preparedness" and cautioned that failure to act "would greatly impair the effectiveness of the Army and Navy and deprive industry of essential supplies in time of war."[30]

The most significant official study of U.S. dependence on foreign raw material supplies in this period was conducted by the Army and Navy Munitions Board.[31] Its 1940 report classified important materials as either strategic or critical. The strategic materials, generally unavailable from domestic sources, were those "so closely knit into our modern industrial structure that the whole trend of modern life would be disorganized without them."[32] Shortages of critical materials would cause serious but not insurmountable difficulties during wartime. The fourteen strategic products listed by the board were antimony, chromium, coconut shell char, manganese, manila fiber, mercury, mica, nickel, quartz crystal, quinine, rubber, silk, tin, and tungsten. The Far East, especially Southeast Asia and India (whose exports were often shipped through Southeast Asian waters), supplied the most important of these materials.

Chromium, according to the board study, "is one of the more important industrial elements for which this country is dependent almost entirely on foreign sources of supply." Commercial-grade chromium comes from the ore chromite. The metal was (and still is) used in alloy steels such as stainless steel, which form the backbone of much technologically advanced industry. Chromium is also useful in chemical applications and electroplating. "For many uses of chromite there are no satisfactory substitutes," the board reported. Two of the United States' chief sources of chromite were located in the Far East, in the Philippine Islands and the French possession of New Caledonia.[33] Discoveries of huge chromite reserves in the Philippines in the 1930s put the islands only slightly behind South Africa as a source of U.S. chromite imports by 1940.[34]

The board considered manganese "indispensable in the present art of steel making," both as a deoxidizer and as an alloy metal in special-purpose steels. "There are no satisfactory substitutes for manganese in steel manufacture," it declared.[35] Domestic reserves of metallurgical-grade manganese ore were almost nonexistent, however. Although supplies in the Western Hemisphere could meet some of its requirements, the United States depended largely on India, the Soviet Union, and the

Gold Coast for its imports. India and Southeast Asia accounted for about one-quarter of all U.S. manganese imports in 1940.[36] Given the insecurity of trade with the USSR, the United States had a strong interest in keeping open lines of supply from Southeast Asia.

Mica was termed strategic because of its value as an insulator in transformers and capacitors, two vital products without which the communications industry could not survive. The United States had only scarce natural supplies. Approximately three-quarters of the world's block mica was mined in India.[37] Manila fiber, made from the leaf stems of the abaca plant, also posed significant problems to War Department planners. "There is no known satisfactory substitute for abaca fiber in making high grade rope that is absolutely essential for marine cordage, oil well cables, and construction work," the board warned. Manila rope had the greatest tensile strength, durability, resiliency, and elasticity of any rope then in use and did not shrink or expand with varying degrees of wetness. The strategic problem lay in the fact that "the entire world supply of high grade abaca is produced in a limited number of provinces in the Philippine Islands."[38]

Quinine joined the list of strategic materials as the only sure cure for malaria. Malaria was then a serious health hazard in the southeastern United States, not to mention the jungles of Asia and Africa. The death rate from malaria during the 1930s averaged 22.2 per 100,000 people in Arkansas, 21.3 in Florida, and 26.0 in South Carolina. "If imports of quinine should be cut off and if no satisfactory substitutes were at hand," warned one authority, "large portions of our population would almost immediately be in serious danger."[39] Virtually all U.S. imports of quinine originated in the Netherlands East Indies.[40]

Defense and economic planners also had to contend with the possible cutoff of tungsten supplies. Although the United States itself mined significant amounts, the nation imported 50 percent more than it produced. Tungsten's superb qualities—including its unsurpassed tensile strength—magnified the seriousness of any potential scarcity.[41] Tungsten was tremendously important in alloy steels, lamp filaments, and industrial chemicals. Outside of that produced in the United States, virtually all of the world's tungsten came from the Far East—chiefly China, Burma, and Malaya.[42]

Of all the metals, none posed more difficulties for government planners than tin. "Tin presents one of our serious strategic mineral problems because the metal is indispensable for so many uses and there is virtually no domestic production even at exorbitant prices," explained the Munitions Board.[43] Another analysis, published by the Institute of Pacific Relations, described some of these "many uses":

> The metal is used in tin plating, solder, babbit, bronze, collapsible tubes, tin foil, piping, tubing, type metal, galvanizing, in chemicals and enamels, electrical equipment, and in many other products. A glance at this list is enough to suggest the calamity that would befall the country if the supply of tin were to be cut off. Our industrial civilization requires that large proportions of fruits and vegetables be canned and tin cans have a monopoly of most of the business. . . . Without tin for solder engineers would have a difficult time in keeping machines functioning. . . . So many other uses might be cited that it is easy to understand why tin has been placed on the list of strategic materials.[44]

The Munitions Board concluded that substitutes for tin were generally not available and that "only a minor part of our requirements of tin during an emergency period could be met by recovering tin from old scrap metal which have a tin content." The Netherlands East Indies and Malaya were by far the largest producers of tin; the Far East as a whole provided the United States with about 90 percent of its imports.[45] Bolivia, the only other major supplier, produced second-rate ore that was mixed with waste material and expensive to process. Its mines were remote, located high in the mountains and far from good transportation. Operated under ghastly working conditions, they were also beset by frequent labor shortages and strikes.[46]

The strategic and economic importance of rubber surpassed that of all other essential raw materials. "There appears to be no question that rubber is almost as essential to national defense as powder [or] explosives . . . and that national defense would be jeopardized should the supply from foreign sources be cut off," the board concluded.⁴⁷ The production of 100 tanks required fully one million pounds of rubber (as well as 66,000 pounds of chromium, 53,000 pounds of manganese, and 3,500 pounds of tin).⁴⁸ Rubber was hardly less important to the civilian economy. "Our domestic rubber goods manufacturing industry is the largest in the world," the Munitions Board noted. "In 1937 it employed 120,000 persons and had a total output value of $883,000,000. On a value basis rubber is about the most important single commodity imported into the U.S."⁴⁹ An independent study of vital raw materials from the Far East drew the obvious conclusion that rubber "enters so widely into American military and business life that a sudden shortage would dislocate the American defense economy."⁵⁰

What made that conclusion all the more troubling was the extraordinary geographic concentration of rubber production. Ninety-eight percent of U.S. rubber imports came from Southeast Asia—largely from British Malaya and the Netherlands East Indies. Alternative sources of natural rubber were not readily available. Complications such as South American leaf disease made it "unlikely that the South American production of plantation rubber will supply a significant part of the demand for rubber within the next decade," the Munitions Board claimed. It estimated that reclaimed rubber could provide at most a quarter of the United States' normal peacetime rubber requirements and that a synthetic rubber industry might need at least four years before it could handle even the barest of U.S. industrial needs. Most observers believed, therefore, that without a crash program of stockpiling the United States would remain totally dependent upon Southeast Asia for rubber.⁵¹

Few official studies in this period drew sharp distinctions between the importance of imports to peacetime industry and their importance to the nation's defense effort.⁵² Materials deemed strategic were vital to both. For an economy struggling to fight its way out of the Great Depression, moreover, the distinction seemed artificial. Foreign threats to the nation's standard of living were as menacing as threats to its physical security. And if war had to be fought, the United States could not afford to lose access to those supplies for long.

The obvious conclusion, at least to military leaders, was to rearm in the hope of deterring hostile powers from severing U.S. lifelines to those materials. As tensions rose with Japan in the spring of 1940, Admiral Stark testified before the Senate Naval Affairs Committee to advocate expanding the U.S. fleet. Without more fighting vessels at sea, he said, the fleet would be unable to "safeguard . . . the supply of vital strategic materials, such as manganese, rubber, tin." In case of war, he warned, the resulting "serious curtailment of our inflow of manganese, essential to our steel industry, or of the inflow of crude rubber and of tin, over 90 percent of which comes from Asiatic waters, would seriously affect our entire economy. Under certain conditions we could protect these vital trade routes. Under other conditions we could not protect them."[53]

Fear of Japan

Stark was not speaking of abstract threats. His boss, Secretary of the Navy Frank Knox, bluntly spelled out the stakes during his confirmation hearing in early 1940: "We should not allow Japan to take the Dutch East Indies, a vital source of oil and rubber and tin. . . . We must face frankly the fact that to deny the Dutch Indies to Japan may mean war."[54]

Japanese leaders and official ideologists made no secret of their goal to create a Greater East Asia Co-Prosperity Sphere, an economically self-sufficient bloc led politically and militarily by Japan to the exclusion of other powers.[55] This bloc ideally would include Southeast Asia. To fuel its war machine and keep its industries productive, Japan wanted unhindered access to the oil and other raw materials of the area. Southeast Asia could also provide markets and room for Japan's expanding population.

In order to prepare for a major advance into Southeast Asia, as well as to extend its encirclement of China, Japan first took steps in 1940 to occupy Indochina. A contemporary account of Japanese foreign policy pointed out that "Indo-China's strategic position, enhanced by the excellent harbor at Camranh Bay, might provide a base of operations for the conquest of the foodstuffs and strategic raw materials of the Netherlands Indies, the Philippine Islands, Malaya, Thailand (Siam) and Burma. Even India, Britain's most prized possession, could not be considered invulnerable if the Japanese were in control of Indo-China, 'crossroads of empire' in Southeast Asia." The interests at stake for the United States in this struggle were great, according to Andrew Roth. "Thus, military possession of Indo-China would place Japan within striking distance of all the 'riches of the Indies'—rubber, rice, tin, oil, coal, iron, zinc, tungsten, quinine, and phosphates. Possession of these resources would not only go far toward the achievement of Japan's long cherished objective of economic self-sufficiency, but would also greatly improve Japan's bargaining position vis-a-vis the United States and other powers even partially dependent on these sources of supply."[56]

If Japan seized control of Southeast Asia and all its resources, would it cut off trade with the United States and the other Western powers? Its deep hostility to the Western powers and aggressive, militaristic foreign policy gave no reason for optimism. When British producer cartels jeopardized the interests of the United States, U.S. leaders knew they could always negotiate with London. But no one could be sure how ideological zealots in Japan would respond to entreaties. Would they charge outrageous prices or extract huge concessions as a condition of doing business if they took over the region? Raymond Geist, chief of the State Department's Division of Commercial Affairs, explained his concerns to the National Industrial Conference Board in 1941: "Arbitrary power by the state, whose dictate would be law, could facilitate acquisition of vast quantities of merchandise far below intrinsic value, inducing chronic scarcity in other areas where there was no opportunity to compete. For instance, rubber from the Far East may become available to the totalitarian states at a fraction of present market price in exchange for goods at abnormally high barter costs, while none might be available to countries of this hemisphere."[57]

In a world of totalitarian powers bent on challenging Anglo-American hegemony in Europe and Asia, the risk of losing access to major raw material supplies altogether seemed only too real. One confidential State Department analysis prepared in late 1941, titled "Japan versus the United States," concluded that the nation could not afford to have its military and industrial capacity left "at the mercy of Japan" lest the world balance of power shift irrevocably:

> From the Far East we derive a major portion of our supplies of rubber and tin, most of our supplies of tungsten and tung oil, all of our supplies of quinine. . . . Under conditions of law and order and peace in the Western Pacific and Eastern Asia we can expect that our need for these commodities will be met. But with any country pursuing in those regions courses similar to those which Nazi Germany is pursuing in Europe, and with such country allied with Germany and Italy, we can have no assurance whatever that we shall not at any moment be denied, temporarily, supplies of those commodities. And if Japan were to gain control of that whole area—as she has already occupied the coast of China, the Island of Hainan, various other islands, and most of Indochina—she would be in position to withhold these supplies from us, from Great Britain and from other countries, to supply them exclusively to her allies, or to dictate to us in what amount and on what terms we might have them.[58]

During the 1930s, the militarist powers, especially Japan and Germany, led a more general international trend toward bilateral trading blocs and state barter deals. As Japan advanced south, U.S. leaders feared it would incorporate all of Southeast Asia into an autarkic, single-currency sphere, the Yen Bloc. Even if Japan did not directly deny the Western nations access to that area, such a bloc would have made the United States financially incapable of maintaining its imports from Southeast Asia.

As part of its program of reviving domestic prosperity within a liberal international framework, the Roosevelt administration put a high priority on restoring the pre-Depression system of multilateral trade.[59] Multilateral trade, as opposed to barter or state trading, would allow capital transfers and currency markets to foster efficient commerce between countries, even if their bilateral trade did not balance. As evidence of the importance of multilateral trade to the industrialized nations, a 1942 League of Nations study cited "the heavy net imports of the United States from South-East Asia arising from the large trade in rubber and tin." If the United States had been obligated to balance its trade with that region on a bilateral rather than multilateral basis, its industrial economy would have been severely crimped.[60] Because the United States exported few products directly to the Asian colonies, it relied on a triangular trade system with England and the Netherlands to supply the foreign exchange to purchase raw materials from that region. Thus, when U.S. policymakers spoke of the need to preserve multilateral trading, they had in mind not just abstract principles but also the need to finance strategic imports.

In 1937, the U.S. trade deficit with British Malaya and the Netherlands East Indies alone approached a staggering quarter of a billion dollars. U.S. imports from Malaya exceeded exports by 2,749 percent; imports from the Netherlands East Indies exceeded exports by 460 percent.[61] To help balance this trade, the United States ran export surpluses with Great Britain and the Netherlands of $400 million and $66 million, respectively.[62] The European countries derived little or no foreign exchange from trade with their Asian colonies. However, their large and profitable overseas investments generated enough income to provide a healthy balance-of-payments surplus, completing the "triangle" of payments. They used investment income earned on the sales of tropical resources to buy U.S. products. The United States, in turn, used its export income to purchase the raw materials it needed from Southeast

Asia. The League of Nations described the pivotal role of Great Britain in this process:

> The explanation of this phenomenon lies in the fact that merchandise trade depends upon each country's commodity needs and the localities where those needs can be met, and not upon their financial claims. British capital has been active in developing primary production in various parts of the world for disposal in the world market and not in the United Kingdom alone; and during the long period of capital exports the United Kingdom export industry adapted itself to meet the requirements of the countries in which the investments were made. The export surplus of these countries, representing largely the yield of British capital, thus arose in trade with other countries which financed their imports of primary goods by an excess of exports to the United Kingdom.[63]

The expulsion of Western interests from Southeast Asia by Japan would lead to a breakdown of the entire multilateral trading process. If Europe no longer received investment income from the Asian colonies, it would buy less from the United States, which in turn would have to curtail its purchases from Southeast Asia. Even if Japan were friendly to the United States, the incorporation of Southeast Asia into the Yen Bloc would worsen the U.S. trade position. The United States' export surplus with Japan, which amounted to $84 million in 1937, could not begin to cover its huge trade deficit with Southeast Asia—$90 million with the Netherlands East Indies alone.[64]

The closed nature of Japan's "Co-Prosperity Sphere" was well known to trade specialists. As one 1940 study observed, "Foreign trade has been diverted strikingly into the yen-bloc area with a consequent reduction in trade with other parts of the world, because the yen-bloc trade does not yield any foreign exchange usable for the purchase of goods from other countries."[65] Administration officials were acutely aware of these considerations. In July 1940, Assistant Secretary of State Henry Francis Grady said the method of international trade was "a matter of great concern for us."

Shall it be conducted on a liberal most-favored-nation or multilateral basis, or on a preferential and restricted basis of bilateral trade balancing?

For instance, shall we, as has always been possible under a most-favored-nation system of world trade, accept raw materials from southeastern Asia as payment for our exports to Europe, or shall we, as a result of bilateralism, be forced to accept instead European products for which we may have less need?

... If our trade with southeastern Asia, for example, were subject to such arrangements, efforts to bring about a more evenly balanced trade might conceivably result in a serious curtailment of our imports of essential raw materials.[66]

Raymond Geist, chief of the State Department's commercial division, also decried the "monopolistic practices of the totalitarian states," which disrupted the "triangular and multilateral flow of goods," including "raw materials essential to our industrial processes."[67]

More broadly, the Roosevelt administration feared that a loss of strategic raw materials could jeopardize the existence of capitalist democracy itself in the United States. For Secretary of State Hull, it was axiomatic that freedom of enterprise went hand in hand with liberal democratic institutions—a worldview shared by most other members of the government. Rising trade barriers, Hull and Roosevelt believed, would lead to "ever-expanding regimentation" of U.S. business and ultimately of American society.[68] Economic isolation forced upon the United States by the autarkic policies of the Axis powers might force extensive state intervention in the economy at home to control industry and ration raw materials. As Will Clayton put it in 1940, "This would involve such far-reaching and radical changes, accompanied by so severe a reduction in our standard of living, that it is very doubtful if democracy would survive the shock."[69] An executive of General Motors offered the clearest exposition of this view in a speech to the National Foreign Trade Convention in 1940:

A vital need of any nation is to establish itself in proper balance in the world economy; to secure for itself ready access to the wealth it needs from abroad, and to use the surpluses it produces in order to acquire that needed wealth. Neither the free enterprise system itself, nor the political freedom from which it derives, can long endure in the United States if maladjustment with the world economy continues to result in our inability to acquire the wealth we need from abroad, or to rid ourselves of the surpluses we have to offer in exchange. An accumulation of these surpluses, and a lack of the goods and raw materials they could be used to buy, bring economic disturbance and social unrest which lead inevitably, if long continued, to demands for political action. Such action can only take the form of deliberate interference with normal economic processes, and this interference—which is the essence of regimentation or totalitarianism—is certain to feed upon itself and to extend over the whole area of the economic body.[70]

But a Japanese military conquest of Southeast Asia would not harm the United States alone. Great Britain also depended on Southeast Asia for raw materials. Indeed, stripped of its empire, Britain had even fewer raw materials than Japan.[71] It could not, therefore, stand to see its richest colonies absorbed by a hostile power. British strategic planners impressed on their U.S. counterparts that the loss of Singapore would sever trade routes across the Indian Ocean that carried men, supplies, and raw materials from Australia and New Zealand.[72] A general strategic review by the British chiefs of staff in 1941 concluded that "the safe passage from Malaya and Dutch East Indies of commodities essential both to ourselves and the United States" was "vital to the successful continuance of our war effort."[73] British Prime Minister Winston Churchill personally warned Roosevelt that loss of Southeast Asia would threaten to cut Britain off "from Indian and Australasian resources."[74] Japan's threat to those outposts of empire, moreover, diverted men and material from Britain's fight for survival in Europe.[75]

The process of triangular trade was as important to Britain as to the United States. The loss of Malaya would deprive Great

Britain of the dollars it needed to finance essential purchases from the United States. American exporters would lose a good market, and Britain's war effort would be jeopardized, threatening U.S. security in turn. "[A]s a source of vital raw materials for the munitions industries of the British Empire and the United States," Asia expert Kate Mitchell observed in 1941, British colonial interests in Southeast Asia "have assumed supreme importance in the Anglo-American war effort."[76]

Numerous commentators viewed U.S. and British strategic and economic interests as inextricably linked in Southeast Asia. "In the Far East," one wrote, "America's measures to safeguard its own rubber and tin life line will be augmented by reason of the necessity of providing similar protection for Great Britain, which cannot under present circumstances experiment with substitutes, and which, furthermore, depends in some measure upon the proceeds of the sale of its rubber and tin to finance its purchases of war materials, especially in the United States."[77] *Newsweek*, in a review of U.S. naval strategy, similarly concluded, "One of the best ways the United States can aid Britain short of war is to act as the watchdog of the Pacific.... For as long as the United States Fleet ... [patrols] the sea lanes that carry such vital supplies as rubber and tin from Asia to America, Britain need have little fear that her possessions in the Pacific will be greatly disturbed by pro-Axis activity."[78]

Such arguments carried great weight within the Roosevelt administration, which for strategic, economic, and sentimental reasons placed supreme importance on ensuring the survival of Great Britain. As Admiral Stark pointed out in a famous strategy memorandum to Roosevelt in late 1940, "the continued existence of the British Empire, combined with building up a strong protection in our home area, will do most to assure the status quo in the Western Hemisphere, and to promote our national interests." If Britain won decisively against Germany, "we could win everywhere," he observed; but if it lost, the United States "might, possibly, not win anywhere."[79] Preventing Great Britain's defeat arguably required protecting its position across the globe in Southeast Asian colonies. The Roosevelt administration ultimately accepted the conclusions of the British chiefs of staff that the loss of Singapore would be "a disaster of the first magnitude, second only to the loss of the British Isles."[80]

Public Opinion and Private Interests

The threat to the United States' industrial lifelines posed by Japan's southward advance was not a closely held official secret. On the contrary, it caught the attention of numerous politicians, private interest groups, experts, and media commentators. Their repeated warnings helped influence public opinion to give the administration greater freedom of action against Japan in the Pacific.[81]

At first, members of Congress moved slowly to face the threat to U.S. economic interests in Southeast Asia. As early as 1936, Congress took steps to protect the United States' tin supply in response to foreign production restrictions. But the country's general isolationist spirit and the obscurity of most technical evaluations of U.S. mineral needs kept the issue of dependence from swaying most legislators. One Far Eastern specialist, indeed, criticized Congress in 1937 for proposing to tie the administration's hands with new neutrality legislation, potentially jeopardizing the country's "access to important raw materials such as rubber, tin, silk, vegetable fibers and oils for which Eastern Asia is our chief source of supply."[82]

By 1938, however, Congress was supporting administration-backed legislation for an aggressive naval expansion program with just such considerations in mind. Senator David Walsh of Massachusetts, the bill's leading defender in Congress, said

> Great Britain has extensive trade routes, reaching into every part of the world, which it is necessary for her to keep open in order that she may survive in case of attack by an enemy. We, too, have trade routes. It is estimated by our experts that unless we are able to keep open certain trade routes the United States of America could not maintain itself for more than two years without being defeated by a powerful enemy. We must have rubber. We cannot

store rubber, because it decays. Can Senators conceive of a situation in time of war in which it would be absolutely impossible to obtain tires for our automobiles, trucks, and commercial vehicles of all kinds and descriptions?

We cannot build battleships in time of war unless we keep the trade routes open to bring in certain essential raw materials. So . . . in very many respects we are in exactly the same situation as Great Britain.[83]

The Senate Naval Affairs Committee, for its part, warned that the United States could be "defeated and conquered" without any physical invasion of the continent if a foreign enemy were to disrupt trade routes or ports "from which we import essential raw materials." Denial of these goods, which were "absolutely essential to peacetime industry" and to "the prosecution of a war," might "easily force us to accept drastic terms to avoid complete collapse," the committee concluded.[84]

Among the most respected commentators on Japan's threat to Southeast Asia was retired Rear Adm. Harry Yarnell, former head of the Asiatic Fleet and commander at Pearl Harbor. A member of such elite groups as the Council on Foreign Relations and the Institute of Pacific Relations, Yarnell was listened to by both the general public and the administration. Appealing to all Americans not to abandon Asia in the face of Japanese aggression, he declared that "we have a vast stake in the Far East:"

> Although the National Defense Advisory Commission is doing what it can to relieve us of our dependence on the Far East for certain essential war materials, it remains true, for example, that practically all our rubber now comes from the Netherlands Indies, Malaya, and Indo-China. In 1939 we used 590,000 tons.
>
> We receive annually 850,000 tons of sugar from the Philippines. We buy more than one-third of the world's output of tin, and most of it comes from the South China Sea area. Bolivia is entirely unable to supply us with tin if the Far East source fails us. We buy more than fifty million dollars worth of copra and coconut oil annually from the Philippines. Abaca, or Manila hemp, is a world monopoly

of those islands. The world's supply of quinine comes from the Netherlands Indies, and we are the world's largest consumer. The largest known chromite deposit in the world is in the Philippines. Of our seven major imports, six are major export products of the Far East.[85]

Many business and public opinion leaders shared this analysis. As early as December 1939, participants in *Fortune* magazine's Fifth Round Table Discussion, "America's Stake in the Present War and the Future World Order," expressed fears for the safety of the Philippines. "[S]hould Japan succeed in controlling the Philippines," they said, "sooner or later the rich resources of the Straits Settlements, Netherlands India, and even the Pacific dominions might fall into its hands."[86]

Three months later, the Sixth Round Table Discussion, on "The United States and Foreign Trade," dealt with these problems in much greater depth. After reviewing the many important raw materials procured abroad for use in U.S. industry, the round table report continued:

> The electric light-bulb, the telephone, the radio, the automobile, and the airplane—most of which Americans regard as essential to modern existence—are produced with the aid of materials imported from overseas.
>
> The extensive use that American technology makes of imports . . . is illustrated by the case of rubber coming from southeastern Asia. It is one of the most important commodities imported into the U. S.; the domestic rubber manufacturing industry is the largest of the sort in the world. Rubber is used in the most plebeian articles, whether they be jar rings or overshoes; there are 280 rubber parts in the modern automobile. Tin also must be imported, entering this country in the form of bars and blocks, smelted for the most part in British Malaya. . . . Chrome ore, employed in ferrochrome, and certain chemicals, is 99 percent imported, coming from South Africa, the Philippines, French Oceania, and Cuba. In years of large use about 60 percent of the tungsten ore, used in manufacturing high speed tools, for hard-facing valve

parts, and lamp filaments, comes largely from China and British Malaya.[87]

Noting that imports had grown considerably over the preceding decade, the report concluded, "*Without these increasing imports the technological progress achieved by American industry in the past ten years would have been difficult if not impossible.*"[88]

Wall Street understood that by a strange accident of geography and history, Southeast Asia was of unique economic importance to the United States. As a publication of the New York Trust Company pointed out in 1940: "Most of the strategic raw materials which the United States cannot do without are available in abundance in Southeastern Asia. In the area surrounding the South China Sea lies one of the greatest deposits of raw material wealth to be found anywhere. Of the 14 strategic raw materials, nine are produced in large volume in this region. . . . It is therefore obvious that the United States has a vital interest in what happens to those nations surrounding the South China Sea."[89] Thomas Watson, president of IBM, summed up the position of many of the nation's most important business leaders when he declared to the National Foreign Trade Convention on July 30, 1940, that raw materials were a higher priority than markets to the U.S. economy. "Our imports are more important to American industry than our exports," he said. "Practically every manufacturing industry in the United States is dependent on imports to keep its wheels turning."[90]

The large business magazines, which began to oppose Japan strongly in late 1940 as the threat to Southeast Asia became obvious, repeatedly cited strategic materials as a key U.S. interest worth defending. *Business Week* justified its support for a tough stance toward Japan in August 1940 by explaining that further Japanese victories could mean the loss of the Philippines and of "our supplies of at least two strategic raw materials—tin and rubber."[91] *Fortune* also took a hard line against Japan's southward military advance. In early 1941, the magazine suggested that Japan might soon invade the South Seas to control its rich resources. The editor suggested that the U.S. fleet defend Singapore and the Netherlands East Indies in order to protect "the supply lines that bring us rubber and tin from the East Indies."[92] In July, the magazine pointed out: "From Malaya and the Indies comes nearly all of our rubber and tin—two of the most vital war materials in which we are dependent on imports. Either by taking the Indies outright or by threatening our commerce with the region, Japan could hold the same whip hand over these commodities that we now have over oil exports to Japan."[93]

The more popular *Time* magazine warned its readers of Japan's intentions in September 1940. "If the Japanese were to accomplish their much-vaunted New Order in this area, the U.S. economy might be severely dislocated," the publication suggested. "Materials for a range of products all the way from tires to electric-light filaments, from tea to teak, from tin for canning to quinine for malaria, would become drastically scarce in the U.S. until substitutes could be produced in sufficient quantities."[94]

Well-informed public opinion leaders in Washington and other major cities read journals such as *Foreign Affairs*, *Foreign Policy Report*, and *Far Eastern Survey*, published by the Council on Foreign Relations, the Foreign Policy Association, and the Institute of Pacific Relations, respectively.[95] These publications repeatedly highlighted Japan's threat to vital American supply lines from Southeast Asia. In a discussion of "America's Stake in the Far East," Miriam Farley informed readers of *Far Eastern Survey* that the United States was "absolutely dependent upon the Far East for the bulk of its supplies of a number of leading raw materials essential to the functioning of its industrial apparatus as well as for considerable quantities of other materials."[96] Robert Barnett, a Far Eastern specialist for the Institute of Pacific Relations, asserted that many imports from the region were "indispensable" and added, "A war situation like that of today emphasizes their strategic importance."[97] Henry Douglas, a frequent contributor to magazines on Far Eastern affairs, declared that a Japanese conquest of "Southeast Asia and the East Indies" would be a "body blow to the industrial and economic functioning of the United States" and "would enable her to dictate, in a very large measure, the economic functioning of highly industrialized countries such as the United States."[98] Another author devoted an entire book to the issue of Japan's threat to the United States' raw material supplies in Southeast Asia, and many others gave more than passing mention to the problem.[99] Newspaper editorials also emphasized the strategic importance to the United States of Southeast Asian resources.[100]

Cumulatively, all of these warnings began to shape the public's consciousness. As journalist I. F. Stone wrote in 1941, "The emergency was beginning to open to our view some strange corners of our economy. . . . We began to worry, like a housewife suddenly out of pepper, cinnamon and celery salt, about many minor but important materials whose presence in the national cupboard we had always taken for granted."[101]

The barrage of alarmist articles, speeches, and books did not go unanswered by isolationists and critics of intervention. Contrary to administration studies, claimed military commentator Hanson Baldwin, "In so far as strategic raw materials vital to the waging of war are concerned, our hemispheric self-sufficiency is . . . more than adequate to practically any demand."[102] Fleming MacLiesh and Cushman Reynolds, authors of *Strategy of the Americas*, also argued that through development of substitutes and a strategy of economic regimentation, the Western Hemisphere could withstand economic pressures from totalitarian aggressors.[103]

The Chicago-based America First Committee, the country's leading anti-interventionist lobby, took pains to address the issue of dependence. The possibility of expanding production of tin and antimony in Bolivia, chromium and manganese in Cuba and Brazil, and synthetic rubber at home, it declared in one study, refuted the "repeated contentions of the alarmists" that the United States would be "crippled should the Axis powers seize far-off lands whose names are strange to Americans." The committee reassured fearful citizens, "We need not go to war for rubber or tin; American boys need not fight and die in Dong Dang [sic] or Bangkok. The Western Hemisphere is self-sufficient in terms of raw materials resources."[104] Nonetheless, the same document took the Roosevelt administration to task for "a serious lack of raw material planning for the defense program (not to mention peacetime production)."[105]

The Grand Area Strategy

No private organization or interest group had a more profound impact on administration policy and thinking in this period than the Council on Foreign Relations (CFR). An elite, invitation-only group founded in New York in 1921 by business leaders and academic experts who had traveled with Woodrow Wilson to Paris to plan the peace after World War I, the council rapidly established itself as the nation's most influential foreign policy constituency.[106] With financial backing from the House of Morgan, the Carnegie and Rockefeller foundations, and other major donors, the CFR established the preeminent journal in its field, *Foreign Affairs*; sponsored innumerable discussion groups, speeches, and books; and gave government officials a convenient means of networking privately with opinion makers in business, law, and academia. Starting in the mid-1920s, every U.S. secretary of state acknowledged its standing by delivering major addresses before it. Countless foreign dignitaries, including heads of state, followed suit.[107]

Serious analysts, not to mention conspiracy theorists, have long recognized its significance as a place where policy ideas are developed, tested, and disseminated.[108] Lester Milbraith, a student of interest-group influence on foreign policy, noted, "The Council on Foreign Relations, while not financed by government, works so closely with it that it is difficult to distinguish Council actions stimulated by government from autonomous actions."[109] Journalist Joseph Kraft observed that "it has been the seat of some basic government decisions, has set the context for many more, and has repeatedly served as a recruiting ground for ranking officials."[110] Among the CFR members who held prominent foreign policy posts in the Roosevelt administration were Adolf Berle, Norman Davis, Herbert Feis,

Joseph Grew, Stanley Hornbeck, Henry Morgenthau, Leo Pasvolsky, Francis Sayre, Henry Stimson, and Sumner Welles. Secretary of War Stimson's aide John J. McCloy, later a famous official in his own right, recalled, "Whenever we needed a man, we thumbed through the roll of Council members and put through a call to New York."[111]

One of the CFR's earliest and most obsessive interests was the impact of the unequal distribution of raw materials on international relations. Its study program in this area was led by indefatigable University of Wisconsin geologist Charles K. Leith, who had advised President Wilson's negotiating team in Paris on minerals questions and later became the top minerals adviser to the Roosevelt administration. The CFR published several books and numerous articles in *Foreign Affairs* on the matter. Nearly all carried the same message: As the world's biggest consuming nation, the United States could not take its raw material needs for granted.[112]

The truest measure of the council's astonishing influence was not felt until the fall of 1939. Within days of the German blitzkrieg through Poland, *Foreign Affairs* editor Hamilton Fish Armstrong and the CFR's executive director, Walter Mallory, visited the State Department with a bold proposition: In view of the department's inadequate resources and overworked staff, the council would undertake to begin postwar planning for it. Secretary Hull, buried in work from the European crisis, accepted with alacrity. He appointed a State Department group to coordinate the secret effort, including council members Undersecretary of State Sumner Welles, Assistant Secretary George Messersmith, special assistant Leo Pasvolsky, economic adviser Herbert Feis, political adviser Stanley Hornbeck, and Jay Pierrepont Moffat, chief of the Division of European Affairs. Welles chaired the committee. The council, for its part, quickly lined up the first of many grants from the Rockefeller Foundation to fund its work. The first organizing meeting was held at Messersmith's home in Washington on December 8, 1939.[113]

In the six years of the program's existence, the CFR produced a total of 682 studies of "American Interests in the War and

Peace" for the State Department and White House. The participants had the time, resources, and independence to step back from day-to-day crises and think conceptually about those interests. Their findings thus carried particular weight. Walter Mallory, a China expert and active participant in the study groups, commented when it was all over, "This project, I believe, represented a new departure in the history of our Government. It marked the first time, so far as I know, in which the services of private individuals, through a private organization, were put at the disposal of the Government systematically and which had a direct and continuing impact on the formulation of policy."[114] Mallory was not simply patting his colleagues on the back. Hull, too, praised the council's contribution in glowing terms.[115]

At the heart of the council's work in 1940 and 1941 was a lengthy and continuing analysis of the implications for the United States of the "division of the world into two great political and economic entities, each almost wholly self-sufficient with a bare minimum of trade between the two giant political and economic blocs." Under what conditions could the United States survive the rapid absorption of the globe into the closed, autarkic trading blocs of Germany, Japan, and possibly the Soviet Union? As one participant put it, the question was how much "elbow room" the U.S. economy needed "in order to survive without major readjustments."[116]

The council's extensive study of trade flows came to one conclusion: The United States could not live bottled up in the Western Hemisphere alone. "A longer-run maintenance of power by the Western Hemisphere or, more specifically, the United States, certainly requires the preservation of the Pacific area and the countries of the Far East," one major analysis of trading blocs concluded in 1941.[117] Council groups coined a term for the "living space" needed by the United States: the "Grand Area." They defined it as "the amount of the world the United States can defend most economically, that is, with the least readjustment of the American economy."[118] It included Great Britain, the Western Hemisphere, and Southeast Asia. The latter region was deemed "more complementary with the United States ... than any other important area of the world."[119] Study after study documented the vulnerability of the U.S. economy to raw material embargoes from that region.[120]

Any shrinkage of U.S. access to the Grand Area would powerfully threaten national interests, council studies asserted: "To maintain a maximum defense effort, the United States must avoid economic readjustment caused by constriction of the trading area.... What such constriction might mean in weakening the defense economy can best be seen by imagining the strain on American supplies of labor, materials and industrial capacity of the attempt to manufacture substitutes for or to do without rubber, tin, jute, and numerous vegetable oils, instead of importing these products from southeastern Asia."[121] To this end, the study groups concluded, "it was essential ... to keep Japan from dominating Southeastern Asia."[122] Should Japan succeed in its aims there, "the position of the free world would then be fraught with greatest danger," and "the United States would be hemmed in, economically as well as militarily, by a unified totalitarian world."[123]

The nature of Japan's intentions thus captured the close attention of council analysts. Owen Lattimore, an Asia expert of whom President Roosevelt had the "highest opinion," concluded that the United States could live with a divided and conquered China if it had to but could not withstand the loss of Southeast Asia. "In island and peninsular Asia," one of his studies warned, "the American interest would be gravely prejudiced by the concentration of imperial power in the hands of an unfriendly or monopolistic nation, because of the need for access to rubber, tin, and other resources, and because of the strategic importance of converging sea and air routes."[124]

A major council study of "American Far Eastern Policy" in January 1941, which Hull received directly from Pasvolsky, declared at the outset, "It is to the interest of the United States to check a Japanese advance into southeastern Asia." Because the colonies there were "prime sources of raw materials very important to the United States in peace and war," it stated, "control of these lands by a potentially hostile power would greatly limit our freedom of action." Japanese aggression there, it added, "would further injure our interests by weakening the British war effort against Hitler." It proposed a series of measures to deter a Japanese advance: offering more aid to China; sending patrol planes, submarines, and torpedo boats to the Philippines, Singapore, and the Dutch East Indies; and tightening the embargo on U.S. sales to Japan of wartime necessities, "using the excuse of our own defense needs" to make it "more difficult for Japanese extremists to take advantage of our action to urge war."[125]

The report, and others that came before, credited China only for its ability to divert Japan's forces from more vital lands to the south: "Should [Japan] be able to negotiate a settlement with the Chungking government, or should she be able to assume a strictly defensive position in China, men, ships, and supplies would be freed for a move toward southeastern Asia. . . . The United States should, therefore, give the Chinese all possible aid in the form of war materials and other supplies."[126]

This policy was driven by realpolitik, not sentiment. Indeed, Lattimore pointedly did not propose giving China enough aid to defeat Japan. Council participants stated explicitly that "America did not desire a full defeat of Japan by China" because "many Americans wanted Japan strong enough to serve as a barrier against Russia."[127] By 1941, the strategy of keeping China afloat with a view to disrupting Japan's timetable for southward expansion had become a central preoccupation of Roosevelt's advisers. As later chapters will show, such expressions both of national interests and strategy permeated the thinking of officials in Washington, many of whom read council studies and participated in their groups.

2

The Rush to Stockpile

> Mobilization of the world's resources has become the essence of modern war. Therefore, the resources available to any state, and its ability to utilize them, determine its success in the gigantic industrial struggle, upon which in a large measure the victory depends.
> *U.S. Military Academy*, Raw Materials in War and Peace, *1947*

Nowhere was Washington's alarm over the future of its access to Southeast Asian raw material supplies more evident than in its frantic efforts to stockpile reserves in the months before Pearl Harbor. As intended, these stockpiles helped the United States win the war against the Axis powers. But Washington never viewed the program as a permanent or satisfactory substitute for maintaining and defending its traditional access to the region's resources.

The push to stockpile long predated the war. In 1933, President Roosevelt created the National Resources Board to study the quality and adequacy of domestic reserves. Its Planning Committee for Mineral Policy soon reported that the United States could not meet its industrial needs without importing large quantities of raw materials from overseas. It recommended stockpiling materials that could not be produced domestically.[1]

The U.S. military had long agitated for such a stockpile program. In 1934 the Army and Navy Munitions Board recommended spending an unprecedented $100 million to build a war reserve of manganese, chromite, tin, tungsten, and other materials. The board suggested that the materials be acquired as repayment for war debts.[2] The State Department, with Roosevelt's approval, proposed to Ambassador Sir Ronald Lindsay that Britain ship Malayan tin to the United States to meet its World War I loan obligations. The British rebuffed these advances and refused to repay the debts, and the deal fell through. But the State Department continued to pressure the British for at least another four years.[3]

The drive to enlarge U.S. raw material stocks in the early 1930s was less a coordinated national program than a campaign by a few concerned government officials who feared that peace might not last forever.[4] As early as 1934, the State Department's economic adviser, Herbert Feis, began privately warning his colleagues of the danger to U.S. rubber supplies in the event of war with Japan.[5] At the same time, Secretary of State Cordell Hull began advocating conservation of raw materials. Urging the president to adopt a stockpiling program, Hull and his colleagues argued that without sufficient reserves, war would bring "grave civilian deprivations" and a "great disturbance of both our economic life and our defense effort."[6]

In the midst of the Depression, huge appropriations were not forthcoming to fund long-range stockpiling programs. Nevertheless, Hull, Feis, and other officials scattered through the bureaucracy continued agitating for greater official attention to the problem.[7] On May 29, 1935, Hull wrote Roosevelt recommending formation of an interdepartmental committee to deal with strategic materials. Once again he advocated an enlarged stockpiling program to take advantage of low world prices.[8] In 1936 a small group of government officials representing the State, War, Navy, Treasury, Interior, and Commerce departments unofficially formed the Interdepartmental Committee on Strategic Materials, which was finally officially recognized in 1939.[9] Feis, who chaired it, recalled that in the view of the participants, "the statistics of rubber supply became an index of American security."[10]

In early 1936, Congress finally heeded their warnings by passing the Tin Protection Act, subjecting exports of tin scrap to licensing arrangements under the control of the State Department.[11] In 1937, Congress passed a naval bill that included $3.5 million toward the purchase of strategic and critical materials.[12] The Navy began buying tin, manganese, tungsten, chrome, optical glass, and manila fiber.[13] The appropriation may have been stingy, but it marked an important first step.

Throughout 1937 the administration, seeking to balance the budget, ruled out expensive stockpiling programs. By 1938, however, as the political situation in Europe and Asia grew more ominous, all relevant departments backed the acquisition of raw material reserves.[14] Hull warned rubber industry leaders to begin building up inventories because "one day we might have a war with Japan."[15] In October 1938, after the Munich crisis, he wrote President Roosevelt that the need for a stockpiling program was becoming "more and more urgent as time goes on." Deploring congressional inaction on programs to neutralize U.S. dependence on foreign supplies of raw materials, Hull said: "It is our feeling that there should be no further delay in initiating steps which would make available with the greatest possible despatch adequate supplies of the few materials which are of the most critical importance. With these supplies in hand we should have greater freedom in deciding the course of action this Government should take in any given international crisis; without reserve stocks we may be exposed to bargaining by the suppliers of these materials, if indeed we could by any line of policy secure all of the supplies required." Hull concluded by citing the consensus of the State, War, and Navy departments that "it is highly desirable to adopt a national policy with respect to this problem and to secure early and effective action by Congress."[16]

Further delay, Feis pointed out at the same time, would only vastly inflate the final cost of amassing an adequate stockpile.[17] Feis's Interdepartmental Committee continued to recommend a crash program of stockpiling strategic materials. A typical report, distributed in December 1938 to the heads of State, Commerce, Interior, War, and Navy and sent directly to Roosevelt by Acting Secretary of State Sumner Welles, read: "It is urgent that the accumulation of necessary reserves of a number of strategic materials be begun without further delay. Failure to act on this matter will continue a vital weakness in the national defense program. Furthermore, this nation will be exposed to grave dangers in efforts to maintain neutrality in the event of a major international war if it has not in advance provided for adequate reserve stockpiles of those materials which otherwise must be secured from distant sources of supply under the control of other nations."[18]

Roosevelt heeded this plea, and on June 7, 1939, Congress enacted administration-backed legislation to authorize $100 million for the acquisition of "certain strategic and critical materials being deficient or insufficiently developed to supply the industrial, military, and naval needs of the country for common defense . . . in times of national emergency."[19] Although the appropriation was far from sufficient to eliminate the risk of foreign supply disruptions, it represented a huge sum in times of fiscal austerity.

Hull set aside his deeply held free-trade principles in 1939 to expedite the stockpiling process. With the secretary of agriculture, he came up with a plan to barter vast U.S. surpluses of wheat and cotton in return for strategic materials. Congress authorized the Commodity Credit Corporation to exchange surplus agricultural commodities for raw materials. The State Department then began negotiating such a state-barter scheme with the governments of Great Britain, Belgium, and the Netherlands. After much arm-twisting, the United States persuaded Britain, on June 23, 1939, to sign an agreement to trade 90,505 tons of crude rubber for 600,000 bales of cotton.[20] Even so, by the end of 1939, the U.S. rubber stockpile amounted to only three months' consumption, or 125,800 tons, compared to supplies of more than 300,000 tons in 1931–1935.[21]

Given the overwhelming importance of rubber to the U.S. economy and the fact that the nations of Europe and Asia were at war, administration leaders could not accept such minimal reserves. On February 13, 1940, at the urging of Hull and other officials, Roosevelt wrote the House and Senate to request the immediate appropriation of money authorized by the 1939 Strategic Materials Act. He cited as justification for his request the report of the Interdepartmental Committee on Strategic Materials, which, he said, emphasized several key points:

1. Commercial stocks in this country of many vital raw materials are now considerably below normal.
2. Prices of most of the desired items are more favorable at present than for some time in the past.
3. Difficulties in both supply and transportation, as well as higher prices, are likely to be encountered if the present war continues and increases in intensity.
4. In the event of unlimited warfare on sea and in the air, possession of a reserve of these essential supplies might prove of vital importance, not only in the national defense, but in strengthening the policy of neutrality.
5. The materials to be purchased can at any time be converted into cash, and in the event of an emergency they will be worth much more than their cost.[22]

The various departments with responsibilities for the stockpile program continued to sound the alarm.[23] On April 17, 1940, Feis circulated a long and pointed memorandum arguing that if the United States failed to take immediate action to purchase sufficient supplies of rubber, the consequences could be disastrous. "The danger was evident," he recalled. "The inflow from the Far East on which we lived could be cut off."[24]

Acting Secretary of State Sumner Welles shared his alarm. On May 1, 1940, he wrote to the president: "The problem of our continued supply of strategic materials has once more come to the fore because of recent developments [with Japan]. The materials which are of greatest concern to us at the present moment are tin and rubber, which come very largely from the [Far] East, and which would be difficult to secure if hostilities broke out in that area or if there were any interruption to shipping over the very long supply routes from the Netherlands Indies and British Malaya." Welles noted that existing stocks of rubber and tin would last only about three months and urged much greater spending to accumulate these and other strategic products.[25]

With Western Europe falling to the Nazis and the Japanese showing ever more aggressiveness, Congress by May 1940 finally began to show "feverish activity" on the stockpiling issue. Talk of spending half a billion dollars to buy adequate reserves became common.[26] The Roosevelt administration, following a special cabinet meeting, decided to treat the matter as one of "urgency and of great national importance."[27] Welles and the Commerce Department worked out a plan to empower the Reconstruction Finance Corporation to centralize the purchase of all raw materials.[28] With Roosevelt's approval, RFC head Jesse Jones went before Congress to seek the necessary legislation. On June 25, Congress gave it the power to form subsidiary corporations for acquiring raw materials designated as strategic or critical by the president. One subsidiary, the Metals Reserve Company, contracted for all the tin it could buy from Southeast Asia and Bolivia, for Chinese tungsten, and for the entire nickel output of the Pacific island of New Caledonia.[29] When Roosevelt added rubber to the strategic list on June 28, the RFC announced the creation of the Rubber Reserve Company.[30] Independent experts lauded the administration for slashing through bottlenecks and red tape, given the urgency of the international situation.[31]

Averting a rubber shortfall was of particular importance. On May 22, 1940, Jones, Feis, and the heads of the major U.S. rubber companies had met to discuss measures for addressing domestic shortages. Feis stressed the threat from Japan as the chief justification for a crash stockpiling program. However, the rubber company representatives convinced Jones that huge open-market rubber purchases would be a grave mistake, because at the first hint of an upward price movement, producers would take their product off the market in hope of garnering yet higher prices. The result would be less rubber at a higher cost. Even so, all agreed that the RFC should begin making significant purchases as soon as Congress authorized them, which it did shortly.[32]

Jones understood that stockpiling might not meet all the nation's growing needs for rubber. Late in the summer of 1940, after discussions with the president of B. F. Goodrich Co., he began to consider setting up a synthetic rubber industry. Numerous rubber, petroleum, and chemical companies had been experimenting with various processes, but none had yet started mass production to achieve economies of scale. Along with Edward Stettinius, Jr. and William Batt of the National Defense Advisory Council, which also handled the problem of raw material supplies, Jones went to Roosevelt to make the case for investing $100 million in synthetic rubber manufacturing. Roosevelt believed the rubber companies would take the risk themselves if forced to but indicated his willingness to spend $25 million. Experts were more skeptical of the ability of the rubber companies to meet the challenge, so Jones privately authorized a $40 million program to subsidize development of a new synthetic rubber industry. The program moved slowly before the war because the major rubber companies had to be persuaded to pool their patents and trade secrets, but Jones had planted the seed that allowed for vast wartime expansion of the industry.[33]

Working closely with Treasury Secretary Henry Morgenthau, Jones devised a way to obtain increased supplies of needed materials while promoting other U.S. foreign policy objectives. He and Morgenthau arranged commercial loans to China in return for shipments of strategic commodities.[34] On December 14, 1938, Jones announced a $25 million loan through the Export-Import Bank to the Universal Trading Corporation of New York in order to finance the exchange of U.S. commodities for Chinese wood (tung) oil used in paints.[35] An editorial in the *Washington Star* explained that the loan "may not be sufficient to save China" but would place "new obstacles in the path of the invading Japanese" and prevent them from "establishing a monopoly of Chinese trade" or from controlling raw materials "which in the hands of the Japanese could give her a grip upon a part of American industry."[36] An internal Treasury Department review noted that increased imports of tung oil had "proven to be of real benefit to the paint, varnish and other wood oil using industries as openly recognized by the National Paint, Varnish and Lacquer Association of the United States."[37]

Greatly encouraged by this initial success, Treasury officials next proposed a loan against Chinese tin. The United States had been importing about 3,000 tons of Chinese tin annually, but it was of low quality, useful only for certain specialized purposes. Some officials thought, however, that the quality could be raised to the standard of tin exported from Malaya and the Netherlands East Indies, whose producers were still restricting output in order to raise prices:[38] "China is the only important producer of tin which has not participated in the international tin agreement. Without being subject to export quota control, China is free to increase her production and export in order to meet the increasing needs of the United States. Annual consumption of tin by various industries in the United States varied from 48,860 long tons in 1938 to 87,000 tons in 1929. Although the proposed shipment of Chinese tin of 10,000 tons a year only fulfills a small portion of the United States requirement, it is important to have such an independent source of supply in view of the war situation and control of the international tin agreement."[39] A commercial loan for Chinese tin, Treasury officials argued further, would "not only supply the urgently needed new funds for the continuation of purchases of necessary materials to the . . . benefit of United States manufacturers" but also "may serve as encouragement of immeasurable value in helping the morale of the Chinese people" against Japanese aggression.[40]

This argument carried the day. On March 7, 1940, the Export-Import Bank authorized a new $20 million loan to China to be repaid with tin. On September 25, 1940, Jones announced that the Metals Reserve Company had agreed to extend a $25 million loan to China for the purchase of tungsten. On November 30, 1940, the administration announced another $100 million loan to finance the acquisition of tungsten, antimony, and tin.[41] By this time, the RFC had contracted to purchase the entire tungsten output of China, the largest producer in the world. In January 1941 it contracted to buy another $39.5

million worth of tin, which had to be flown out of China over the Himalayas after the closing of the Burma Road.[42]

Yet all of these efforts produced far less dramatic results than the administration had hoped for. The enormous sums spent on stockpiling produced relatively small growth in actual reserves because industrial demand was soaring. In mid-1940, one influential authority warned: "Despite our ambitious projects for stockpiling and our barter agreements with Great Britain, we have as yet accumulated very limited reserves of either rubber or tin. It is estimated that the present supplies of both commodities in this country would not last for more than three or four months at the normal rate of consumption. The extent of our anxieties in this direction is indicated by the fact that imports of rubber since the beginning of December, 1939 have been the heaviest in history."[43]

In mid-1941, Charles K. Leith, the government's top raw materials adviser, lamented that the stockpile program had been started "much too late for successful completion under present conditions." The greatly expanded demands of industry, the shortage of shipping, and the loss of some foreign sources of supply left industry and government stocks "far short of our objectives."[44] By December 7, 1941, the United States had accumulated only 116,000 tons of tin, or thirteen months of consumption, despite having several times that amount on order.[45] The rubber situation looked even worse. When Japan took Singapore in February 1942, cutting off over 90 percent of the world's supply of natural rubber, the United States had less than ten months' supply in the stockpile.[46] The government's stocks met only 24 percent of national objectives for tin, 30 percent for rubber, and 16 percent for chromium and manganese.[47]

These shortages caused more than minor hindrances to the war effort. The loss of rubber from Southeast Asia, Assistant Secretary of State Breckinridge Long noted in early 1942, "threatens to change our whole transportation life—and we all ride on rubber."[48] The Baruch Committee, appointed by President Roosevelt that year to report on the country's rubber needs, predicted dire results unless a crash program of synthetic rubber production, reclamation, and rationing were undertaken. Noting that "the demands now placed upon us are enormous," the committee warned that the nation's transportation systems could literally collapse if such an effort were not successful. But creating a huge synthetic rubber industry from a small base would not be easy. "Normally such a development would require a dozen years," the committee cautioned. "To compress it into less than two years is an almost superhuman task." Yet the "safety of our nation and the success of the Allied cause" depended on the outcome. "If we fail to secure quickly a large new rubber supply our war effort and our domestic economy both will collapse. Thus the rubber situation gives rise to our most critical problems."[49]

What had gone wrong? Much of the blame rested on the decision to begin stockpiling on a mass scale only in 1940. Bureaucratic foul-ups, foreign supply bottlenecks, and lack of shipping ensured that even a crash stockpiling program could not meet the administration's objectives.[50] The impossibly compressed timetable reflected the understandable difficulty decisionmakers had in foreseeing the direction, extent, and pace of Japan's ambitions. Only by 1940, when Japan started its southward advance in parallel with Nazi gains in Europe, did the urgency of protecting the United States' raw material supplies become widely apparent.

Even so, the administration might have acted earlier but for budget constraints. By 1938, the Roosevelt administration was nearly united in appreciating the need for a comprehensive program to accumulate strategic materials. The State, War, and Navy departments and the Bureau of Mines were all on board. But there was one crucial holdout: President Roosevelt. As Feis recalled, "When it came to formulating and attempting to put through a stockpile program . . . a stubborn obstacle was found to be the President's fiscal program. . . . [A]s the record of 1939 and 1940 shows, it repeatedly interposed to prevent the allotment of sufficient funds to meet even the minimum stockpile needs."[51] Roosevelt was committed to balancing the budget, and spending for stockpiles created few jobs. In 1939, against the wishes of his own departments, Roosevelt instructed Congress to drastically hold down stockpile appropriations, from $100 million for four years to only $10 million for one year. He finally compromised by allowing the higher appropriation but attaching strings to limit near-term spending.[52] Later that year, however, he changed his mind and asked for the full appropriation.[53] Once Germany overran France in May 1940, Roosevelt became a born-again stockpiler, complaining that newspaper columnists and "self-constituted experts" did not appreciate the great energy he was devoting to the cause.[54]

Congress, too, initially lagged in its appreciation of the problem. Despite expert assessments to the contrary, the common popular assumption until 1940 was that the United States was self-sufficient in basic materials. Government advocates of stockpiling programs met what one official evaluation later called "the deadweight of public complacency" until the "latent growing danger had suddenly become a clear threat to our existence."[55] As one trade journal observed in mid-1941, "the country is not yet alive to the meaning of an 'all-out' program of national defense. . . . The critical aspects of the situation filter all too slowly to the masses of the people and even to some segments of industry." The stockpile program was hardly unique in this respect, the journal acknowledged: "Shortages of everything plague Washington."[56]

By late 1941, when few authorities any longer doubted the critical link between the United States' economic health and military developments in the Far East, national leaders could only regret that they had not acted earlier. As Senator Alben Barkley of Kentucky observed in October 1941:

> Undoubtedly, we as a people have been short-sighted in the past, not only about manganese, copper, and chromium, and all those things which are now regarded as so indispensable, but we have been short-sighted as to steel, which we do produce in the United States, and we have been shortsighted as to aluminum, which we do produce in the United States. If, 10 or 20 years ago, we could have foreseen what we now know, I am satisfied that even if private

industry had not been willing or able to produce more than was being consumed currently, so as to create piles of stock against the day when they might be desperately needed, the Government of the United States would have taken some action toward that accomplishment. But it is just one of those situations in which everybody's business is nobody's business. Neither private industry nor the Government was farsighted enough to see that the time might come when we would be desperately in need of these things, and be in a terrifically great hurry, and resort to all sorts of expedients in order to get them.[57]

Congressional isolationists also impeded progress on stockpiling programs, believing that such programs—like rearmament—could be used by the administration as easily to promote intervention as to create a neutral Fortress America.[58] In the debate over the 1939 Strategic Materials Act, Congressman Leo Allen of Illinois acknowledged the seriousness of U.S. dependence on foreign raw materials but suggested that "this bill which provides for the piling up of war supplies will but further agitate our own, as well as foreign, nationals."[59] Congressman Charles Faddis of Pennsylvania, author of the bill and a "very good soldier" for the administration and for his state's steel interests, replied to Allen:

> It does not necessarily follow that we contemplate using these materials in war time, as far as their use in lethal weapons is concerned, but it is highly probable that the day may come when the world will be so torn with strife that it will be impossible for us to secure enough of these essential commodities to enable our industry to function even though we may not be engaged in any hostility ourselves.
>
> To illustrate: We are the largest consumer of tin in the world. . . . Every pound of this tin comes from abroad. The largest percentage of it comes from the Malay Straits. . . . We do not at the present time in the United States have one single smelter that could smelt tin ore, could we acquire the tin ore. We are the largest consumer of manganese in the world and annually consume in normal times in the neighborhood of 1,000,000 tons of

ferromanganese. Without manganese our steel industries could not function. We are also the world's largest consumer of chromium and tungsten. Without these materials our steel industry could not function. Prior to this time we have imported practically all of our chromium and tungsten as well as our manganese.[60]

Intense lobbying by domestic mining interests also undermined the cause of preparedness. Well-organized and vocal producers of low-grade domestic ore worked determinedly to convince Congress that U.S. security could best be maintained by exploiting their uneconomic deposits of strategic minerals rather than by expanding imports. These promises were generally fraudulent and were exposed as such even by the mining trade journals, but many members of Congress nonetheless respected the mining industry's political clout and voted against appropriations to import high-grade foreign ores. Leading the fight for the "exclusively domestic" policy were two powerful members of the House Committee on Military Affairs: Rep. James Serugham from the mining state of Nevada, and committee chairman Andrew May, president of the Greenbrier Mining Co. of Virginia, which bid on government contracts for manganese.[61]

Representative Faddis, irked by a decision of the appropriations committee to cut stockpile funding for fiscal year 1940, accused the committee of having "fallen victim to the same line of propaganda and the same lobbying activities of the American Manganese Producers' Association which has been evidenced in the past five years while this matter has been before Congress." Noting that the proposed $10 million appropriation would not purchase even half the manganese consumed in a year, "to say nothing whatever about tungsten, chromium, and a great many other of these essential commodities which we do not produce," Faddis carried the day and won back the full $100 million appropriation. But the manganese lobby kept fighting until Pearl Harbor.[62] It was no wonder the valuable element's reputation as "political metal no. 1" equalled its reputation as "critical metal no. 1."[63]

Despite apathy, isolationism, miserliness, and the power of special interests, Congress did rally in the last year of peace to support a strategic materials program to blunt the Japanese threat. On October 30, 1941, Senator Elbert Thomas, a Utah Democrat, reminded his colleagues of the high stakes:

> So long as the American people live on rubber and out of tin cans, the ship lines and the sources of rubber and tin will be vital to the American people, and the American people will see to it that nothing interferes with those lines. Everyone knows how great is our need for rubber and tin. . . . [Manganese and chromium] alone, the most essential for our whole defense effort in the making of steel, come in the main from areas that would be unsafe if we could not count on keeping shipping coming through the Indian Ocean. The minute the Japanese control the Malay Peninsula and the great protecting naval base that commands the Straits at Singapore, they will have control of the Indian Ocean. . . . [A]t any time that we are cut off from the Dutch East Indies and the Malay States, both of which the Japanese now threaten by the occupation of Indochina and of Siam . . . [Japan] would have a stranglehold at our very throats to use in whatever way she wanted. The whole automobile industry and many other industries dependent on rubber would have to skimp, and many people would be thrown out of employment in the industries dependent on automobiles. . . . The only way to protect our position in tin is to keep the sea lanes open to Singapore. Americans as a whole have not been aware of many other materials . . . that are in some ways even more vital to our industrial structure. . . . The present crisis has led us to the understanding of the importance of the Atlantic bases. I think it is time that we emphasize, too, the Pacific, which is even more important from the defense supply standpoint.[64]

Bureaucratic inefficiency contributed to the sluggish response to the crisis. Jurisdiction for the administration of economic defense measures was divided between the State, War, Navy, and Treasury departments, as well as the Reconstruction Finance Corporation and the vaguely defined Advisory Commission to the Council of National Defense. Because of Roosevelt's preoccupation with his reelection campaign, the rivalry and infighting of these agencies went unchecked through most of 1940. "The Administration has been too prone when difficult problems arose to easily dispose of them by creating another board, only to add to the confusion of the assortment of agencies we now have," the House Committee on Military Affairs complained. "We are now plagued with, and will continue, evidently, to be harassed because of the absence of a coherent organization."[65]

Personal conflicts also complicated matters. As Baruch observed in the case of rubber stockpiling, "the incompatibility of Jones and Ickes, each of whom had a voice in the rubber program, was legendary in Washington. But their private feuds . . . distracted energy and attention from the problem of getting rubber."[66] Production curbs by the rubber and tin cartels during the Depression further aggravated the administration's difficulties in accumulating adequate supplies. The authorities in charge of these schemes refused to raise their export quotas in the face of rising U.S. demand resulting both from industrial recovery and the stockpiling program.[67]

Tin restriction began in 1931, in the face of a Depression-induced collapse of world tin prices. World demand for the metal fell from 180,000 tons in 1929 to 140,000 tons in 1931; prices dropped two-thirds between 1927 and 1930. The unprecedented severity of the crisis foiled private efforts by the Tin Producers' Association, which represented mining firms in Malaya, the Netherlands East Indies, Bolivia, and Nigeria, to prop up prices. Soon the respective governments, whose revenues depended in part on tin sales, stepped in to promote production and control exports. An international committee composed of representatives from the major tin-producing countries was formed to create and police a worldwide tin cartel. The first international Tin Restriction Scheme took effect March 1, 1931.[68]

At the request of the Tin Producers' Association, the International Tin Committee ultimately reduced world production quotas to only a third of 1929 levels. The resultant scarcity of tin forced prices back up dramatically by June 1933 to a level

11 percent higher than 1929 prices. In contrast, the price of unrestricted metals such as copper and lead remained far below previous highs.[69]

Some of the price rise could be traced to growing U.S. demand for tin. U.S. industrial requirements rose from an annual rate of 41,000 tons at the end of 1932 to 60,000 tons at the end of 1933.[70] The scarcity and high price of tin outraged U.S. leaders. At the 1933 London Economic Conference, Secretary Hull announced his opposition to the cartel and asked for a new arrangement that would be more "equitable to the consuming countries." And the House Foreign Affairs Committee undertook its famous "Tin Investigation" to seek ways of countering foreign production controls. In response to mounting criticism, the International Tin Committee agreed to let one nonvoting representative from the United States attend its meetings. The action, of course, was purely symbolic; if anything, it only legitimized the "ruthless high-price policy" then being pursued by the committee. In 1935, for example, production quotas were still at only 40 percent of 1929 output. Prices remained much too high, world tin stocks declined, and trading and consuming interests protested even more vociferously but to no avail.[71]

The outbreak of World War II in Europe saw the beginning of frantic efforts by the consuming countries to purchase more tin. The International Tin Committee, recognizing the surge in wartime demand, attempted to increase production quotas, but it hopelessly complicated the situation by issuing a maze of complex regulations and quota instructions that mired producers and traders in red tape. Prices and output fluctuated wildly, and wartime dislocations caused large increases in the costs of production, shipping, and insurance, further hindering U.S. stockpiling efforts.[72]

In the beginning of 1940 Washington opened negotiations with the International Tin Committee in the hope of raising production quotas to allow the purchase of adequate tin supplies without sending prices skyward. The committee agreed on July 1, 1940, to raise its quotas, and the United States agreed to buy 75,000 tons of tin.[73] In 1941, the United States contracted for another 75,000 tons of tin, although the quota was larger than most producers could meet.[74] By September 1941, the U.S. had more than 400,000 tons of tin ore and concentrate on order. The following month, the Reconstruction Finance Corporation began building a large smelter in Texas City to give the United States the ability to refine low-grade tin ore from Bolivia when other sources were cut off.[75] However, the overall effect of these measures was inadequate: When the Japanese attacked Pearl Harbor, U.S. stockpiles held only 116,000 tons. New reserves simply could not keep up with rapidly rising wartime demand.[76]

Rubber cartel schemes posed similarly severe difficulties for U.S. economic defense planners. The International Rubber Restriction Agreement, accepted by all of the rubber-producing countries in Asia (representing 99 percent of the world's output), took effect on June 1, 1934, to end the disastrous price slump caused by the Depression. Prices, which had peaked at 25 pence in 1925, fell to an all-time low of 3 pence in 1931. As with the tin committee, the United States received only a token, nonvoting representative on the governing board of the rubber cartel, despite Hull's vain protests on behalf of the consuming nations.[77]

By 1936, world industrial production—and with it world demand for crude rubber—had reached new highs. But rubber shortages developed as the cartel severely limited available supplies. Stocks of crude rubber held by U.S. industries fell to less than six months' consumption. Export quotas still remained at only 75 percent of 1929–1932 levels.[78] With demand still rising, prices reached 26.6 cents per pound in 1937. The U.S. Department of Commerce complained, "The effect of . . . International Rubber Regulation thus far is in the direction of a reduced volume of international trade at an unreasonable price, when the world needs increased volume at a reasonable price."[79] But in the face of the 1937–1938 U.S. business recession, the cartel slashed export quotas to 45 percent of 1929–1932 levels by the third quarter of 1938. U.S. officials lodged vigorous protests, but the producers interpreted all demands for higher quotas and increased stockpiles simply as a desire to break the cartel.[80]

When the German armies marched into Poland in 1939, U.S. rubber stocks amounted to only 160,000 tons, adequate for only a few months. The outbreak of war in Europe alerted U.S. rubber manufacturers for the first time to their precarious position. They, along with speculators from other nations, deluged producing countries with orders for rubber and sent prices soaring.[81] The Roosevelt administration continued its fight to raise its export quotas, which remained as low as 75 percent in the last quarter of 1939. Little progress was made, however, because the rubber cartel feared the upsurge in demand would only last a short while. The State Department warned the British government that "any further delay in the accumulation of such stocks would be viewed with great concern in the light of the present world situation." Finally the cartel relented—and raised the quota cautiously to 80 percent.[82]

Jesse Jones and A. L. Viles, president of the Rubber Manufacturers Association, met with a representative of the British rubber interests in June 1940 to fight the delay in raising quotas. Although the cartel representative insisted that the maximum the United States would be allowed to purchase was 150,000 tons, Jones managed with great difficulty to raise the quota to 180,000 tons. The Dutch similarly balked at raising production but finally relented under U.S. pressure and accepted an 11 percent quota hike. After years of restriction, however, producers had great difficulty meeting even those limited increases.[83]

Supply shortages were compounded by rapidly accelerating civilian demand. Even though Jones spent $300 million to acquire a rubber stockpile of some 673,000 tons,[84] rising domestic consumption was wiping out many of his achievements: "Between the twenty-eighth day of June in 1940 and Pearl Harbor Day, we piled up in the United States, or had afloat, the largest stock of rubber that had ever been accumulated at any time in any country, but nothing like enough to feel comfortable. What we had brought in, however, was accomplished despite a shipping shortage and the slowness of the rubber people to ship rubber. Making the situation more uncomfortable were the increasing demands for rubber by American civilians for nondefense purposes—mostly automobile tires—reaching an all-time high rate in 1941 of more than 900,000 tons a year."[85]

Feis raved against the depletion of vital stockpiles for civilian purposes, and others in the State Department backed him up. Welles asked Roosevelt to instruct all relevant government agencies to act to preserve U.S. stockpiles, and Hull wrote the head of the Office of Price Administration, "If our imports are constantly consumed in current production and in a large measure by civilian use, as appears to be the case today with many commodities—such as chrome, manganese and rubber—our situation will remain as grave in the event of a war emergency as though we had never made an official effort to import supplies of these materials."[86] Competition for rubber supplies from the European powers seriously cut into the U.S. stockpiling program as well. The rush for rubber supplies was worldwide. The Soviet Union in particular, because of its low stockpiles, entered the market in 1941 to buy all the rubber it could. It was also a major competitor for scarce tin supplies.[87]

The shortage of available shipping further impeded the U.S. preparedness effort. When war broke out, the European countries recalled much of the merchant shipping normally available for the transportation of commercial raw materials from Southeast Asia to the East Coast of the United States. U.S. raw materials imports in 1941 were approximately double the quantity purchased in normal years of peace, placing a further strain on available ocean fleets. Writing in 1941, journalist I. F. Stone noted, "The shipping shortage intensified the raw material shortage, and at the end of the first year of defense the combination of the two shortages began to dispel illusions about our ability to live in independence of the rest of the world."[88]

Ships were diverted to the Pacific Coast in order to cut transportation delays (although this approach ultimately cost an extra $30 million to $50 million), and bottlenecks were patiently worked out at the West Coast ports. All available ships were diverted to the Far East to load up with raw materials, including commercial ships and army transports.[89] Jones later described the chain of events:

> In August [1941], anticipating possible hostilities with Japan, we had begun to hold weekly meetings in which the State Department, the RFC, the Maritime Commission, and two or three other agencies took part. The object was to speed up shipping from the Orient.
>
> Instead of bringing the Far Eastern tin and rubber and abaca to the Atlantic coast in the normal way, we decided to have it unloaded at our Pacific ports so the ships could make a quicker turn-around.
>
> At that time the transcontinental railways did not appear to have enough cars to handle promptly all freight that would be coming in at Pacific instead of Atlantic ports. We would have to hire storage space. Railroad rates from the west coast would make the cost of delivery to eastern industrial centers much higher than usual. . . .
>
> Beginning in 1940, and continuing as long as possible after the Japanese struck us, Admiral Emory Scott Land, Chairman of the United States Maritime Commission, and his chief of traffic, F. M. Darr, had actively sped along our program to obtain shipping space and even divert vessels from the regular runs in order to fetch all possible rubber and tin out of British Malaya and the Dutch East Indies, chromite and manganese ore from India and China, and Manila fiber and other strategic materials from the Philippines.[90]

Some noninterventionists actually cited this immense stockpiling effort as reason to believe that the United States could survive any economic blow caused by Japan's imminent occupation of Southeast Asia. Rep. Hamilton Fish of New York, for example, argued that Jones's successful efforts to buy up all surplus tin from Southeast Asia and Bolivia and the entire rubber supply of the Far East proved that the United States did not have to be "forced into a war in order to acquire these essential defense articles." He proclaimed on the floor of the House in late 1941, "it is not necessary for us to go into a rubber war . . . or a tin or a manganese or a nux vomica war."[91] But most authorities believed the effort had not met its goals. As one official history of raw materials later observed, "The United States had been caught once more in the position of the homeowner trying to take out fire insurance while a three-alarm blaze was raging in the next block."[92]

The administration knew the nation's limited stockpiles could not buffer the economy for long if Japan struck south. "Would a lack of rubber compel the United States to draw back from positions that otherwise seemed advisable? Or would it be compelled to accept an uncalculated risk that these positions might prove disastrous? At the end of 1940 the size of our rubber supplies stirred queries of this sort in the minds of both civilian and military officials concerned with our foreign policy." Thus did Herbert Feis describe the mounting desperation of U.S. leaders as they watched Japan advance towards Southeast Asia.[93]

In order to delay—or better yet, deter—such a Japanese thrust, administration officials bent every effort to achieve through diplomacy and all sanctions short of war what they could not achieve through stockpiling. They hoped to avoid war with Japan; Roosevelt and most of his advisers preferred to maintain the status quo in the Far East while they dealt with critical challenges in Europe and the Atlantic. To this end they engaged in tedious negotiations, appeased Japan by continuing shipments of oil and scrap metals, aided China to bog down Japanese troops, and finally, when all else had failed, embargoed Japan to punish its southward expansion. But when Japan continued on its aggressive course, the administration stood ready to fight.

3

The Emerging Threat
1940

> No nation, not even the United States, can find its livelihood entirely within its frontiers. Domestic supplies of essential materials may be conserved by export embargoes and by limiting consumption. Artificial substitutes may be found for those that are lacking. Materials which must be obtained abroad may be imported and stored for use in emergencies. But these emergency measures do not wholly eliminate the need for imports, while on the other hand they involve new restrictions against trade, new obstacles in the way of free access to world supplies of raw materials. Thus these restrictions intensify the struggle for control over world markets and raw-material sources and result in further frictions, discriminations, and retaliations and in the increasing aggravation of international relations.
> *Assistant Secretary of State Henry Francis Grady, January 25, 1940*

By 1940, Americans were a deeply troubled people. Millions still suffered from unemployment and poverty as much of the promise of the New Deal went unrealized. Worse yet, the United States now faced a challenge even more frightening than the Depression—the threat of a new world war encompassing Europe, Africa, and Asia.

In Asia, the United States was embroiled for reasons that extended far into the past. Americans had traded with China since

1784 and won most-favored-nation rights in 1844. By the time of the Spanish-American War, the U.S. government had become actively involved in advancing the interests of U.S. businessmen and missionaries in China. Secretary of State John Hay's famous Open Door notes of 1899 and 1900 set a precedent for future U.S. policy in the Far East. Signed by the major powers interested in China, these documents sought to assure the United States equal access to the China market without resort to war.

Japan began to emerge as a major regional power in its own right around that time. It defeated China in the Sino-Japanese War of 1894–1895, then dealt Russia a devastating blow in 1905. The United States welcomed Japan's rise as a counterweight to Russian influence in the Far East, but soon Japanese and U.S. interests began heading on a potential collision course. Japan took advantage of the outbreak of World War I to grab a foothold in China. It seized German concessions in China and ultimately issued a list of twenty-one demands on China itself. The Wilson administration fiercely opposed Japan's efforts to nullify the Open Door policy. Some members of the administration—including Franklin Roosevelt, assistant secretary of the navy—actually talked of war.[1]

Japan had complaints of its own against the United States. Its "defeat" at the 1921–1922 Washington Naval Disarmament Conference, which established the 5:5:3 naval ratio for the United States, Britain, and Japan, confirmed Japanese suspicions that the West still relegated it to second-class status. U.S. restrictions against Japanese immigration further wounded Japan's pride.

These were normal frictions between proud and ambitious nations, however, not harbingers of war. Even as it elbowed its way into their club, Japan was generally careful to play by the rules of other industrial powers, embracing the standards of parliamentary democracy, international treaties, and diplomatic protocol that earned it the respect of more established powers. At home, politics in Japan during the 1920s were, if anything, trending in a democratic, antimilitary direction.[2]

Then the Great Depression struck. Already weakened by a financial panic in 1927, Japan was shaken by the implosion of the world economy after 1930. As unemployment grew in the cities and crop failures hit the countryside, urban and rural labor riots broke out. In the midst of this economic ferment, violent right-wing and ultranationalist groups flourished, emasculating parliamentary government and strengthening extremist cliques within the armed forces that demanded a militant foreign policy.

The extremists struck first in Manchuria. The Kwantung Army created a minor incident on the South Manchurian Railway in September 1931 in order to justify invading the coveted region. With overwhelming force, Japan's troops conquered the territory by early 1932 and transformed it into the puppet state of "Manchukuo." A pattern was set of military adventurism and civilian submission to the army's faits accomplis.

The United States condemned Japan's aggression as a violation of international law and a direct challenge to Western interests in China. When Japan paid no heed, then Secretary of State Henry Stimson announced that the United States would refuse to accept any alteration of the status quo by means of force and would continue to uphold the principle of the Open Door—a message designed less to intimidate Japan than to protect "the material interests of America and her people" in China.[3] President Hoover vetoed Stimson's idea of imposing economic sanctions against Japan as too risky. U.S. interests in Manchuria, he argued, were not worth fighting to save.[4]

Neither Japan nor the United States allowed the tensions generated in this period to ease. Japan pulled out of the League of Nations in 1933 and the Washington Naval Disarmament Treaty in 1934, further isolating itself. The breakdown of the London Naval Disarmament Conference of 1935–1936 highlighted its growing differences with the Anglo-Saxon powers. Britain and the United States insisted on large navies to defend their coasts and possessions and pushed for naval ratios disadvantageous to Japan. The West thus reinforced Japan's view that it could not through peaceful means win recognition as a first-rate power.[5] Japan's ominous response to its growing isolation was to edge closer to Nazi Germany in 1936 with the signing of the Anti-Comintern Pact.[6]

Japan's sense of isolation was compounded by commercial restrictions and boycotts that met its trade offensives in China and Southeast Asia in the early 1930s. Japan, an island nation with few resources and a growing population, sought to overcome its vulnerability to foreign economic pressures by forcefully expanding its economic sphere and "living space." The promotion of pan-Asianist and anti-Western ideology among ultranationalist groups provided the rationale. Beginning in the summer of 1937, Japan turned its military operations southward into China, ultimately announcing its intention to crush all resistance throughout the country. And on November 3, 1938, the government of Prime Minister Konoe Fumimaro announced Japan's intent to create a "New Order in East Asia."

The United States refused to acquiesce silently in Japan's attempt to push Western powers out of China. At stake was a large potential market for U.S. goods, substantial philanthropic interests, and more general principles of international conduct. All these contributed to Washington's diplomatic stand against Japan. However, despite hundreds of Japanese depredations against U.S. property and interests in China, the Roosevelt government did little but protest. A committee of experts within the State Department, convened in late 1938 to study possible responses to Japan's aggression, concluded that none of the nation's interests in China was important enough to justify a campaign of retaliation that could "involve serious risk of armed conflict."[7] Outside of small loans to China and Roosevelt's call for a "moral embargo" on weapons sales to aggressor nations like Japan, the administration made no substantive attempts to rescue China. By its inaction, the administration made its position clear: The United States would not fight to save China.

The public was not eager to reverse that position. Americans faced too many problems at home to welcome a bloody struggle for marginal interests in China. A September 1937 poll showed that 54 percent of the American people preferred to withdraw troops protecting U.S. citizens in China rather than risk an incident. When people were asked about which country, Japan or China, they sympathized with, 55 percent responded "neither." By February 1938, almost two-thirds of the public still opposed allowing shipments of arms or ammunition to China. As late as June 1939, only 6 percent were willing to go to war to protect U.S. interests in China.[8]

If the plight of Chinese peasants and American missionaries was not enough to sway the public further, neither were the interests of American business enough to sway Washington. If anything, U.S. trade with Japan was much more significant than that with China. China absorbed less than 3 percent of all U.S. exports, a share that failed to grow during the 1930s; Japan's share, by contrast, jumped from 4.9 percent in 1929 to 8.6 percent in 1937.[9] Japan, in fact, was the United States' third best customer, behind only Great Britain and Canada.

Nor was China a significant haven for U.S. investment. Private U.S. long-term investment in China was only a third as great as that in Japan and less even than that in the Philippines.[10] As one critic of intervention noted, "the total is less than the cost of two battleships," and "only a few days of war in the Pacific would cost more than a generation of profit on our China investment."[11] Indeed, the entire Far East accounted for only about 6 percent of total U.S. investments abroad.[12]

Given the relative paltriness of these stakes, few businessmen clamored for hostile action against Japan. Most businessmen feared the destabilizing effects of war and hoped that diplomacy would secure needed markets without recourse to armed conflict. Between 1935 and 1940 most exporters firmly opposed sanctions against the island nation.[13] Even those involved predominantly in trade with China opposed a U.S. embargo against Japan as late as 1940.[14] One commentator, influential Far East expert Tyler Dennett, even maintained that American business might prosper more in China if the Japanese won the war. "If Japan has her way in China," Dennett explained in *Foreign Affairs*, "she will be in the market for many years to come for capital goods, for raw materials, and for loans.... If Japan can secure capital, create order and develop Chinese resources, the market will blossom like a rose. Japan might become rich by the new trade, and so might some Americans. Extraterritoriality would go, but it is already on its way out."[15]

U.S. business journals and organized trade groups echoed all of these concerns. "Fortunately for us," the *Wall Street Journal* wrote in mid-1937, "our relations with China are less important to us than our relations with Japan." Delegates to the National Foreign Trade Convention later that year denounced government threats to invoke the Neutrality Act and place controls on war exports to Japan. The U.S. Chamber of Commerce warned in 1938, "A proposal to break off an important trade connection suggests resentment rather than mature reflection; if an embargo is declared on Japanese goods, American industry will suffer." Most businessmen could only scoff at the notion of respecting a voluntary "moral embargo" on sales that could help Japan's war effort. As one oil company executive declared with impeccable logic, "If we don't sell to Japan, the British and Dutch will."[16] As late as 1940, a poll by *Fortune* magazine found that only 19 percent of important businessmen favored intervening in the Pacific to stop Japan.[17]

But attitudes were changing as Japan's ambitions grew. Peter Hoffer notes that the Japanese drive into Southeast Asia beginning in 1940 brought the war into "a new and ominous stage" that "all but snuffed out any hope of commercial amity between the United States and the Japanese Empire. With the threat of war becoming more real each day, businessmen were compelled to reassess their attitude towards Japan." By late 1941, Hoffer concludes, "[t]he Japanese appeared to most businessmen as a substantial threat to American interests in the Pacific. . . . Businessmen's magazines which had been friendly to Japanese economic aspirations were now sufficiently apprehensive of Japanese military movements to perceive that 'new and ominous decisions are being made in Japan.' Japanese occupation of Indo-China moved one business journal to exclaim: 'Japan has thrust a dagger into the Allied stronghold of southeast Asia.' In the months before December 1941, business newspapers decried Japanese 'duplicity'; the commercial journals were now prepared for war."[18]

Japan's First Probes to the South

With most of its military resources tied down in China, Japan waited long before making the critical decision to move south and risk a conflict with the Western colonial powers. It had no detailed plan or timetable of expansion, following instead a path of least resistance as opportunities and challenges arose. Even its direction was uncertain. The Japanese Army always looked north, viewing the Soviet Union as its main threat. Along the Manchukuo-Soviet-Mongolian frontier, it engaged in frequent skirmishes with the Red Army after 1934. These escalated into a multidivision-sized clash at Changkufeng (or Lake Khasan), just over the border in Siberia, in July–August 1938. In the summer of 1939, units of the Japanese Army pushed into Soviet-occupied Outer Mongolia, chafing to test their adversary. But in a stunning defeat at Nomonhan–Khalkin Gol that August, the Japanese suffered more than 50,000 casualties.[19]

Japan's fearful setback, followed shortly by the Hitler-Stalin pact, dashed the army's plans of expansion to the north. However, with the fall of France and the Low Countries in 1940, the prospect of a southward advance against their colonies became an enticing alternative. Unable to read Japan's intentions or appreciate its internal debates, U.S. leaders tended to assume the worst. Years of frustration with Japanese expansion taught administration officials to eye all of Tokyo's moves and pronouncements with suspicion.

Although U.S. officials had long fretted over Japan's intentions toward the Western possessions in Southeast Asia, not until 1939 did Japan's probes to the south provoke close scrutiny. On February 10, Japan invaded and occupied the island of Hainan, claimed by France and only 125 miles from the port of Haiphong in Indochina.[20] In response to French protests, Japanese Foreign Minister Arita Hachirō announced that Japan had no intention of annexing Hainan or threatening Indochina; Japan's sole intention, he said, was to tighten its blockade around China. Remarked Hull, "We received this with lively skepticism"—and with good reason.[21] A famous Japanese naval authority had already mapped out the strategy: "If Japan will construct a naval base in the port of Yulin in Hainan Island, and concentrate a powerful naval force in that vicinity, she can thus reduce the military value of Hongkong, cut off the French navy from Saigon, and dominate the sea route of an American expeditionary force. The sea power in the South Seas will thus fall into the hands of Japan. Japan will thus become the master of the South Seas."[22] Only three days after the Japanese seized the island, the semiofficial newspaper *Asahi* editorialized, "The French, British and American territories are now within our reach, and we have now almost all the South Seas in our hands."[23]

On March 31, Japan occupied another area claimed by France, the strategically located Spratley Islands in the South China Sea. "With Hainan, the Spratley group dominated the route between Hongkong and Singapore, placed Japan within reach of the Netherlands Indies and further blocked the southern approach to the Japanese empire," one contemporary analyst noted.[24] Already, in the eyes of some U.S. leaders, "the outlines of Japan's expansionist ideas were becoming ever clearer."[25]

When the United States expressed its disapproval of Japan's apparent violations of international law in seizing French property, Arita hastened to allay fears that "Japan entertained some territorial designs toward the South Seas."[26] His attempts were in vain. During mid-April, despite rising tension in Europe, Roosevelt ordered the fleet from the Atlantic back into the Pacific. His order clearly signaled his concern over Japanese expansionism.[27]

Already administration leaders and influential news commentators framed the problem of Japan's southward expansion in terms of raw materials. In early 1939, when the Navy was seeking funds from Congress to build new naval bases in the Pacific as a barrier against Japan, Adm. William Leahy testified that fortification of Guam was needed to protect tin, rubber, and tungsten trade routes from the Netherlands East Indies.[28] The distinguished columnist Walter Lippmann warned of a Japanese "stranglehold on the supply of rubber if it were allowed to command the maritime highways over which the United States receives rubber and other necessary materials."[29] The *Washington Evening Star* editorialized in favor of fortifying Guam to protect "our lines of communication for strategic war materials from the East Indies."[30] Ultimately, however, Congress defeated appropriations for the Guam base to avoid provoking Japan.

The issue of Japan's threat to the United States' strategic materials sources was kept alive within the State Department by an extraordinary dispatch from Erle Dickover, American consul general in Batavia, capital of the Netherlands East Indies. Distributed throughout the State Department and to various intelligence agencies, Dickover's report on the "Protection of Sources in the Pacific Area of Essential Raw Materials" won a high rating from his superiors. Citing numerous statistics to prove his point, he wrote:

> It appears to be becoming increasingly realized in the United States that our industries and our economic organization are dependent to a remarkable degree on raw materials originating in Malaysia. Should the war and the interruption of supplies continue more than a year, the lack of adequate supplies of rubber alone would throw our whole industrial and economic organization into chaos.... To lay in adequate reserve stocks of all these essential materials would require an immense amount of money. It would appear, therefore, that it would be most difficult and expensive to endeavor to build up and maintain stocks of tropical products sufficient to keep our industries running on a normal basis for any extended period of time.

Proposals to fall back on Latin America ignored the fact that rubber trees take years to grow and that U.S. facilities were not suited to refining low-grade Bolivian tin. Citing the Japanese seizure of Hainan as evidence that "the Japanese Navy is preparing for military action in these seas in connection with its 'southward advance' policy," Dickover declared that "the United States [should] take immediate steps to protect its trade interests in and trade routes to this part of the world." Congressional isolationists and Britain-haters would no doubt object to a defense of Southeast Asia, he acknowledged. But they would have to be convinced that "as a purely business proposition," looking at the question "from a cold-blooded, common-sense point of view, and discarding all sentiment and idealism," the United States had no choice but to stand firm and "protect its sources of supply in Malaysia from the threatened aggression by one or more of the totalitarian states."[31]

Secretary Hull and Undersecretary Sumner Welles conferred on the afternoon of June 26, 1939, to discuss the general state of world affairs. Both were convinced that Germany would soon move in Europe. Therefore, they agreed that "the best thing to be done was to try to keep the Japanese out of it" and tentatively decided to relocate the fleet at Pearl Harbor.[32] (There was a precedent for such action: In February 1932, the Hoover administration moved the fleet to Hawaii to prevent an "outbreak southward" by Japanese forces.[33]) That fall, Admiral Stark, chief of naval operations, finally received permission from Roosevelt and the State Department to move a naval detachment from the West Coast to Hawaii. The ships were transferred in October.[34] The purpose was explicitly to influence and moderate Japanese foreign policy.[35]

The Japanese, however, only escalated their pressure on the European positions in China and fed their press a series of jingoistic threats against the Western colonial position in Southeast Asia. So in February 1940, when the Army and Navy Joint Board evaluated the strategic situation in the Pacific, a southward advance by Japan looked possible, even probable. "Japanese control of the Dutch East Indies would involve 90% of the U.S. rubber and tin supply," the analysts noted bleakly. With England and France bogged down in Europe, "the United States is the one nation in a position to supply any deterrent." The Joint Board members concluded that the United States should send naval rein-

64 The Emerging Threat

forcements to Hawaii and investigate "increasing the army air component and naval aviation strength in the Philippines as an additional deterrent to further Japanese expansion plans."[36]

Hoping to intimidate the Japanese or at least to cool their ardor, the administration decided in early 1940 to hold annual fleet maneuvers off Hawaii. Admiral J. O. Richardson, commander of the Pacific Fleet, moved ships from West Coast bases to Pearl Harbor. Meanwhile, he requested from his superiors further details on the U.S. diplomatic situation with Japan, the better to evaluate his military challenge. "I believe the situation in the Far East is continually deteriorating so far as our relations with Japan are concerned," Stark wrote Richardson on April 8, two days before the latter reached Hawaii. "I think you should continually keep uppermost in your mind the possibility of trouble in the Orient and the means to meet it."[37]

Scramble for the Indies

German victories in Europe in the spring of 1940 emboldened Japanese military leaders, who saw opportunities to profit from the distress of colonial powers in Southeast Asia. On April 12, powerful section chiefs within the Japanese Navy General Staff declared that "the time has come to occupy the Dutch East Indies." Plans were actually laid to send the Japanese Fourth Fleet south, but fear of a U.S. reprisal embargo on petroleum products held the navy back.[38] But the Foreign Ministry and its press allies showed little rhetorical restraint. On April 13 and 14, editorials in the Japanese press expressed the country's "concern" for the Indies resulting from the German invasion of the Netherlands.[39] Then, on April 15, Foreign Minister Arita startled reporters at an official press conference when he declared that all of Southeast Asia was "economically bound [to Japan] by an intimate relationship of mutuality in ministering to one another's needs." Should the European war extend to the Indies, he continued, the peace and stability of the South Seas, a region of vital importance to Japan, would be threatened. "In view of these considerations," he concluded, "the Japanese

Government cannot but be deeply concerned over any development accompanying an aggravation of the war in Europe that may affect the status quo of the Netherlands East Indies."[40]

As Hugh Byas pointed out in the *New York Times*, this statement, taken at face value, merely echoed long-standing U.S. policy. "By basing his action on Japan's concern for peace and stability in the Pacific," he observed, "Mr. Arita has taken a ground that other nations can share." But he sensed the unspoken view held by many in the capital: "It is admitted that while Americans do not talk of 'lifelines' in other nations and territories the United States also has important economic interests in Netherlands India."[41]

Soon after the State Department heard Arita's message, Hull called in Assistant Secretary of State Breckinridge Long for a "private chat." They discussed the strategic significance of the Netherlands East Indies and agreed the United States could not overlook any threat by Japan, however veiled, to change its status: "Japan has given every indication that she will resent British or American occupation of the Dutch East Indies in case the Netherlands is attacked by Germany and has left the intimation that she would occupy the islands. Almost all of our tin and most of our rubber come from there. The trade routes of the United States would be crippled, and industry in America would be most importantly affected by the occupation of those islands by Japan. The Secretary has in mind to do something to prevent it."[42]

On April 17, two days after Arita's statement, with Feis privately hammering on the extreme precariousness of the United States' rubber supplies,[43] the secretary of state responded directly and forcefully in a public announcement. As he had in private, Hull stressed the importance of Southeast Asian raw materials to the U.S. national interest:

> Any change in the status of the Netherlands Indies would directly affect the interests of many countries.
> The Netherlands Indies are very important in the international relationships of the whole Pacific Ocean. . . .

> They produce considerable portions of the world's supplies of important essential commodities such as rubber, tin, quinine, copra, et cetera. Many countries, including the United States, depend substantially upon them for some of these commodities.
>
> Intervention in the domestic affairs of the Netherlands Indies or any alteration of their status quo by other than peaceful processes would be prejudicial to the cause of stability, peace, and security not only in the region of the Netherlands Indies but in the entire Pacific area.[44]

Hull's reply laid the diplomatic basis for future U.S. policy toward the Japanese threat to Southeast Asia.[45]

The interventionist press similarly played up the issue of the Indies' raw materials. The *Washington Star* warned on April 17 that "Japan appears to be paving the way for her own protectorate in the Dutch islands," adding, "The raw materials of these islands are important to the United States, and this country could not look with approval on a wider Japanese monopoly of the products of the Far East." A *Washington Post* editorial the same day declared that the United States' "supply of essential raw materials, notably rubber and tin, might be cut off were the Dutch East Indies to be occupied by a nation with a military and economic policy like that of Japan." The *New York Times* editorialized on April 19: "Riding the Equator east and west for three thousand miles, a distance as great as the whole span of the United States itself, the Netherlands Indies support a population of sixty million and produce commodities—oil, tin, and rubber—which the modern world cannot do without. They are an empire in themselves, and no Pacific Power can be indifferent to their future."[46]

Hull's warning to Japan provoked an immediate world reaction. The Japanese press reacted with shock and anger, but President Roosevelt backed up Hull, lending further official weight to his statement. And the British and French authorities announced preparations to defend the Indies against a Japanese invasion.[47] Within the administration, anxieties were running high at the Department of Commerce as well as at State. Secretary of Commerce Harry Hopkins called a hurried conference of department officials to discuss the economic implications of a possible Japanese invasion of the Dutch East Indies, which led to the issuance of a timely public report on the vital raw material riches of the Netherlands East Indies.⁴⁸ Hopkins later called a meeting with the Business Advisory Council, made up of captains of industry, which called "in the strongest terms at its command" for a massive expansion of the stockpile program.⁴⁹

Prompted by the flap over Arita's remarks, Feis and the other members of the Interdepartmental Committee on Strategic Materials formally presented Hull with a tough memorandum on the need to speed up the stockpiling of materials acquired from the Far East, such as rubber, tin, and quinine. If war broke out, they warned, "supplies of all three materials would be pitifully inadequate." Feis later explained, "The headlines of the past fortnight had impressed many hitherto unperturbed figures. Overnight the appeal of the [stockpiling] enthusiasts received the magical support of authority. The Acting Secretary of State [Welles] on May 1 sent the ... memorandum to the White House with an urgent recommendation that a comprehensive program for accumulation of strategic and critical materials be undertaken at once."⁵⁰

Roosevelt, smarting politically from attacks in the press, the business community, and his own administration over the slow progress of the stockpiling program, tried to paint a less dire picture of the situation. On May 23, he told members of the Business Advisory Council that U.S. rubber stockpiles would allow six to eight months for the creation of a synthetic rubber industry. "Now, I am told that that is a practical thing. . . . That synthetic rubber, as we know, does cost more, but the damn thing works." The United States could also put its low-grade manganese mines to work to replace lost foreign supplies, albeit at greater expense. And should tin shipments from Singapore be cut off, "we will still have something to fall back on and that is the Bolivian mine. . . . If we are cut off from that by water, we have got to do two things: We have got to do what the Germans did, which is go around the country and collect all the old tin we can find. . . . Furthermore, with the help of the metallurgists, we have got to try to use 'ersatz' stuff as the Germans are doing: in other words, other metals as substitutes for tin."[51]

But such German techniques were the desperate measures of a command economy at war. The administration was united in striving to forgo them at home by deterring Japan if possible. Still smarting from Arita's interest in the fate of the Netherlands East Indies, the administration decided to show the flag more prominently in the Pacific. Already, in the course of a year, the fleet had been moved from the Atlantic to a base almost 2,500 miles into the Pacific. Now the fleet began a series of extensive maneuvers off the Hawaiian coast involving 140 ships, 500 planes, and thousands of seamen.[52] The Japanese were duly impressed.[53] Then, in order to emphasize the point, Roosevelt ordered a delay in the scheduled departure of the fleet from Pearl Harbor. On May 7 Admiral Richardson received his orders from Stark to postpone departure for two weeks.[54] The same day, Stark wrote Richardson a letter with the latest word from Roosevelt: "When the Fleet returns to the Coast (and I trust the delay will not be over two weeks, but I cannot tell) the President has asked the Fleet schedule be so arranged that on extremely short notice the Fleet be able to return concentrated to Hawaiian waters."[55] The Navy Department, meanwhile, issued a bland press release to the effect that the fleet would remain in Hawaii indefinitely to "carry out further tactical exercises."[56]

Admiral Richardson complained that from a purely military point of view, the fleet should be moved back to the West Coast, where better docking, supply, repair, and recreation facilities were available. But Admiral Stark quickly informed him that when the decision to retain the fleet at Pearl Harbor was made, "it looked as if . . . a serious situation might develop in the East Indies, and that there was a possibility of our being involved."[57] The same day, May 22, Richardson wrote to ask why his ships could not return to the mainland, now that the threat seemed to have subsided. "You are there because of the deterrent effect which it is thought your presence may have on the Japs going into the East Indies," Stark replied on May 27. "We believe that both Germany and the Italians have told the Japs that so far as they are concerned she, Japan, has a free hand in the Dutch East Indies."[58]

High-ranking U.S. officials hoped that by presenting a show of strength against further expansion by Japan to the south, war could be avoided. By the same token, however, war might result if deterrence failed. The U.S. ambassador in Tokyo, Joseph Grew, reported to Hull on May 14 that he believed Japan's prime minister and foreign minister were "not deluded by theories of American restraint" in the event of a Japanese occupation of the Indies.[59] Not ready to take any chances, Secretary Hull spoke with the Japanese ambassador two days later in order to condemn any threat to the status quo in the Netherlands East Indies. He was distressed that Japan, already at war with China, "would not be content unless it extended itself three thousand miles beyond to modestly take in the great archipelago comprising the East Indies presumably with a view of shutting out all equality of trade opportunities among nations." Hull later declared, "If we had not adopted a firm attitude from the very outset . . . Japan might well have made a decisive move toward the East Indies in the summer of 1940."[60]

In the face of such opposition, Japanese leaders held themselves to pointed rhetoric. On May 29 the minister of overseas affairs, Gen. Koiso Kuniaki, maintained that the "South Seas regions are very important in conjunction with the further expansion of Japan's economic strength. . . . In the light of the progress of the China affair and the increasingly tense international situation caused by the second European war, careful and appropriate measures are required for the execution of Japan's South Seas development policy."[61] On June 3, Foreign Minister Arita spoke before the Pacific Society, an expansionist-oriented Japanese association. Grew summarized his speech for Hull: "Fundamental policy of Japanese Empire based upon mission as stabilizing force East Asia. Obviously Japan concerned not only with China continent but also with South Seas areas. . . . Japan has deep concern not only for political status Netherlands

East Indies but also for economic resources, trade, industry and development those islands. Can nations avoid conflict friction when there exist tariff walls, immigration restriction, other barriers preventing smooth interchange of goods between nations which are complementary in economic sense."[62]

Grew would not let the issue drop. On June 10, he told Arita that Japan's desire to see trade barriers eliminated was indeed admirable but that "if the Japanese Government could associate itself with the American Government in bringing about a free flow of commodities between nations, substantial progress might be made toward removing the causes of unrest, reflected in the conflicts both in Europe and in the Far East." Grew expounded at length on "the unsoundness of economic blocs and of the creation of barriers to trade, devices which can never constitute a permanent basis for a progressive world economy."[63] Arita, of course, had heard such theories expressed innumerable times in the speeches of Cordell Hull.

As the position of the Western colonial powers deteriorated in Europe, it became increasingly clear to members of the administration that Japan could not be restrained by words alone. In response to this growing menace, the State Department's political adviser, Stanley Hornbeck, and his assistant Alger Hiss prepared a series of memoranda—the most extensive of their kind to that time—on the nature of U.S. interests in the Far East.[64] These analyses, prepared in mid-June, were distributed to such top officials as Cordell Hull, Sumner Welles, and Assistant Secretary Adolf Berle. They demonstrated a deep, almost obsessive interest in strategic materials.

In their first report the two experts addressed "The Importance of the Far East as a Market for American Products." Whereas future trade prospects in Europe could "not be considered bright" and opportunities in Latin America were similarly limited, Asia was another matter altogether—but as a source of raw materials, not as a market.

> From the standpoint of world trade, the area of east Asia and Oceania is of tremendous importance. It supplies most of the world's *tin, crude rubber, silk, jute, copra, and tea*....

In addition to being the major source of raw materials consumed in large volume by the United States and other industrial nations, the Far East is the major source of other equally necessary products which are required in smaller volume. The Far East has a complete monopoly of the production of *manila fiber* and a practical monopoly of *quinine;* it produces the bulk of the world's output of *tungsten;* and normally supplies half or more of the world's output of *antimony.* It is also an important source of *mica* and *spices.* Its *wool, sugar* and *tobacco* enter largely into world trade and in regard to such commodities as *rice,* petroleum, butter, cheese, cotton, chrome ore, silver, and even coal, iron ore, nickel, aluminum and *manganese,* the important volume of the Far Eastern production offers additional supplies for the world market.

Hornbeck and Hiss concluded that "many of our most important raw material import desiderata are to be found in commercial quantities only in the Far East."[65]

The next analysis, produced by Hornbeck on June 15, consisted of "Brief Notes on the Economic and Strategic Importance of the Dutch East Indies and Adjacent Regions." He began, "It is difficult to overestimate the economic importance, particularly to the United States, of South and East Asia and Oceania." Once again he ran down the laundry list of irreplaceable raw materials for which the region was "today practically the sole source of world supplies." Finally Hornbeck summed up the strategic implications:

Were the Dutch East Indies or French Indochina to be occupied by any major power hostile to Great Britain, the threat to Singapore and hence to the Malay States, to Thailand (Siam) and to Burma would be most serious. . . . Australia and New Zealand would be menaced and, in general, the availability to the British of the vital resources of the entire region of the western Pacific and southern Asia would be definitely lessened. . . .

Were the Dutch East Indies or French Indochina to be occupied by any major power hostile to the United States, our position in the Philippines would be threatened. In addition, and ultimately of far more importance to our national well-being, our access to the tin, the rubber, the vegetable oils and other indispensable resources of the entire western Pacific area would be jeopardized.[66]

Hornbeck's final memorandum, an examination of the "Economic and Strategic Importance of the Far Eastern Area," simply reprinted an article by the distinguished geographer and Far East expert Robert Burnett Hall in the April 1940 *Geographical Review* on "American Raw Material Deficiencies and Regional Dependence." Hornbeck called it "the most interesting, incisive and concise exposition that I have seen anywhere of the tremendous economic importance, especially to the United States, of the Far Eastern area." The article declared:

> By "a pyramidal error of geography" the United States finds itself so vitally and overwhelmingly dependent on southeastern Asia that our entire foreign policy must be adjusted to that fact. . . . It is not an exaggeration to say that the United States would be compelled, for its existence as a major industrial state, to wage war against any power or powers that might threaten to sever our trade lines with this part of the world. . . . Only on the lands west of the Pacific, and especially on southeastern Asia, is our dependence so vital and complete that our very existence as a great industrial power, and perhaps even as an independent state, is threatened if the sources should be cut off.[67]

Hornbeck's emphatic and detailed analyses of U.S. interests in the Pacific could hardly have failed to influence Hull's thinking. As the secretary's political adviser, with years of experience and unquestioned expertise on the Far East, Hornbeck exercised great influence in the department, even if Hull occasionally had disagreements with him over tactics.[68] And Hornbeck was writing to the converted: Hull and Welles had already displayed personal great concern over precisely the issues that Hornbeck stressed—U.S. dependence on Southeast Asia's raw materials.

Meanwhile, the administration's worst fears were being realized, as German successes in Europe incited Japanese leaders to press into the heart of Western colonial power in Asia. On June 17 Japan took its first major step toward dominating French Indochina. Suing for peace after their defeat by the German Army, French authorities were in no position to resist Japanese demands. Japan threatened to "wean Indo-China away from hostility to Japan" unless the French halted all supply shipments to China along the strategic Yunnan-Indochina railroad. And while the Japanese Army maneuvered near the Indochina border, Japan's vice minister for foreign affairs insisted that his nation be allowed to station observers along the railroad to ensure that all military traffic did stop. The French were forced to accept these conditions. On June 20 they announced an agreement allowing the Japanese free rein in southern China (formerly influenced by the French) and a measure of control in Indochina.[69]

The rapidity of Japan's moves left the United States in a weak position. Hull instructed Ambassador Grew simply to inform Arita, through an exchange of notes, that the United States desired to come to an understanding with Japan as to the future of the South Pacific. "In the proposed notes," he told Grew, "there would be expressed the agreement between the Government of the United States and the Japanese Government that they have a common desire that the status quo, except as it may be modified by peaceful means, be maintained with regard to the possession and territories of belligerent European powers in the Pacific area." He stressed to Grew that such an agreement would be "intended as a preventive rather than a curative measure."[70] Clearly, Hull wanted to buy time for the United States and keep Japan out of Southeast Asia as long as possible.

But the Japanese government did not bite.[71] Instead, War Minister Hata Shunroku declared to his staff on June 25, "We must not indulge in pedantic words and miss this rare opportunity. Every action must be based on the great spirit of the Imperial Way and, if necessary, Japan must act drastically against the Powers who obstruct our policy."[72] In a June 29 radio broadcast, Arita said: "Japan, while carrying on vigorously her task of constructing a new order in East Asia, is paying serious attention to developments in the European war and to its repercussions in the various quarters of East Asia, including the South Seas region. I desire to declare that the destiny of these regions in any development therein, and any disposal thereto, is a matter for grave concern to Japan in view of her mission and responsibility as the stabilizing force in East Asia."[73]

Hornbeck, citing these events, characteristically insisted that "nothing short of or less than the language of force, either military or economic or both, will exercise effectively restraining influence upon Japan's present leadership."[74] Impressed by his adviser's fighting mood, as well as Japan's aggressive rhetoric, Hull was reluctant to humor the Japanese further in return for a paper agreement to respect the status quo. Thus, when British Ambassador Lord Lothian came to the secretary on June 27 to propose a compromise by which the United States would offer economic assistance and other concessions to Japan in return for an agreement to stabilize the situation in Southeast Asia, Hull refused. He saw no reason to trust the Japanese. Tokyo, he believed, was simply biding its time, seeking to exploit any signs of Western weakness to expand further. Offering concessions to Japan, Hull believed, would only encourage its militarism.[75]

Hull and other Washington policymakers did not know it, but in late June the Japanese Army was busy making its first formal commitment to an aggressive southward advance. At a series of general staff and division chief conferences prompted by Hitler's rapid march through France and the Low Countries, Japanese military leaders drafted an outline of major foreign policy principles. The army believed Japan must take the Netherlands East Indies as part of its program to "free itself from its dependence upon Britain and the United States . . . through the establishment of a self-sufficient economic sphere." Sentiment was strong in the army for pursuing the southward advance even at the risk of sacrificing opportunities in China. Dazzled by German victories in Europe, Japan's military leaders believed they could seize the European colonies of Southeast Asia in a lightning strike without drawing the United States into war. The navy, less sanguine about the consequences of aggression, was firmly resolved to wage war against Britain "or even against the United States" for these objectives but demanded vast resources to prepare for a large and costly conflict with the Western powers.[76]

Serious as the Japanese threat was, however, the Nazi onslaught commanded even more attention from Washington. A debate now opened within the administration over the disposition of the fleet, pitting those whose priority was Europe against Asia-firsters. On June 16, Assistant Secretary Long described the basic conflict in his diary: "Our fleet is at Hawaii. I propose it be sent to the Atlantic seaboard—at least half of it—even if the movement is piece-meal and clandestine. Berle and Grady are now in and Hackworth and Hornbeck are sent for. The last named opposes the transfer. He has a private war on with Japan and argues that to divide the fleet is to announce we do not mean business anywhere and to transfer it to the Atlantic is to turn the Pacific over to Japan and invite occupation by Japan of the Dutch East Indies. Welles agrees with me."[77]

As he did so often, Hornbeck won out. On June 22 Admiral Stark wrote Richardson at Pearl Harbor to explain that "tentatively decision has been made for the fleet to remain for the present where it is"—at Pearl Harbor.[78] As Hornbeck had hoped, the Japanese were highly conscious of, and concerned by, its continued presence there.[79]

On July 9 Richardson traveled to Washington to press his case for a removal of the fleet from its inadequate and exposed harbor in Hawaii. He discussed the matter with Hull, who again stressed the diplomatic importance of a forward-positioned fleet. "He felt that we should take a very strong position with respect to Japan and that the retention of the fleet in Hawaii was a reflection of that strong attitude."[80] Two days later Richardson talked with Hull's political adviser and finally located the source of his troubles. "I was distinctly of the impression that Dr. Hornbeck was exercising a greater influence over the disposition of the fleet than I was," he later recalled. The admiral recorded in his diary that day that Hornbeck "was the strong man on the Far East and the cause of our staying in Hawaii where he will hold us as long as he can."[81]

Hornbeck's motives for taking such an uncompromising stand on the fleet's disposition came through in a fifty-page memorandum dated July 4, entitled "Reflections on Certain Features of the Far Eastern Situation and Certain Problems of U. S. Far Eastern Policy."[82] He opened with several fundamental assumptions: the "notorious" fact that "a strong element in Japan's leadership" was advocating seizure of the Dutch East Indies; that "the presence of the U.S. Battle Fleet at Pearl Harbor" was a major deterrent to such a thrust against the Indies; and that continued Chinese resistance was the best defense against further Japanese "imperialistic expansion." Withdrawing the fleet from Pearl Harbor, he maintained, might disastrously weaken Chinese morale, give the Japanese Navy a free hand, and encourage Japan's leaders to think seriously "even of closing in upon Singapore and of stirring up trouble in India" making their nation "the one and only great power exercising effective influence in the area of the Pacific and the Indian Ocean." The result would give Japan "full possession of vastly important natural resources" and sea lanes at the expense of the United States and its West European friends.

Finally, Hornbeck argued against wasting too much effort trying to change the course of events in Europe: "The United States can do little today toward preventing Hitler from becoming supreme in Europe. The United States could do much today toward preventing Japan from becoming supreme in eastern Asia. The United States can (may), of course, fall back upon and fortify its position within the Western Hemisphere. If it chooses to do this, and only this, the probability will be that, before long, weakened economically and cut off from valuable markets, especially those from which essential raw materials are derived (in the Far East), the United States will be confronted by material pressures, including those of armed force . . . by Germany and Japan."

With Horneck's logic guiding it, the administration kept its naval pressure on Japan. The Japanese, in turn, were still waging their war of nerves against the Netherlands East Indies. Japan's Foreign Office released to the press on June 28 a statement calling for "further promotion of close commercial relations" between Japan and the Indies and demanding that the Netherlands and its colony "actively take appropriate measures in order to definitely assure the exports of the desired quantity of required goods of the Netherlands East Indies, and also dispose promptly [of] the questions regarding the Japanese enterprises and the entry of Japanese."[83] Secretary Hull responded on July 4 through the embassy in Tokyo. In a telegram to Ambassador Grew he cited detailed trade statistics to demonstrate why the Netherlands East Indies were of even greater economic importance to the United States than to Japan.[84] When Grew spoke with Arita on July 11, he delivered much of Hull's message almost verbatim, stressing the importance of exports from the Indies "in the economy of many countries." Later he warned the Japanese not to commit themselves to "policy of acquiring territory by force."[85]

A new crisis for U.S. leaders arose that month when the British government, hoping to appease Japan and blunt its ambitions to the south, signed an agreement with the Japanese government temporarily halting the flow of certain war materiel over the Burma Road into China. Secretary Hull quickly protested the British decision, which appeared to invite more Japanese pressure on the weakened European powers, in a press conference on July 16. Claiming that "this Government has a legitimate interest in the keeping open of arteries of commerce in every part of the world," Hull decried the closing of the Burma Road and the Yunnan-Indochina railroad as "unwarranted interpositions of obstacles to world trade." His real concerns were to keep alive China's resistance to Japan, a struggle vital to the United States' effort to keep Japan out of Southeast Asia, and to prevent any halt in the flow of U.S. imports of tungsten and other strategic materials from China—imports already delayed by the closing of the Yunnan-Indochina railroad.[86]

On July 17 a Japanese faction led by War Minister Hata Shunroku overthrew the cabinet of Adm. Yonai Mitsumasa, marking the beginning of a more militant policy for Japan. Prince Konoe Fumimaro, who had led Japan when it invaded southern China in 1937, became premier on July 22; the pro-Axis Matsuoka Yōsuke took over as foreign minister, replacing Arita, whom the army deemed too indecisive. Within days, Matsuoka had prepared a draft policy paper, "On Strengthening Cooperation Between Japan, Germany, and Italy," for the Konoe cabinet. Appendix 3 specified: "The sphere to be envisaged in the course of negotiations with Germany and Italy as Japan's living sphere for the construction of a New Order in East Asia will comprise: The former German islands under mandate, French Indochina, the Pacific islands, Thailand, British Malaya, British North Borneo, the Dutch East Indies, Burma, Australia, New Zealand, and India, with Japan, Manchuria, and China as the backbone."[87]

Hull did not need to see that document to be convinced by recent events that on top of "driving us out of business in the area of China she occupied," Japan was "obviously preparing other moves, this time southward, toward French Indo-China, British Malaya, or the Dutch East Indies, possibly even the Philippines."[88] The U.S. government determined to act against the threat.

On July 2, President Roosevelt had signed into law H.R. 9850, the National Defense Act, which gave him legal authority to control exports of certain strategic materials, semifinished products, and vital machine tools. All such exports were placed under a licensing system, giving the president great flexibility in regulating foreign trade. The act provided Roosevelt with the increased leverage he desired against Japan, a nation heavily dependent upon the United States for petroleum, scrap metal, and machine tools.[89]

Now came the time to use that authority, although the administration divided on the question of just how severe the restrictions against Japan should be. On July 18, British Ambassador Lothian, upset by Hull's attack on his government's decision to close the Burma Road, suggested to Secretaries Stimson, Knox, and Morgenthau, all hard-liners, that the

United States embargo petroleum exports to Japan; for their part, the British would destroy the Indonesian oil wells. These steps, he suggested, would quickly bring Japan to its knees. Lothian may simply have intended to call Washington's bluff, but Morgenthau enthusiastically carried the proposal to Roosevelt, who showed interest in its promise for preventing further Japanese expansion. He called a meeting of Stimson, Knox, and Acting Secretary Welles to discuss the possibility of an embargo, and on July 25 he placed petroleum and scrap metals under licensing restrictions.

Welles, following the State Department line, vigorously opposed sanctions on the grounds that they could provoke the very thing the United States most wanted to avoid: an attack on the Netherlands East Indies, Japan's major alternative source of oil. Admiral Stark and Gen. George Marshall, the chief of staff, supported Welles on the grounds that the U.S. military was not yet prepared to come to the defense of the Dutch or British colonies. These arguments impressed Roosevelt, who reversed his decision on July 26, limiting his embargo only to the highest grades of aviation gasoline and iron and steel scrap. Interior Secretary Harold Ickes commented bitterly: "In other words, we are pretending to be holding back on exports of gasoline for Japanese planes while we are doing nothing of the sort." Roosevelt had limited his sanctions in order to prevent a new Japanese drive to the south; Japan could still buy and refine lower-grade petroleum products and function with other grades of scrap metal.[90]

But the Japanese government now saw that Roosevelt had a powerful economic weapon at his disposal, one he could bring into action at any time. When the president, citing "the interests of national defense," actually applied the export embargo on high-octane aviation gasoline to all areas outside the Western Hemisphere on July 31, the Japanese embassy protested: "As a country whose imports of American aviation gasoline is of immense volume, Japan would bear the brunt of the virtual embargo. The resultant impression would be that Japan had been singled out for and subjected to discriminatory treatment." Japan had learned that it could not keep advancing with total impunity.[91]

While the White House tersely announced the news to Japan, Netherlands Minister of Embassy A. Loudon lobbied Joseph Ballantine, assistant chief of the Division of Far Eastern Affairs, for a promise of assistance from the United States to help prevent a Japanese invasion of the Indies. Appealing to racial solidarity as well as the pocketbook, Loudon said:

> [T]he situation of the Netherlands East Indies was critical in that the future now lay between two alternatives. The Islands must either become absorbed in the East Asiatic economic bloc or be retained as a source of wealth for the white race. He suggested that the Dutch Government could do much to increase its value for American trade. Although Americans knew of the Indies as a source of rubber and tin he felt that they did not realize its potential importance as a market for American manufactured products. He said that Java was already partially industrialized but if the Indies continued to remain in Dutch hands they could be further developed in the interests of the white race.[92]

Loudon's urgent appeal for help acquired special relevance a few days later when General Koiso, the newly appointed Japanese delegate to the Netherlands East Indies, spoke of incorporating the islands into Japan's Co-Prosperity Sphere. On August 3 Tokyo's representative summarized his country's policy toward the Dutch colony: "Japan-Manchukuo-China insufficient, construction economic zone great East Asia necessary [including] South Seas. Netherlands Indies long exploited as colony and placed under administrative pressure. From moral viewpoint, freeing Oriental races necessary and destined to be realized. Friction with the United States may be unavoidable, Japan's resolute determination necessary."

Koiso expressed similar views in greater detail the next day.[93] But events were forcing the State Department for the moment to turn its attention back to Indochina, where Japanese encroachments continued. Early in August, the United States learned that during a secret discussion with the Vichy French government, Japan had demanded the right to pass troops through Indochina and to use air bases in the French colony. It claimed only to want to fight China, not to occupy Indochina.[94] But the implications of Japan's demands were obvious. On August 6 Welles instructed Grew to reemphasize to Tokyo the United States' commitment to the status quo in the entire Pacific. "The same belief and the same observation naturally apply to French Indochina likewise," he reminded Grew. "This Government is seriously perturbed, therefore, over the demarche which it is reported that the Government of Japan has made to the French authorities." Grew met with the Japanese foreign minister the next day and gave him the essence of Welles's message.[95]

In order to strengthen the resolve of the Vichy government to resist future Japanese demands, James Dunn, Hull's adviser on political relations (Europe), called on the French ambassador on the morning of August 6. He told the ambassador that the United States was "doing everything possible . . . to keep the situation in the Far East stabilized" by exerting "economic pressure on Japan," basing the fleet in Hawaii, and steadfastly asserting its interests through diplomatic channels. But when asked by Dunn to delay talks with the Japanese, the French ambassador, the Count de Saint-Quentin, replied that the current level of support from the United States was inadequate "to enable them to withstand the pressing demands made by the Japanese Government for the establishment of certain rights in Indochina." The ambassador "did not think it would be practicable for the French Government to delay the negotiations because the Japanese themselves stated at the time of making the demands that if the French Government did not acquiesce in the granting of these rights, the Japanese Government had every intention of taking the necessary action to acquire them."[96]

Partly as a result of U.S. pressure, however, the French did begin to stiffen their attitude toward Japan, particularly over the continuation of shipments to China, still beleaguered by Britain's refusal to open the Burma Road.[97] By holding out for a guarantee of the territorial integrity of Indochina during discussions with Japan, the Vichy colonial government managed to keep Japanese troops out of Indochina—for the time being.[98] The French, bargaining from a position of weakness, could only hope to delay the inevitable.

In late August, the French and the Japanese worked out a tentative agreement granting the Japanese various military privileges in Indochina, subject to further discussions. On September 2, however, the Japanese demanded that the French immediately allow all Japanese troops the right of free passage through the colony. French authorities resisted this ultimatum, but they recognized the hopelessness of their situation.[99] The United States provided what diplomatic support it could. On September 3, Hull wired Grew instructions to meet with the Japanese foreign minister and castigate Japan for aggravating the Indochina situation. Grew spoke with the vice foreign minister the next day, to little avail.[100]

The international situation grew extremely tense as the major Pacific powers parried and thrusted. On September 4, U.S. officials announced that the U.S. fleet would remain in the Pacific instead of being transferred to the Atlantic.[101] They also informed the press that an Anglo-American exchange of destroyers for naval bases had been worked out. Hull told Japan in a press conference to keep its hands out of Indochina. These moves, along with militant statements by representatives of Britain and Australia, served to put increasing pressure on Japan.[102]

But the State Department now learned just what the August 30 agreement between France and Japan entailed. The French had given Japanese troops free passage through Indochina, allowed the establishment of military bases in the north, and recognized the predominance of Japan's rights and interests in the Far East—in effect leaving Indochina ripe for the picking. Further negotiations between the French and the Japanese soon began.[103]

Hull protested Vichy's concessions in a discussion with the new French ambassador, Gaston Henry-Haye. "[T]he French Government cannot imagine our surprise and disappointment when it took this step without any notice whatever to us," Hull complained. He argued that Japan was bent on dominating the Far East "on the sole theory of enriching Japan . . . while all foreign nationals would be driven out and could only return to the Pacific area by paying sky-scraping preferences." For this reason, the secretary said, "the United States had contested in every way short of military activities every inch of the Japanese movement of aggression."[104]

Yet U.S. efforts had failed to halt Japan. Mark Gayn, a journalist on special assignment for the *Washington Post*, summed up the situation. "Japan's victory in the last weeks' diplomatic poker game in Indochina was an event of world shaking importance," he wrote. Comparing it to the Battle of Britain, Gayn added, "The State and Navy Departments could not but regard Japan's entrenchment in Indo-China as a very definite threat to vital American interests in the Pacific." From Indochina, he concluded, "Japan would be able to heighten her intimidation of Thailand and the Dutch East Indies, as well as of Britain concerned for the safety of Malaya and Burma. Both the East Indies and Malaya are of tremendous importance to the United States, for there she secures the bulk of her tin, rubber and quinine."[105]

With such considerations in mind, Grew fought for a harder policy against Japan that would deliver economic sanctions as well as diplomatic protests. In his famous "green light" telegram to the State Department on September 12, Grew insisted that the Konoe government was bent on its policy of southward expansion and now saw a "golden opportunity" to pursue its ambitions. Carefully imposed economic sanctions, he asserted, were the only means short of war to control Japan. "Japan is today one of the predatory powers," he wrote. "Her policy of southward expansion is a definite threat to American interests in the Pacific and is a thrust at the British Empire in the East."[106]

The next day the White House announced that export licenses would be required for all equipment used in the production of tetraethyl lead or aviation gasoline and all technical information relating to aircraft and their engines.[107] Grew's forcefully stated position definitely influenced this decision. As usual Hull and Welles, along with military leaders, fought against even stiffer sanctions, proposed by Morgenthau, on the grounds that the United States was still unprepared to fight Japan in Southeast Asia. Their disagreement was over tactics—the balancing of threats and risks—not the broader national interest.[108]

Similar tactical debates were unfolding in Japan, where secret negotiations for a military pact with Germany and Italy aroused the Imperial Navy's concern that Tokyo was forcing events faster than warranted by the country's military position. At a meeting of top military and political leaders on September 14, Kondō Nobutake, vice chief of the Navy General Staff, said, "The navy is not yet prepared for war against the United States, but preparations will be completed by April of next year. By that time we shall have equipped the vessels already in operation and shall have armed 2.5 million tons of merchant ships. After we have completed this, we will be able to defeat the United States, provided we carry on blitz warfare." But the navy did not block the negotiations, which Japanese leaders hoped would keep the United States from standing in the way of their advance into Southeast Asia.[109]

And advance they did, undeterred by the administration's mild export controls. On September 19 Hull learned from the U.S. consul in Hanoi that the Japanese were demanding the right to station their troops in Hanoi, the port city of Haiphong, and five strategic airports. Japanese troops threatened to invade Indochina on September 22 unless the Vichy authorities agreed to Japan's demands. Hull asked Grew on the same day to make the Japanese government aware of his "great surprise" at the ultimatum in view of previous Japanese agreements to respect the status quo. The next day Grew spoke with Foreign Minister Matsuoka, who claimed that the ultimatum was necessary because the French had acted in bad faith during recent discussions.[110]

Hull addressed the issue of Japanese encroachments in Indochina at a press conference held on September 23, but his words seemed worn and weak in the face of Japan's aggressive moves. "Events are transpiring so rapidly in the Indochina situation that it is impossible to get a clear picture of the minute-to-minute developments," he said. "It seems obvious, however, that the *status quo* is being upset and that this is being achieved under duress. The position of the United States in disapproval and deprecation of such procedures has repeatedly been stated."[111]

The Tripartite Pact

On September 22, the French colonial government under Admiral Decoux caved in to Japanese demands. Even so, the Japanese Army invaded Indochina with 30,000 troops, touching off a major crisis. The United States watched it unfold without aiding the French, for fear of letting equipment fall into Japanese hands.[112] But on September 25 the administration did announce a new $25 million loan to China in return for tungsten, and the next day Roosevelt extended his licensing powers against Japan to steel and iron scrap, effective in October.[113] These actions signaled both the administration's real hostility to Japan's southward encroachment and its reluctance to risk war with Japan until the United States' rearmament program had advanced further.[114]

Coinciding with bold moves by Japanese troops to consolidate their hold over northern Indochina came the announcement of the signing of the Tripartite Pact by Germany, Italy, and Japan. The three partners pledged "to assist one another with all political, economic, and military means" if any one was attacked by a power not yet at war—such as the United States. As *Asahi* saw the situation that day, "It seems inevitable that a collision should occur between Japan, determined to establish a sphere of influence in East Asia, including the Southwest Pacific, and the United States, which is determined to meddle in affairs on the other side of a vast ocean by every means short of war." Coming from a mouthpiece of Japanese ruling circles, the prediction seemed ominous.[115]

The Roosevelt administration publicly betrayed no shock— only recognition that the pact made formal a relationship that the State Department had long assumed. Secretary Hull told reporters on September 27: "The reported agreement of alliance does not, in the view of the Government of the United States, substantially alter a situation which has existed for several years. Announcement of the alliance merely makes clear to all a relationship which has long existed in effect and to which this Government has repeatedly called attention. That such an agreement has been in process of conclusion has been known for some time, and that fact has been fully taken into account by the Government of the United States in the determining of this country's policies."[116]

Secretary of War Stimson privately shared that view. He even welcomed the signing of the Pact, which clarified the world situation and handed the administration a propaganda advantage: "It is a very serious proposition of course but it is so evidently evidenced by fear on the part of the Axis and so clearly represents only what they would do without a treaty, that I personally have not been much worried by it and I don't think the President has. . . . So in substance the new arrangement simply means making a bad face at us. It will be pretty useful, I think, however, in waking up our people to the effect that at last they have got what they have been talking about—isolation. . . . Clamors are being made for an alliance with Great Britain already."[117] As Stimson sensed and hoped, the announcement of the Tripartite Pact did result in a major stiffening of public opinion against the Axis.[118]

Yet the Pact was not a mere exercise in public relations. Germany valued the fact that it diverted U.S. attention away from Europe to the Pacific. Japan was reassured that Germany would not contest its moves toward the Western colonies of Southeast Asia. Japan also knew that the growing threat of a two-front war would soften the U.S. response to its southward thrust. A United Press dispatch from Shanghai reported alarmingly, "With the great source of her scrap iron supplies cut off by the United States embargo, Japan must look to the East Indies for a great part of her war materials needed to fulfill the clauses of the new triple alliance." The September 28 dispatch also quoted "authoritative quarters" as predicting an immediate Japanese drive to the East Indies.[119]

Such considerations weighed on Hull more than he let on. His fears of an imminent Japanese move on the colonies of Southeast Asia were in fact strongly renewed.[120] Grew also believed that the Pact signaled an effort by Japan "to push the southward advance and to provoke war with the United States."[121] The *Washington Post* characterized the issues that had U.S. leaders most concerned: "Chief cause of what immediate apprehension was expressed in the Capitol yesterday over the new alliance was consideration of this country's need for importing tin and rubber. The possibility of Japan seeking to take over the Netherlands East Indies . . . was not minimized in informal discussions on Capitol Hill. Such a move by the Tokyo Government might have the effect, if not indeed the objective, of cutting off American supplies of those two critical materials."[122]

Joseph Alsop and Robert Kintner, writing in their syndicated column "Capital Parade," picked up a similar angle in their survey of Washington opinion. Noting that the U.S. loan to China and export embargo on scrap metals were "intensely offensive to Tokyo," the two men reported that "now there is talk of Japanese reprisals against the United States, possibly in the form of closing off our vital supplies of rubber and tin."[123]

Despite the danger of Japanese reprisals against U.S. sanctions, Hornbeck fearlessly pushed for a hard line against further Japanese expansion. "The Japanese are now definitely on the move southward," he asserted in a memorandum analyzing the Tripartite Pact. "[T]he Japanese will move southward unless and until they meet with or find interposed positive obstacles which they cannot or which they estimate that they cannot overcome."[124] Loans to China and embargoes might not pose obstacles big enough to halt Japan, he added. Only the clear threat of war, produced by a strong military posture in the Pacific, could prove to Japanese leaders that the United States meant business.[125]

In early October, Jay Pierrepont Moffat temporarily left his diplomatic post in Ottawa to visit his superiors in Washington. There he gauged the change in attitudes wrought by the signing of the Tripartite Pact. Hull expressed his growing anxieties over the future of Japanese-American relations. "Every indication pointed to the fact that Japan was planning to advance in the southern Pacific," Moffat recorded in his diary after their talk. "We were on the point of calling home our own citizens, of completing our naval mobilization in Hawaii." Although Hull's mind "was clearly on the Far East," the secretary wished to avoid a war that would cut into U.S. aid to Britain.[126]

Sumner Welles, too, worried about the consequences of having to fight Japan. "He could never lose sight of the fact that Japan's aggression might well be a baited trap for us," Moffat wrote. "If we went to war with Japan all our efforts would have to be directed toward supplying our ships and our troops in the field and England would correspondingly suffer."[127] However, Norman Davis, ambassador to the Vatican, close confidant of Roosevelt, and leader of the Council on Foreign Relations' postwar planning effort, believed that the United States "shall in effect be the heirs of the Empire and it is up to us to preserve its vital parts." One of these was Singapore, "a key point which we could never let go." Of all the people Moffat talked to in Washington, "Norman Davis was the one who would view a war with Japan with the greatest equanimity."[128]

Finally, Moffat met twice with Hull's chief adviser. Hornbeck believed "that we were already at war though if we adopted a firm and uncompromising stand we might yet avoid a 'shooting war.'" For Hornbeck, Singapore was "a vital interest to the United States for which we should, if need be, fight." Moffat came away with the impression that "Stanley regarded Japan as the sun around which her satellites, Germany and Italy, were revolving."[129]

On October 7, Breckinridge Long found Hull deeply worried about the likelihood of war. "Chances were about 50–50 as to whether the Japanese would attack Singapore," Long learned. Wives and children of U.S. military officers in the Far East were being asked to return home as soon as possible; "accommodations on the regular liners were booked up until the first of December." The Navy was concentrating its fleet at Pearl Harbor to prepare for "instant action" and "any eventuality." Long himself had no doubts as to Japan's intentions. "I can see very plainly the fearful trend of present events. . . . Singapore is the objective of Japan."[130]

To block Japan's ambitions, the United States began discussions with Britain and Australia, through their ambassadors, to lay the groundwork for further talks on mutual defense agreements to protect Southeast Asia and Oceania.[131] Prime Minister Churchill sent a telegram to Roosevelt on October 4 asking whether he might not "send an American squadron, the bigger the better, to pay a friendly visit to Singapore" in the hope of deterring Japan from expanding the war, particularly if Britain decided to reopen the Burma Road.[132] Stimson wanted to go even further and move part of the Pacific Fleet to Singapore. Then, if any hostilities broke out between Japan and the Western powers, "it would produce a situation in which the Japanese were the avowed aggressors and any resulting action by our naval forces would have behind them the full sentiment of sympathy from our population."[133] Roosevelt was not willing to risk so much, but he kept the fleet at Pearl Harbor over the pragmatic and tactical objections of Admiral Richardson. Roosevelt wanted the fleet in a forward position to restrain Japan.[134]

Washington's fears were amply reinforced by further news. On October 11, the U.S. consul in Hanoi reported that Japanese troops were preparing to seize Camranh Bay and strategic airports in the south of Indochina for later use "against Manila and Singapore." He also confirmed reports that the Japanese were constructing a military base in the Spratley Islands in the center of the South China Sea. Naval intelligence informed senior administration officials on October 16 that the Japanese Foreign Office was facing pressure "to take steps to effect the military seizure of the Dutch East Indies at the earliest opportunity."[135]

Hull now had little hope that the Japanese could ever be brought around to a less militant policy. His growing despair would reflect itself in later negotiations, which often resembled nothing more than a waiting game. As Breckinridge Long noted, "The Secretary said that he had done every reasonable thing to bring Japan to an understanding and that he had worried and thought and tried every expedient but that Japan made it impossible to proceed with any order. He did not throw out the possibility of an understanding but did not know how to proceed to attain it without sacrificing principle and felt that every time we relaxed in our rigorous attitude toward Japan she took advantage of the relaxation in the misconception that we were weak or were willing to permit her to carry out her designs to establish a 'new order' in Asia and in the islands of the sea."[136]

In this mood Hull responded more agreeably to the advice of hard-liners such as Hornbeck. On November 6 Hornbeck told Stimson that Hull had approved of a plan to defend Singapore by sending submarines and aircraft to the island base. Several days later Stimson, Knox, and Hull discussed the idea further at their usual weekly meeting in the State Department. The Australians, Knox reported, had agreed to supply Singapore with an additional fifty planes, and the U.S. Navy was willing send the British ten submarines. Stimson wrote after the meeting, "This constituted a reinforcement of the defense forces in regard to the New Netherlands [sic] which the State Department thinks is the best that we can do." Hull wanted to do more but the United States, not yet fully rearmed, could not afford to give much away.[137]

The Navy agreed with this strategy of reinforcement. "There seems no doubt that Japan is resolved on a southward movement—employing force if necessary," wrote Adm. Thomas Hart, head of the Asiatic Fleet, to Stark on November 13. Hart suggested that the United States, Britain, and the Netherlands advertise their willingness to resist an attack on Southeast Asia. "A Japanese attack on British or Dutch possessions, or both, is a most likely development, unless the Japs are fairly certain that we will intervene," he argued. One could safely assume that "the only consideration that our rights and interests in the Netherlands East Indies, as elsewhere in the Far East, will receive from the Japanese will be what we are able to force upon them; and that if we wish to maintain those interests, the occasion approaches which will be our last chance to do so except entirely on our own and starting from scratch."[138] War, in short, seemed dangerously near.

In case any laggards still questioned whether the stakes made war a necessary last resort, Hornbeck prepared his most extensive analysis of U.S. strategic interests in the Far East on December 4, 1940. Its characteristically long title was "The Importance of Singapore to the Defense of the British Isles and the British Empire and to the Interests of the United States."[139] He began with a discussion of Southeast Asia's economic importance to Anglo-American defense requirements:

1. The importance of Singapore to the immediate defense of the British Isles lies in its command of the means of access to the raw materials and man power of Malaya, the Dutch East Indies and India. While the British Isles could doubtless do without direct access to these materials and to this man power, the effect of such a loss upon the economic and financial resources of the British Empire—a vital factor in the defense of the British Isles—would be considerable. Such a loss by seriously weakening our own economy (rubber, tin, jute, quinine, vegetable oils, tungsten, antimony, mica are among the supplies that might be lost to us) would adversely affect the extent of our economic aid to the British Isles.

If Japan took Singapore, Hornbeck continued, China's collapse would be ensured, and the United States would lose all ability to defend its interests in Asia. With the riches of Southeast Asia at its disposal, Japan could threaten India and challenge the United States in other areas:

At the same time our general diplomatic and strategic position would be correspondingly impaired and our economic position would be considerably weakened—by our loss of the Chinese, Indian and South Seas markets for our exports (and by our loss of much of the Japanese market for our goods, as Japan would become more and more self-sufficient) as well as by inevitable restrictions upon our access to the rubber, tin, jute and other vital materials of the Asian and Oceanic regions.

Finally, Hornbeck countered the suggestion that Japanese control of Southeast Asia would make no real difference to the

U.S. economy. Japan's autarkic Co-Prosperity Sphere would inevitably exclude the United States:

> It has been suggested that Japan would be only too glad to sell to the British and to us the products of the region, and that in fact, therefore, our (and the British) economic situation would not be adversely affected. The fate of British and American trade in Manchuria and in North China is persuasive evidence that our (and British) export trade would certainly suffer.... The present and the immediate future are times of war, and ... the United States is openly aiding Great Britain and China.... Consequently, were Japan to acquire control of Singapore (i.e., control of the vast natural resources of Asia and the South Seas) she could not be expected freely to sell to the British or to us—Britain's greatest armorer and supplier—our severally and jointly expanding requirements of the strategic materials of the Orient.

Hornbeck's analysis struck other officials as a definitive statement of Anglo-American interests. He showed it to Admiral Stark on December 5 and to Hull the next day, and soon officials such as Sumner Welles were distributing it widely. Hull liked it so much that he sent it to President Roosevelt on December 10. Demand for the memorandum prompted Hornbeck to prepare revised editions on December 9, 1940, March 29, 1941, and May 9, 1941. A later edition found its way to Roosevelt adviser Lauchlin Currie, who passed it to the president on May 10, 1941. Hornbeck's treatise received rave reviews from those who read it. "This memo seems to me conclusive and unanswerable," wrote Lynn Edminster, special assistant to the secretary of state. Ambassador Grew wrote that Hornbeck's memorandum could "be accepted as final and fundamental."[140]

Even after reading Hornbeck's memo, however, Grew had understandable doubts about the United States' capacity to fight on two fronts. He wrote Roosevelt questioning "whether getting into war with Japan would so handicap our help to Britain in Europe as to make the difference to Britain between victory and defeat," adding that "the principal point at issue ... is not whether we must call a halt to the [southward expansion] but when."[141] Significantly, Roosevelt let Hornbeck draft his response. The reply simply reiterated the line already taken in Hornbeck's Singapore memo: that Britain depended on the resources it drew from the Far East to sustain its war effort at home.[142]

In this same period, ironically, British military representatives in Washington were under instructions from their government to stress a mirror-image argument for a U.S. naval intervention to deter a Japanese advance into Southeast Asia. Such a move by Japan, they were reminded, "would constitute a threat, not only to British vital interests, but equally to those of the United States of America," which was "depending upon supplies from [there] pending the building up of her stocks of raw materials."[143]

For frustrated U.S. policymakers, however, there was still no way around their limited means to safeguard such important interests. The country's rearmament program—including its stockpiling of strategic materials—was far from complete. The specter of a two-front war haunted military experts. The best that could be hoped was that patient diplomacy and economic leverage could still persuade Japan to turn back from its southward course. At least such tactics might slow Japan down.

But the Roosevelt administration did gain one new weapon by late 1940: public opinion. Since the announcement of the Tripartite Pact, public opposition to the Axis powers was hardening. As the State Department's Joseph Ballantine explained in a lecture to the Naval War College late that year:

> Until a few months ago American attitude toward Japan was largely influenced by considerations of sympathy for China as the victim of aggression and of injuries which Japan was doing to American rights and interests in China. However, following upon indications of Japanese designs in Malaya and the Dutch East Indies and Japan's entry into a formal alliance with the Axis powers, the American public had seen cause for concern over the possible effects of these developments upon this country's more vital national interests. Not only do Japan's objectives constitute a po-

94 *The Emerging Threat*

tential menace to the trade routes which afford us access to strategic raw materials, especially rubber and tin, but consideration of the possibility of collusion between Japan and Germany in employing against us what is popularly referred to as a squeeze play has given rise to no little apprehensions for our national security. As a consequence, there has been a marked stiffening in the attitude of American public opinion toward Japan.[144]

Looking back on 1940 in his memoirs, Cordell Hull defended the administration for going "well beyond the use of words to express disapproval of Japan's actions." The application of embargoes, the "vast program of rearmament," the stationing of the fleet at Pearl Harbor, and various forms of aid to China "were all part of our policy of firmness."[145] But for the moment, at least, that policy had failed to halt Japan. Government leaders knew that they would face greater challenges from across the Pacific in the coming year.

4

War of Nerves

January–June 1941

> In the international controversies that are likely to arise in the Orient growing out of the question of the open door and other issues the United States can maintain her interests intact and can secure respect for her just demands. She will not be able to do so, however, if it is understood that she never intends to back up her assertion of right and her defense of her interest by anything but mere verbal protest and diplomatic note.
> *President Taft, inaugural address,*
> *March 4, 1909*

"Japan entered the year 1941 determined to wrest what further gain she could from the war in Europe, but still undecided as to when and where."[1] Secretary Hull's perception was reasonably on target. Tokyo still did not know how far it could go before provoking war with the United States—whether it could call Washington's bluff and take the Indies and Singapore without an all-out conflict. Japan inched its way into Southeast Asia through Indochina and Thailand, not yet prepared to launch a major invasion. By midyear, however, it was ready to commit to a concerted offensive into the region.

Trouble in Thailand

A border dispute between Thailand and Indochina provided Japan the leverage it needed to punish recalcitrant Vichy authorities in Indochina. Japan, which hoped to secure bases in southern Thailand, backed Bangkok's claim to parts of western Cambodia and Laos. The dispute took a violent turn in November 1940 when Thai troops attempted to cross the border. The French retaliated, and a small war broke out. In December the Thai government refused a French offer to have the matter arbitrated by a neutral third power.[2]

On January 4, 1941, the U.S. minister in Thailand reported to Hull that "a Japanese fifth column movement is being organized for any eventuality that may arise in this area making it possible for Japan to control this country in its own interest and for use as a base for [operations] against Singapore." He cited reports of Japanese troop infiltration, the arrival of Japanese officers in Thailand, and a Japanese agreement to supply Thailand with 400 planes in return for raw materials.[3]

On January 6, the British embassy sent the State Department its own analysis of the situation in Thailand. The British believed Japan was backing Thailand in order to prolong the hostilities and weaken European interests in the entire region, creating a power vacuum that Japan could fill. If Japan chose to mediate the dispute, it would gain a foothold. "The strategic position which Japan no doubt hopes to acquire in both countries is one from which it can menace the integrity of other territories lying to the south," the report said. Allowing Japan to win allies in Thailand would thus be "to the detriment of Indochina, Thailand, the Netherlands East Indies and the British possessions in the Far East."[4]

Thailand declared martial law along its border with Indochina on January 8, declaring: "[W]e must now settle accounts with the French." Thai troops soon invaded Cambodia, forcing the French back many miles and inflicting heavy casualties.[5] The British, frantic to see a settlement reached before the Japanese solidified their position, pleaded with the United States to relax its position against the Thais and help settle the conflict "in view of the importance of Thailand as a base for operations against Burma, Malaya and Singapore." Grew, who relayed this message to the State Department, agreed with the British.[6]

London's fears were well founded. While Thailand battled France over the border, Japanese troops reinforced their "temporary" positions in Indochina, made new demands on the French, and even allowed the Thais to use airfields the French had ceded to Japan.[7] The British soon gave the United States more bad news, reporting that "about the middle or later part of February, coincident with attempted German invasion of the British Isles, Japan is to attack in the south, possibly Burma, 'to knock out' the British Empire; action is to be taken before the United States is prepared and so quickly that the United States will not be given time to make decision for or against intervention—the United States in any event would face dilemma of deciding between military operations in Atlantic and Pacific."[8] Such warnings came often. By now, U.S. leaders believed a Japanese strike to the south could come almost at any time.

Hull warned the Thai ambassador on January 13 to end the fighting, declaring that Japan's sole interest was in dominating all of Asia and that it would swallow up Thailand when ready.[9] Japan kept the Western powers off guard by offering to settle the conflict on January 21; both sides quickly accepted. A cease-fire was arranged for January 28, and negotiations began the next day. The parties finally reached a settlement on January 31.[10]

Yet the British remained dissatisfied. In another aide-mémoire to the State Department, they cited new reports suggesting that come April Japan and Thailand would coordinate attacks against Indochina. Japan would seize Vietnam, letting the Thais slice off Laos and Cambodia as their prize. "Japan would then have reached, with the minimum of effort, a position extending to the boundaries of Burma and providing powerful bases for operations against that country, Malaya and the Netherlands East Indies." The British memorandum asked the United States to warn Japan off.[11]

Ominous intelligence reports were coming in from all quarters. On January 27, for example, Grew informed Hull of a possible "surprise mass attack on Pearl Harbor . . . planned by the Japanese military forces, in case of 'trouble' between Japan and the United States." The secretary distributed this "fantastic" report to the War and Navy departments.[12] On February 4 the Navy Department warned of a possible large-scale offensive by Japan against Southeast Asia to be coordinated with a German attack on Great Britain on February 10.[13] The Japanese press, meanwhile, continued to play up the chauvinistic speeches of government officials.[14] For Grew, it was now clear that "if definitive action [to stop Japan] is to be taken, it may have to be taken before too long."[15] The outlook for U.S.-Japanese relations, he wrote, "has never been darker."[16]

The Drought-Walsh Mission

It was with warnings like these in mind that the State Department approached the diplomatic efforts of two private citizens—Bishop James Walsh and Father James Drought of the Catholic Foreign Mission (Maryknoll) Society. The two men had visited Japan in November 1940 on their own peace-seeking mission and managed to obtain interviews with influential Japanese officials, including Foreign Minister Matsuoka. Impressed by the possibilities for peace, the priests returned to the United States with several documents summarizing their view of the Japanese negotiating position. On January 23, 1941, Roosevelt gave them an audience.[17]

Walsh began the conversation by stressing that he had no illusions about the power and influence of the military in Japan. He emphasized the need to strengthen the liberals in Japan by coming to an understanding that would undercut the military, but his words cast serious doubt on whether such an understanding could last. The peaceful elements in Japan, he noted, "feel that if some constructive cooperation is not realized with the United States before March or April, the Fascist element will take control in both China and Japan, no matter whether England or Germany wins in the spring offensive." At the same time, the United States could not push Japan too far, for "the loss of the China War and the imminence of an American War, would put the radical nationalists, civil and military, in complete control." Finally, the bishop stressed the need for absolute secrecy, owing to the fragility of Japanese politics. "If our efforts became known in Japan," he warned the president, "the Konoe government would be toppled and war would immediately break out in the southwestern Pacific."[18]

Based on recent experience, Hull and other policymakers were not inclined to put much faith in negotiations, except as they might delay Japan's military progress. Although Walsh's impressions of the Japanese negotiating position seemed hopeful, Hull later observed, "The President and I, of course, had heard such opinions emanating from the liberal group in Japan before. Whatever the intentions of the liberals, the military group had virtually always been too strong for them." The proposals presented by Walsh stood "in drastic contrast" to what Hull assumed to be the real state of opinion in the Japanese government. He believed there was "no likelihood" of Japan's taking a conciliatory position. Furthermore, with Japan still jockeying for position in Thailand, Hull could "view the approach of Bishop Walsh and Father Drought only with caution."[19]

Roosevelt sent a copy of Walsh's memorandum to Hull on January 26 with a note asking for guidance. The secretary responded at length on February 5. Obviously discomforted at the prospect of sensitive negotiations bypassing the State Department, he cast doubt on "the practicability of proceeding on any such line at this time." He pointed out that the Japanese government was sending a new ambassador, perhaps with new proposals for negotiation, and therefore "we should not I think, resort to other agents and channels before we have even talked with the ambassador and while we can work through Mr. Grew in Tokyo."[20] Roosevelt, however, would let no avenue for peace go unexplored. He overruled Hull and proposed letting Walsh and Drought continue their efforts.[21]

But Roosevelt did listen to Hull's more substantive criticisms of the proposals Walsh brought. These reservations concerned the threat posed by Japan to U.S. interests in Southeast Asia. "[I]f through the good offices of this Government an arrangement were worked out which would extricate Japan from its present involvement in China," the secretary wrote Roosevelt on February 5, "the likelihood would be that Japan would extend and accelerate her aggressions to the southward rather than that Japan would change her present course of aggression to one of peaceful procedures."[22] There could be no clearer evidence that Hull's view of China was not clouded by sentiment or abstract principle. He was a realist whose real priorities lay in Southeast Asia. China was the flypaper that tied up Japanese divisions and prevented them from jeopardizing U.S. interests to the south.

Hull sent along to the president a longer memorandum by Hornbeck that explored this logic in greater depth. Hornbeck opened his analysis with a "fundamental" assertion that Japan's dominant military group could only be stopped by "the resistance of a stronger obstacle or . . . a greater force." Short of entering the war itself, the United States could look only to China to provide that force and safeguard U.S. economic interests in Southeast Asia: "Many of Japan's leaders earnestly desire now to extricate Japan from its present involvement in China in order that Japan may be in a better position than it is at this time to embark on conquest to the southward in areas which are richer in natural resources than is China and from which Japan might, if successful in conquering these areas, enrich herself more rapidly than she can in and from China. Any arrangement which would help Japan to extricate herself temporarily from her involvement in China would be of doubtful soundness from the point of view of the United States."[23]

The ultimate logic of this analysis was that negotiations were useless unless Japan wrapped up its military adventures altogether, not piecemeal. For all the reasons Hornbeck had outlined in December, the United States could not compromise the security of Western interests in Southeast Asia. But to safeguard those very interests in the Indies, Washington could not compromise too much on China for fear of freeing the Japanese military to engage in further conquests. This reasoning lent itself to the show of negotiations but no real concessions. Unless Japan backed down all the way, this logic would lead to war.

Further evidence that Japan was bent on grabbing the resources of Southeast Asia unless forcefully stopped came from a British aide-mémoire delivered on February 7. It amassed evidence pointing to an imminent Japanese advance on the region, starting with Camranh Bay and air bases in southern Indochina.[24] While Japanese officers set up shop in Saigon, the British began transferring their forces from Singapore to northern Malaya.[25] On February 10, Assistant Secretary Long recorded in his diary: "The Japanese are preparing for a southward movement and it looks very much as if they would cross the Malay Peninsula and attack Rangoon, Saigon and Penang. Rangoon controls the southern lead to the Burma Road, and Penang controls the northern end of the Straits of Malakka which leads to Singapore. . . . [I]t looks as if they were preparing this move . . . simultaneously with the German move against England which is expected in April at the latest."[26]

Tensions between Japan and the Western powers grew as Roosevelt announced on February 11 that U.S. supplies would continue flowing to Britain even if the United States became involved in a Far Eastern war.[27] But Japan still had the initiative. By February 14, Ambassador Grew was able to report without hesitation, "The French are finished in Indochina."[28]

With the Japanese threat to Southeast Asia mounting daily, Roosevelt, Hull, Stimson, Knox, Stark, and Marshall met on February 11 and decided to warn all Americans out of such sensitive areas as Rangoon, Burma, and Singapore. But the decision was rescinded owing to the arrival of the new Japanese ambassador, Admiral Nomura. Even if the chances of peace were as slim as one in a hundred, the administration would give negotiations a chance.[29] Roosevelt attended the first meeting of Nomura and Hull on February 14 to impress Nomura with the United States' determination to achieve peace. If a settlement proved impossible, the private administration agenda was to keep talking and delay the conflict—"to slow down the Japs," as Stimson put it.[30]

Roosevelt appreciated the Japanese government's gesture in sending Nomura, a friend from the president's days as assistant

Navy secretary in the Wilson administration. Unfortunately, Nomura was not an experienced diplomat and spoke little English. These shortcomings caused serious difficulties in later discussions between the two governments. Although gracious to his old friend, Roosevelt firmly outlined the U.S. position. Noting that the American people were "seriously concerned . . . at the course of Japan," Roosevelt referred to the "movements of Japan southward down to Indochina and the Spratley Islands and other localities in that area" as matters of "very serious concern." Roosevelt warned that another incident like the 1937 sinking of the U.S.S. *Panay*, in the light of the American public's hostility towards Japan, could lead to war.[31]

The same day that Roosevelt spoke with Nomura, the U.S. counselor of embassy in Japan, Eugene Dooman, exchanged views with a high-ranking Japanese diplomat. Declaring that "a Japanese threat to occupy lands from which the United States procured essential primary commodities would not be tolerated," Dooman added,

> It would be absurd to suppose that the American people, while pouring munitions into Britain, would look with complacency upon the cutting of communications between Britain and the British dominions and colonies overseas. If, therefore, Japan or any other nation were to prejudice the safety of those communications, either by direct action or by placing herself in a position to menace those communications, she would have to expect to come into conflict with the United States. . . . The United States cannot but be concerned by the various initiatives taken by the Japanese in Indochina and elsewhere for the reason that if Japan were to occupy these strategic-important British and Dutch areas, it could easily debouch into the Indian Ocean and the South Pacific and create havoc with essential British lines of communication.

Dooman explained candidly that the United States' piecemeal approach to economic sanctions reflected a desire not to provoke Japan into threatening regions of vital economic importance to the United States: "The United States . . . [is] well aware that an alternative source of supply for Japanese purchase of petroleum and certain other products of the United States is the Netherlands East Indies, and for that reason it has been reluctant to impose embargoes on the sale to Japan of commodities of which it has a surplus; but the Japanese must clearly understand that the forbearance of the United States springs from a desire not to impel Japan to create a situation which could lead only to the most serious consequences."

Dooman concluded by implying that the future of peace in the Pacific hinged upon whether or not Japan chose to continue its expansion into the South Seas, saying "it was quite possible to pass over the present critical period without war, but that one essential condition to this more or less happy issue out of our difficulties must be the realization on the part of the Japanese that they cannot substantially alter the status quo in Southeast Asia, particularly, without incurring the risk of creating a very serious situation."[32] Dooman could hardly have drawn the line between peace and war more clearly. Although coming from a second-tier diplomat, this blunt message had Grew's approval. Washington never disavowed it and almost certainly gave its approval a few days later.[33]

The next day the British ambassador, Lord Halifax, and the Australian minister of embassy, Richard Casey, called on Hull for a briefing on the conversation with Nomura the day before. The meeting had evidently not lifted Hull's spirits. He told the visitors of his fear that a militaristic group within Japan would either launch an attack against the Netherlands East Indies or Singapore or "inch by inch and step by step, get down to advance positions around Thailand and the harbor of Saigon, Indo-China. This would leave the peacefully disposed elements in Japan, including the Japanese Ambassador to the United States, to express their amazement and to say that such actions were without their knowledge or consent." Once again, the United States' chief negotiator was suggesting that negotiations might be in vain.[34]

All three powers took the threat outlined by Hull seriously. On February 16 the British announced they were prepared to mine an area of 4,000 square miles around Singapore without advance notice. A major Australian military force reached Singapore two days later—the "largest and most powerful reinforcement of men, guns and machines ever to arrive at that base in a single convoy." On February 20 Washington announced that it was sending a number of modern U.S. bombers via Hawaii to strengthen the British defenses at Singapore. At the height of the crisis, the *New York Times* called for firmness: "The possibility of a Japanese attempt to seize Singapore is a threat to which the United States cannot afford to remain indifferent. . . . Of the rubber which the United States imports, all but an unimportant share comes from plantations in the regions dominated by Singapore. Much the greater part of our equally indispensable supply of tin comes from Malaya and the Dutch East Indies, under the shadow of Singapore. With that port in unfriendly hands, our imports of these and other essential commodities, and our trade with an important section of the world, would be jeopardized."[35]

Apparently the Japanese government did not expect such a show of force. *Asahi* denounced the "encirclement" campaign by the United States, Great Britain, Australia, and New Zealand. In a more conciliatory statement, the Japanese said that although their interests in the South Seas were "a matter of life and death," any attempt to seize the area by force would only "cause destruction and bring no favorable result to Japan." The statement promised that Japan would "seek a settlement by peaceful means" unless the other powers sought to "stifle" Japan.[36] This enlightened pragmatism failed to dampen the State Department's suspicions, however. Acting Secretary Welles replied coldly in public on February 18, "In the very critical world condition which exists today the Government of the United States is far more interested in the deeds of other nations than in the statements that some of their spokesmen may make."[37]

The war of words did not escalate further, and Japan took no military action. Washington concluded with relief that the appearance of a strong front by the Western powers had prevented a devastating confrontation. From the evidence of Japanese troop movements and naval preparations, an official Australian analysis concluded that Japan must have planned to launch a major invasion to the south between February 16 and 20. The report, sent to the State Department on March 6, argued that the sum of Roosevelt's warnings to Nomura on February 14, the publicity given to mutual defense consultations of Australia, Britain, and the United States, and the extensive coverage of Far Eastern affairs by the American press convinced the Japanese that further aggression would be met by force. The Australian analysis concluded that next to sending the U.S. fleet to Singapore, the most effective U.S. response to Japan's expansion would be a massive publicity campaign spotlighting and condemning Japan's every aggressive move.[38]

In the wake of the February crisis, the U.S. minister in Thailand, Hugh Grant, assessed Tokyo's slightly chastened attitude: "Japan is not going to attack Malaya now and will attempt to avoid a conflict with the United States and with Great Britain because of her economic situation but she will continue her program of expansion through intrigue and sabotage."[39] Indeed, Japan continued to apply pressure to the French in Indochina. As mediator of the border dispute between Thailand and Indochina, Japan proposed that the French cede one-third of Laos and Cambodia to Thailand. The Vichy authorities rejected this proposal on February 21, pledging to fight before giving up such a vast portion of their colonial holdings. Decrying France's obstinacy, Foreign Minister Matsuoka told the Japanese Diet that "the white race must cede Oceania to the Asiatics." On February 28 Japan declared that France must accept its proposal or face the consequences. The Vichy government finally capitulated on March 11.[40]

Still searching for the one chance in a hundred that peace could be preserved through negotiations, Hull held the first of a long series of informal discussions with Ambassador Nomura on March 8.[41] Hull lost no time in making clear that the United States would remain hostile as long as "Japanese troops, planes, and warships are as far south as Thailand and Indo-China, accompanied by such threatening declarations as Japanese statesmen are making week after week."⁴² Roosevelt met with the ambassador again on March 14 to reinforce that message, declaring that the United States could not tolerate Japan's drive toward "Singapore, the Netherlands East Indies and the Indian Ocean." Through peace, he emphasized, Japan too could benefit from the region's resources if it joined the United States in upholding the principle of free trade and open markets: "The President came back to the matter of the great work the United States has been doing for economic equality of opportunity, and said that if Great Britain wins, she must be willing for Germany to have equal access to all raw materials and equal trade opportunities. He then remarked that the United States and Japan do not produce rubber and tin and numerous other commodities produced by the British Empire, and that by international arrangements, access to each and all of these must be equal to each country alike."⁴³

Unswayed, the Japanese continued their military buildup in Indochina. On March 20 Grew reported that Japan had 135,000 troops stationed on Hainan and another 15,000 in Indochina. The German government, he wrote, was pressuring Japan for an immediate attack on British Malaya and the Netherlands East Indies, but Japan was not ready. Nevertheless, Grew believed that soon Japan would use Thailand as a base from which to seize Singapore, Malaya, and surrounding areas, depending on "Japan's estimate of the correlations of forces both in Europe and the Far East and the consequent risks involved."⁴⁴

A British aide-mémoire on April 8 supported Grew's belief that Japan's position in Thailand would soon pose a grave threat to the nearby European colonies. "Japan's general position as mediator and guarantor," the memorandum argued, "gives her ample opportunities for keeping naval forces in Indo-China and Thai waters and even military forces in South Indo-China." With such bases Japan could easily strike south to Malaya and the Indies. The aide-mémoire concluded that the Western powers should resist Japan to save Singapore and to "prevent loss to ourselves and gain to the Axis of an important source of supply of rubber and tin."⁴⁵

Anglo-American Naval Cooperation

Faced with an impending Japanese move southward, U.S. and British naval officials had for some time been discussing the possibility of joint operations in the Pacific in case deterrence failed. These efforts culminated in late March 1941 with the signing of the "ABC-1 Staff Agreement," which essentially pledged the United States to cooperate with Britain's defense of Southeast Asia.

Anglo-American staff conversations began late in 1937 as an indirect result of Japan's invasion of southern China and the forging of the Anti-Comintern Pact. Roosevelt and Hull foresaw the possibility that the United States ultimately would engage in a two-front war with Japan and Germany. They instructed Adm. William Leahy, the chief of naval operations, to draw up contingency plans, assuming Britain as an ally. Soon the director of Britain's War Plans Division was contacted to discuss further the possibility of naval cooperation. In January 1938, officials from both navies agreed to recommend joint action to stop a thrust by Japan to the south.[46]

Although representatives of the two countries kept in contact, serious staff conversations resumed only in September 1940 in London. Delegations from Britain and her dominions of Canada, Australia, and New Zealand traveled to Washington to initiate more formal joint staff conferences on January 29, 1941. A disagreement soon developed. The British delegation believed the defense of Singapore was of fundamental importance and that the United States should transfer part of the Pacific Fleet there in order to deter Japan from cutting Britain's lifelines. Adm. Richard Turner, spokesman for the U.S. naval delegation, opposed the idea of dividing the fleet and "resisted the demand" made by the British, according to the conference minutes. "It was agreed that for Great Britain it was fundamental that Singapore be held; for the United States it was fundamental that the Pacific Fleet be held intact."[47]

On March 27 the various delegations finally came to an understanding known as the ABC-1 Staff Agreement. A worldwide strategic accord, the document asserted the primacy of the European war effort and recommended a defensive effort against Japan. Incorporated directly into the Joint Army and Navy Basic War Plan, known as "Rainbow 5," the agreement specified the duties of the U.S. Navy in the Pacific: "If Japan does enter the war, the military strategy in the Far East will be defensive. The United States does not intend to add to its present military strength in the Far East but will employ the United States Pacific Fleet offensively in the manner best calculated to weaken Japanese economic power, and to support the defense of the Malay barrier by diverting Japanese strength away from Malaysia."[48]

As Admiral Turner pointed out later, "It would be a grave error for anyone to get the idea that the war in the Central Pacific was to be purely defensive. Far from it."[49] In fact, the ABC-1 agreement provided for a whole series of U.S. tactical offensives against Japan, with the primary goal of diverting Japan's naval forces and supporting British forces in the South Seas.[50]

Knox and Stimson accepted the ABC-1 Staff Agreement on May 28 and June 2, respectively. Although Roosevelt himself never explicitly endorsed its content, he made known his general approval and allowed all future military planning to be governed by its provisions. Because the agreement was in no sense a treaty, the United States was not bound by it, yet Britain and its dominions had every reason to expect the United States to abide by its terms. The joint accord presented the administration with a firm *moral* obligation to come to Britain's aid in case of war in Southeast Asia. Later conferences at Singapore, whose resolutions were not officially accepted, hardened the administration's resolve—always conditional on an unpredictable Congress—to follow Britain into war if Japan breached the West's stronghold in Southeast Asia.[51]

Attempts at a Negotiated Settlement

War was still the last thing anyone in London or Washington wanted. Negotiations to stave off or at least delay that eventuality remained a high priority for policymakers, however pessimistic their view of Japan's ultimate intentions.

The arrival of Col. Iwakuro Hideo in New York on March 21 seemed a hopeful sign. The State Department knew him to be a representative of the Japanese War Ministry, extremely influential with the younger officers. As the principal assistant to the head of the Military Affairs Bureau, Iwakuro obviously carried great clout. He immediately joined the Walsh-Drought team to help draft a proposal for an "understanding" as a basis for negotiations between Japan and the United States.[52] Walsh and Drought had so misread Japanese intentions during their stay in Japan that Iwakuro was forced to rewrite the preliminary drafts they prepared before his arrival. Even, so the colonel's draft made an incautious attempt at reconciliation with the United States. Roosevelt saw it on April 5 and Secretary Hull on April 9.[53]

For the next few days the State Department carefully reviewed the terms of the plan. The proposed agreement allowed Japan to remain bound by the Tripartite Pact and essentially pledged the United States to neutrality in the European war. Japan would negotiate an accord with China to withdraw Japanese troops, but if China refused the terms, the United States would have to cut off aid to it. Japan agreed to respect the Open Door, but the United States would have to recognize Manchukuo. Both countries would cooperate in the acquisition of Southeast Asian raw materials. Finally, Japan expected the United States to help exert diplomatic pressure "for the removal of Hongkong and Singapore as doorways to further political encroachment by the British in the Far East."[54]

Hull was immediately struck by the lack of guarantees that Japan would follow through on its proposals for China. Without such guarantees, a U.S. accord with Japan would undermine Chiang Kai-shek, especially if he were denied U.S. aid. "How could we ask Chiang Kai-shek to negotiate when there were so many loopholes for Japanese interpretation, and how could we agree to discontinue aid to China if he refused?" Hull later asked.[55] Faced with the possibility of conflict both in Europe and in Asia, the United States could not risk losing China; it was too important as a quagmire that kept Japan from its more dangerous regional aims.

In reaching these conclusions, the State Department's Division of Far Eastern Affairs appreciated a sharp analysis by Stanley Hornbeck, which dealt "succinctly" with "the fundamental question presented."[56] Hornbeck noted that the agreement said nothing about the presence of Japanese troops in Indochina and did nothing to protect the European colonies from Japan. He presumed that Japan's real goal was to "get a considerable part of that army out of China and to have . . . her resources available for possible activities in some other direction (which might be against British interests or Dutch interests or even American interests—or Soviet interests)." Under the circumstances, "Japan's present involvement in China is to the advantage of the United States and Great Britain."[57] As always, Hornbeck was an unsentimental, hardheaded realist on the China question.

Maxwell Hamilton, chief of the Division of Far Eastern Affairs, prepared his own appraisal of the situation on April 14. His analysis closely paralleled Hornbeck's. Like Hornbeck, he suggested continuing aid to China, explaining that if another year passed with Japan still bogged down in China, "then there is a distinct possibility that the present balance of Japanese opinion in regard to Japan's future course of action may be decisively turned." U.S. policy, he continued, "has had as one of its effective purposes the attrition of Japan's energies and resources by steps undertaken gradually on a basis designed to obviate creating the impression that they were in the nature of overt acts directed primarily at Japan." Hamilton concluded that the United States could best prevent further Japanese expansion by continuing to confront Japan "with determination, without element of bluff."[58]

Washington received another blow when it learned that Japan and the Soviet Union had signed a neutrality pact on April 13. After the public announcement, Hull issued a bland statement pointing out that the pact changed nothing and that its significance "could be overstated."⁵⁹ In reality, however, the administration feared that with the Russian threat removed from Japan's rear, the threat to Southeast Asia increased. "The pact will tend to stimulate and support the Japanese extremists who advocate a vigorous prosecution of the southward advance," Grew theorized, "because it guarantees Soviet neutrality in case Japan gets into war with a third country (i.e. the United States)."⁶⁰ Secretary of the Navy Knox told the American Newspaper Publishers Association on April 24 that the latest pact would enhance "the likelihood of an expansion of hostilities by Japan into a region which is one of the sources of critical war materials for both Great Britain and ourselves."⁶¹

When Nomura and Hull discussed the terms of Iwakuro's draft proposal on April 16, the secretary expressed his mixed reaction. Some of its conditions might be acceptable, he suggested, but "[t]he one paramount preliminary question about which my Government is concerned is a definite assurance in advance that your Government has the willingness and ability to go forward with a plan for settlement."⁶² Hull handed the ambassador a list of four essential principles of reasonable international conduct that would have to form the basis for further negotiations. These points included:

1. Respect for the territorial integrity and the sovereignty of each and all nations;
2. Support of the principle of noninterference in the internal affairs of other countries;
3. Support of the principle of equality, including equality of commercial opportunity;
4. Nondisturbance of the status quo in the Pacific except as the status quo may be altered by peaceful means.

If the Japanese government would accept these rules of conduct, Hull said, friendly and earnest negotiations between Japan and the United States could begin immediately. The fact that no great power had ever respected all four points did not bother the secretary; failure to *profess* these principles would, in his eyes, demonstrate Japan's evil intentions.

After some thought, Nomura told the secretary that the principle of equality might indeed provide a good starting point for discussion. Hull shot him down. "We could not think of entering into negotiations if your Government should even hesitate in agreeing to this point," he snapped. "No country in the world would get more from the doctrine of equality than Japan." In no mood to argue, Nomura turned instead to the fourth point—nondisturbance of the status quo. Could not acceptance of this point interfere with Japanese operations in Manchuria? But Hull was really only concerned with preventing any new disturbances—such as an invasion of Southeast Asia. He replied that "the question of non-recognition of Manchuria would be discussed in connection with the negotiations and dealt with at that stage, and that this status quo point would not therefore, affect 'Manchukuo,' but was intended to apply to the future from the time of the adoption of a general settlement."[63]

Nomura personally saw merit in the U.S. case. He cabled home to advise that "since there is danger that an advance southward militarily by our Empire would lead to war between the United States and Japan," his government should pursue its ends "by peaceful means without resorting to the sword." The United States, he added, had promised to "support our [peaceful] economic penetration thither."[64]

Despite Nomura's goodwill, however, his lack of training as a diplomat and his poor English led to serious difficulties in the negotiations. When he sent to his superiors in Tokyo a copy of the unofficial "Draft Understanding," he failed to convey along with it Hull's objections or even the secretary's four principles. Instead Nomura left the impression that the draft represented an official *U.S.* position paper. Hull had hoped the Japanese government would accept the draft as a starting point for their side of the negotiations and that further discussion would make the entire package more acceptable to the United States. Japan had the same idea from the opposite angle. Each side, therefore, adopted a position more uncompromising than the original proposal; this hardening, in turn, caused each side to believe that the other was reneging on prior commitments. This shared and fundamental misunderstanding caused much disappointment and distrust in both camps.[65]

But diplomacy was proving a thin reed upon which to rest hopes for peace, given the chasm that separated the interests of the United States and Japan. While Hull talked with Nomura, the Japanese military pushed its political offensive in Thailand, and the British continued to pester Hull with their predictions that Japan would strike at Singapore from new bases in that country.[66] What to do about the situation was an unresolved tactical question. Hull feared that Japan already controlled Thailand and believed that mere verbal protests would do little good unless backed up by force, which was impractical.[67] Grew, by contrast, argued that extremist Japanese leaders should quickly be disabused of their notion that the United States would not fight if Japan attacked Southeast Asia.[68]

One alternative to direct military intervention was already under way: aid to China. On April 25, Lauchlin Currie offered Roosevelt his arguments for stepping up military assistance to China in order to keep Japan safely bottled up there:

> Singapore is the key to the Indian Ocean, Australasia and Oceania. It is as indispensable to the continuation of Britain's war effort as it is to Japan's dominance of the East. It may be assumed, therefore, that Japan will move against Singapore whenever conditions appear favorable.
>
> Japan would be prepared to offer China peace on very favorable terms for the purpose of releasing large numbers of men and planes and quantities of material . . .
>
> Therefore the defense of Singapore should be a cardinal feature of our strategy and the British strategy.
>
> The best defense of Singapore is in China. Were China put in a position to assume the offensive, Japan would have to strengthen her forces in China, rather than weaken them. The assumption of a vigorous air offensive by the Chinese against the Japanese in China and in Japan and in Indochina, would also effectively tie up the Japanese air force.[69]

Echoing these sentiments, Hornbeck on May 5 reiterated his belief that Japan was seeking a way to disengage from China only to divert to "other fields a portion of her resources and reserves." Any treaty giving Tokyo an easy out would only assist Japan "toward an improving of her position for pursuit of a policy of further adventuring southward or adventuring even against us," increasing the likelihood that the United States would have to "fight in *two* oceans."[70] Heeding such arguments, President Roosevelt on May 6 declared the defense of China to be vital to the defense of the United States and authorized shipments of lend-lease supplies to China.[71]

The next day, Nomura, armed with a long-delayed communication from his government, met with Hull for another informal discussion. The ambassador informed Hull that his superiors wished simply to sign a nonaggression pact with the United States rather than pursue the April 9 draft proposal. The idea was a nonstarter; it would commit the United States to holding back if Japan attacked British or Dutch territories in Southeast Asia. Such a pact "would have meant our agreeing to refrain from war with Japan no matter what she did in the Far East," Hull understood.[72]

The secretary was especially suspicious because a day earlier Japanese and French authorities had announced the completion of an economic agreement virtually incorporating Indochina into the Yen bloc. France agreed to grant Japan most-favored-nation status with respect to "the entry, the establishment, the acquisition and possession of movable and immovable property, the exercise of commerce and manufacturing industry, the imposition of taxes of various kinds and the treatment of companies." Furthermore, Vichy authorities agreed to give Japan highly favorable tariff treatment. U.S. leaders saw the accord as just one more piece of evidence that Japan would soon try to consolidate its hold over all of Southeast Asia.[73]

Nomura called on Hull again on May 12 with a draft of a new peace proposal. Hull was no more impressed than before, noting with disapproval the "modification of the provision in his original document about Japan's keeping out of the South Sea area in a military way." In this new draft, Japan referred only to its well-known "peaceful nature." As Hull saw it, "very few rays of hope shone from the document."[74] He could not have been encouraged by Grew's subsequent talk with Matsuoka in Tokyo on the May 14. Japan would carry out its southward advance by peaceful means, Matsuoka assured the U.S. ambassador, unless "circumstances render this impossible." Such circumstances apparently included Britain's troop build-up in Malaya, which Matsuoka claimed was inflaming public opinion in Japan.[75]

With the Japanese threat looming larger, officials in Washington took great interest in Grew's analysis of the situation. On May 22, Sumner Welles sent Roosevelt an excerpt from Grew's diary of March 30, 1941, already distributed throughout the department by Hornbeck. Grew's basic assumption, like Roosevelt's, was that "the future safety of the United States, our future way of life and all that, are inextricably bound up with the safety of the British Empire." It followed necessarily that "we cannot in our own interest and security afford to see Singapore fall" to Japan. "The fall of Singapore into Axis hands," he maintained, "would, first and foremost, result in the rapid severance of Britain's most important life-line" to the men and materiel in its Asian colonies and the dominions. Grew argued that "the risks of not taking positive measures to maintain our future security in the Far East . . . are likely to be much greater than the risk of taking positive measures as Japan's southward advance proceeds (whether by nibbling or with a direct thrust)." He advocated strong action to neutralize Japan's "challenge to our whole economic and political position in Asia and Australasia," which, if successful, would mean "the incalculable loss of the Chinese, Indian and South Seas markets for our exports as well as our access to vital materials (rubber, tin, jute, etc.) produced in those regions." Grew thus proposed that the administration inform Japan that any advance on Singapore would bring the United States into the war.[76]

Hornbeck bolstered Grew's strategic-economic analysis of Anglo-American interests in Southeast Asia with another long memorandum, "Better To Give Aid on Two Fronts and Fight on

One Than to Withhold Aid on One and Have to Fight on Both." Like Grew, he accepted as axiomatic the U.S. interest in saving the British Empire. Again like Grew, he viewed control of Singapore as a vital element in preventing Japan from dividing the Empire and severing supply routes to Britain. To protect this key Western outpost, Hornbeck advised, "we should do all that we can toward discouraging Japan from making an attack upon Singapore; we should generously assist China—thereby keeping Japan busy with China—and we should dispose of certain increments of our armaments products and our armed forces so that what is visible in British hands in Malaya, in Dutch hands in the Netherlands East Indies, and in American hands in the Philippines will deter the Japanese from taking the risks of a major movement south of Manila." But Singapore was ultimately as important to the United States as it was to Britain, he maintained. "To be effective as an arsenal [of democracy], both for supplying of other nations and for meeting our own needs, it is vitally necessary that we have access to essential raw materials from all over the world." That meant keeping Japan out of Southeast Asia at all costs. "[W]e cannot under existing conditions give effective assistance to Britain and get along without rubber and tin, etc., from the Singapore area."[77]

With threats growing daily on two fronts, however, tactical disputes once again flared within the administration over where to deploy U.S. military forces. In late April, Stimson, Knox, and Marshall began arguing that the U.S. fleet should be sent back to the Atlantic Ocean in order to protect sea lanes to Britain. As Marshall observed, "if the Atlantic is lost all the raw materials in Malaysia will be of no avail. If the Atlantic is lost, the Pacific is also lost."[78] But the State Department and the leading admirals opposed the move. Hull still believed that the presence of the fleet in the Pacific would help pressure Japan into signing an agreement favorable to U.S. interests. "Further, he and his advisors believed that the disappearance of the American fleet from the Pacific would be taken by the Japanese as a go-ahead signal for their southward expansion; from such expansion there might well result a situation in which the United States would be forced to fight," Stimson later recalled.[79] Roosevelt explicitly accepted Hull's analysis.[80] The president was firmly convinced that the Pacific Fleet must remain based in Hawaii to protect Singapore, the Netherlands East Indies, Australia, and New Zealand.[81] In the final compromise, three battleships and an aircraft carrier were transferred to the Atlantic, but the main body of the fleet, including nine battleships and three aircraft carriers, remained at Pearl Harbor.[82]

The truth was that the United States simply did not have enough warships to cover both fronts. On June 4, Assistant Secretary Long bemoaned the fact that "we are not prepared—not enough planes, guns, explosives, shells. Not a sufficient supply of those articles." With Britain tied down in Europe, the United States would have to fight a Pacific war alone. "If we were ready to start I would not worry so much about it all," Long confided in his diary, "but the combination of circumstances means we almost must face the world alone—for Japan will soon be starting on her road to oil in Java, with tin and rubber to torment us with. But as a result of it all I am very depressed."[83]

Hull's mental state was not much different. When the Japanese ambassador visited on June 2 to claim that except for minor phrasing, the positions of the two governments were very close, Hull could hardly contain himself. Severely challenging Nomura's judgment, he questioned whether Japan "seriously desires" to enter into a peace settlement and help revive the Open Door in Asia. "The kind of statements that Matsuoka and others are making daily sharply raise the question I just put to you," Hull told the ambassador. "I'm forced to inquire whether Japan really is seeking this sort of agreement, or whether she is only seeking a way to get out of China and then go forward in other directions with methods and practices entirely contrary to the principles that would have to underlie our settlement."[84] Taking up the line Hornbeck preached daily, Hull was not about to jeopardize Southeast Asia by pulling Japan out of its Chinese quagmire. An impasse had been reached, and Hull made little progress with Nomura and his associates in later negotiations that month.[85]

For several months the Japanese had been negotiating with the Dutch to secure a favored commercial position in the Netherlands East Indies. Understandably reluctant to join Japan's "Greater East Asia Co-Prosperity Sphere," authorities in the Indies resisted Japanese demands, despite the clear risks.[86] On June 9 Grew reported to Hull that the Dutch had refused the latest Japanese requests for special privileges for immigration, business opportunities, and mineral resource exploitation. The Dutch officials asserted the principle of commercial equality, demanded assurances that no materials be re-exported to Germany, and refused to let the Indies fall under the Japanese sphere of influence, in marked contrast to Vichy's acceptance of Japanese hegemony in Indochina.[87] Japan broke off negotiations on June 17.[88]

Elsewhere in the region, the State Department was devising a plan to wean Thailand away from Japan. On June 17 Assistant Secretary of State Dean Acheson wrote the British minister in Bangkok, who had requested U.S. assistance in denying Japan the rubber and tin of Thailand. Acheson simply proposed to buy up all stocks of the two strategic materials. "We believe, with you, that a serious situation exists in Thailand and that it is desirable that efforts be made to the end that Thailand's political independence and normal economic relations be maintained," Acheson wrote. "The defense needs of the American Government are such that, irrespective of other considerations, we should be glad to purchase all of Thailand's rubber and tin, or as much as might be obtainable."[89] Welles said much the same: "This Government attaches great importance to the acquisition of tin and rubber."[90] The State Department proposed that the United States loan Thailand $3 million and reconsider export restrictions affecting Thai goods in order to expedite the deal. The British enthusiastically supported the plan, believing it would significantly reduce raw material exports to Japan and improve Thailand's relations with the West. But negotiations with the Thai government moved slowly, and the U.S. proposal was effectively killed when Japan occupied southern Indochina in late July.[91]

On June 22, Germany invaded the Soviet Union, presenting administration leaders with yet another crisis and more tough questions. Besides the enormous implications for Europe, what did it mean for Japan? Would it now go north to seize Siberia, or plunge into Southeast Asia, now that its rear was secure? Hamilton, chief of the Division of Far Eastern Affairs, hoped the invasion would "result in a postponement for at least a few months of any Japanese attack upon British and Dutch possessions to the southward" as Tokyo reassessed its position: "In my judgment the strongest motive which would impel Japan not to attack British or Dutch possessions in the Pacific is the likelihood that such action by Japan would result in war with the United States. It seems to me that there is much less likelihood that a Japanese attack on Russia would result in war with the United States and I would therefore be very skeptical of a Japanese pledge not to attack the Soviet Union."[92]

At least some members of the department fervently hoped Japan would go north and ease pressure on the Western position in Southeast Asia.[93] It was not to be, however. Instead, a decisive turning point in U.S.-Japan relations was reached in early July, when Japanese leaders made their fateful decision to prepare for a major push into the prized territories of Southeast Asia. These intentions were no mystery to the United States, whose leaders spent the last few months of peace trying to delay Japan until the U.S. position in the Pacific could be fortified. With full knowledge of the risks, Japan was backing both countries into a corner from which they could not escape.

At an Imperial Conference attended by top major military and political leaders in Japan on July 2, factions looking south for greater glory carried the day. An invasion of the Soviet Union was not ruled out, but the army and navy won permission to acquire bases in southern Indochina and prepare for further conquests. The "Outline of National Policies in View of the Changing Situation," approved at the conference, declared that in order to "guarantee the security and preservation of the nation" and achieve its goals in the "southern regions," preparations for "war with Great Britain and the United States will be made. First of all . . . various measures relating to French Indochina and Thailand will be taken, with the purpose of strengthening our advance into the southern regions. In carrying out the plans outlined above, our Empire will not be deterred by the possibility of being involved in a war with Great Britain and the United States."[94]

Prime Minister Konoe, the first to speak at the conference, stressed the urgency of the situation and the need for Japan to embark steadfastly on this new program of empire building. If the Western powers stood in the way, Japan must push them aside and "remove all obstacles."[95]

Navy Chief of Staff Nagano Osami spoke forthrightly on the need "to push steadily southward." If the Western colonial powers continued their obstructionist tactics, he argued, Japan would "finally have to go to war with Great Britain and the United States. So we must get ready, resolved that we will not be deterred by that possibility." Against the United States specifically, the admiral believed that Japan should not flinch from its "policy to establish the Greater East Asia Co-prosperity Sphere, even if this ultimately involves the use of force."[96]

Only two days later, Ambassador Nomura sent Secretary Hull a simple but astounding note. "I am glad to inform you," he wrote, "that I am now authorized by the Foreign Minister to assure you that there is no divergence of views in the Government regarding its fundamental policy of adjusting Japanese-American relations on a fair basis."[97] In the light of what was to come, U.S. leaders could not help but question such declarations of peaceful intent. Japan's credibility would soon reach a new low.

5

Japan Moves South

July–December 1941

> The demand for mineral raw materials by the so-called "have-not" nations has now become one of the major threats to world peace. . . . A realistic view of the international minerals situation . . . seems to indicate that sooner or later war may have to be fought collectively by the "have" nations if they are to preserve their material . . . positions. . . . The democratic Powers possess the might necessary to uphold their interpretation of the right. Are they willing to use it?
> — *Charles K. Leith, U.S. government minerals consultant, April 1938*

Although the policy deliberations of Japan's leaders were a tightly held secret, Roosevelt administration officials guessed rightly that their foes' next moves would bode ill for Western interests in Southeast Asia, starting with French Indochina.[1]

The military intelligence agencies of the United States and Britain in fact produced remarkably accurate evaluations. On July 3, for example, the Navy Department notified its attaché in London, "The unmistakable deduction from information from numerous sources is that the Japanese Government has determined upon its future policy which is supported by all principal Japanese political and military groups. This policy probably involves war in the near future. An advance against the British and Dutch cannot be entirely ruled out, however the

Chief of Naval Operations holds the opinion that Japan activity in the south will be for the present confined to seizure and development of naval, army and air bases in Indo-China." The Navy pointed out that the Japanese government had ordered all Japanese shipping back into the Pacific and was requisitioning merchant ships.[2] The United States also knew that the Japanese Army had suddenly called up over a million men and that the government had begun censoring the mails.[3]

The U.S. naval attaché in London passed this news to the British chiefs of staff, who agreed with the general conclusions reached by the Navy Department. They believed Japan's program to be:

a. to seize Indo China, naval and air bases for which shipping and military forces are held ready;
b. for the expansion southward, to take advantage of any opportunity that arises;
c. for the present, to take no military action against the Soviet [Union].[4]

In the Foreign Office, one analyst warned that if this scenario came to pass and Southeast Asia were overrun, "both we and the States would probably run out of rubber in under a year, if we pooled all available supplies." He also noted that England had exported from Malaya so much tin to the U.S. stockpile that "there would appear to be only 2 months reserves in this country of tin, and 2 months of concentrates. In consequence, America will have to look, at any rate for the next year, almost entirely to the danger zone [Southeast Asia] to fulfill her requirements."[5]

State Department experts shared exactly the same concern. Willys Peck, back in the State Department after serving as ambassador to China, asserted, "A Japanese attempt to conquer Malaya and the Netherlands East Indies, even if not successful, would inevitably cut off supplies vital to the United States of rubber, tin and other commodities." In line with the previous judgments of Hull, Hornbeck, Hamilton, and Currie, Peck argued, "It is more than ever urgent that China's resistance to

Japan shall be intensified, to the end that more and more of Japan's armed striking force shall be immobilized and dissipated in the 'China Incident.' " By "dragging Japan into deeper and deeper involvement in the China hostilities," he proposed, "the United States can work powerfully toward the achievement of some of her principal objectives, among them the maintenance of the status quo in the Far East, the preservation of our rubber and tin supplies, the safeguarding of the Philippine Islands, the aiding of Russia against Germany, and the aiding of Britain."[6]

The United States soon received confirmation of what Japan had in mind from a highly reliable source. A cryptographic intelligence breakthrough, code-named MAGIC, allowed the United States to break the Japanese "Purple" cipher used for top-level diplomatic correspondence between the Japanese government and its embassies. On July 8, the State Department began receiving deciphered intercepts of Japanese messages outlining the official policy. One message from Tokyo to Berlin declared: "1. Imperial Japan shall adhere to the policy of contributing to world peace by establishing the Great East Asia Sphere of Co-Prosperity, regardless of how the world situation may change. 2. The Imperial Government shall continue its endeavor to dispose of the China incident, and shall take measures with a view to advancing southward in order to establish firmly a basis for her self-existence and self-preservation."[7]

Later that day Matsuoka sent a diplomatic circular to Nomura containing more bad news for the United States: "Preparations for southward advance shall be reinforced and the policy already decided upon with reference to French Indo-China and Thailand shall be executed.... In the meantime, diplomatic negotiations shall be carried on with extreme care. Although every means available shall be resorted to in order to prevent the United States from joining the war, if need be Japan shall act in accordance with the three-Power pact and shall decide when and how force will be employed."[8]

Washington could not know from MAGIC that interservice rivalries within Japan still precluded an absolutely final decision over how far, and even whether, to press the southward advance.⁹ But by July 12, the United States had learned from its intercepts of new Japanese demands on the French for military bases in Indochina.¹⁰ Three days later U.S. officials knew for sure that Japan was demanding that the French cede two great ports—Saigon and Camranh Bay—along with eight air bases scattered through southern Indochina and Cambodia. Confirmations of this intelligence soon arrived from Grew and other conventional sources. If the French did not accept the ultimatums, Japanese troops were prepared to take the country by force.¹¹

U.S. leaders naturally saw Japan's encroachments on Indochina as merely the first steps in an accelerated program of expansion southward to a vital area, "the producers of which are of special importance to the United States and many other nations," as Hull put it in a talk with Hamilton on July 18.¹² Hull pointed out that Japan's objective in acquiring bases in *southern* Indochina was not to defend itself against encirclement by the Western powers but was "preliminary to going south." This judgment was hardly speculation anymore. After all, a Japanese dispatch only four days earlier had declared in blunt language: "After the occupation of French Indochina, next on our schedule is the sending of an ultimatum to the Netherlands Indies. In the seizing of Singapore the Navy will play the principal part. . . . [W]e will once and for all crush Anglo-American military power and their ability to assist in any schemes against us."¹³

More bad news came in on July 17, when the old Konoe government was dissolved and a new, even harder-line cabinet was formed under the prince's leadership. "Japan's cabinet switch dashes Roosevelt's June hope that 'moderates' would get control," reported the *Wall Street Journal*. "Dutch East Indies, not Siberia, is the 'ominous' spot, State Department thinks."¹⁴

Acting Secretary Welles met with the Japanese minister of embassy on July 21 to discuss the Indochina situation. Welles conveyed the administration's extreme concern over Japan's ultimatum to the French and asked what Japan's next step would be. The Japanese official denied any knowledge of plans to occupy Indochina but nonetheless asked what effect such a move would have on the negotiations. Welles said further conversations between the United States and Japan would, in his view, be "completely illogical" if Japan continued to aggress against the countries around it. Hull agreed that the only way for Japan to demonstrate its desire for peace would be to "desist from any reported plans to go ahead with the acquisition of military and naval bases in French Indochina."[15]

Mere words did not deter Tokyo. Japanese troops began to occupy southern Indochina on July 21. As Hull put it, Japan had finally succeeded in taking "possession of the whole of France's strategic province, pointing like a pudgy thumb toward the Philippines, Malaya, and the Dutch East Indies."[16] Two days later, Japan's Foreign Office sent out a cable, decoded by MAGIC, reporting on a new propaganda campaign in Indochina to "facilitate lightning action whenever it becomes necessary and to ultimately oust US and UK from SEA." The cable cautioned, however, that duplicity was the order of the day. "We must not . . . give the impression that we intend to make further military penetrations to the south."[17]

The same day, Welles called Hull for instructions on how to receive Nomura, who had requested an interview. The secretary of state replied that Japan's occupation of the French colony "looked like Japan's last step before jumping off for a full-scale attack in the Southwest Pacific." He instructed Welles to continue negotiations with the Japanese ambassador no further, and Welles informed Nomura of the secretary's decision the same day.[18]

Tired, distraught, betrayed, and angry, Hull probably felt the talks served no useful function. In his view, Nomura would simply continue to feed the administration lies about Japan's intentions, whereas the United States might, during the course of discussions, inadvertently reveal important intelligence that would aid Japan in its expansionist policy. By breaking off the negotiations, the United States served notice on Japan that it would fight to protect its interests lying in Japan's path.

Hull's drastic step proved just how great was his assessment of the threat from Japan's occupation of southern Indochina. Official State Department historians later summed up the significance of Japan's thrust: "By this further expansion in southern Indochina Japan virtually completed the encirclement of the Philippine Islands and placed its armed forces within striking distance of vital trade routes."[19] Japan now "threatened essential supplies of American defense materials from the South Pacific," another department history observed.[20] From here until December 7, the United States worked not so much for a hopeless peace as to prevent a complete collapse of its position in the Pacific.[21]

The British government had similar concerns as it sized up the changing military picture in the South Seas. On July 23, Foreign Secretary Anthony Eden expressed "grave concern" that Japan's new foothold in Indochina would be "potential daggers aimed at Singapore, Britain's Far Eastern fort, and her tin and rubber producing ally, the Netherlands East Indies."[22] Hull and Welles met the same day to discuss the implications of Japan's most recent act of aggression. Both concluded that any U.S. reaction must be based on the assumption "that by its actions and preparations Japan may be taking one more vital and next to the final step in occupying all the South Seas area." Hull defined the central issue as the potential loss of "trade routes of supreme importance to the United States controlling such products as rubber, tin, and other commodities. This was of vital concern to the United States."[23]

The next day Welles handed the press a statement observing that Japan was giving "clear indication" of its desire to expand by force into Southeast Asia, using the excellent bases, ports, and airfields provided by the French for a Japanese invasion force. These developments, he said, "tend to jeopardize the procurement by the United States of essential materials such as tin and rubber which are necessary for the normal economy of this country and the consumption of our defense program. . . . The Government and people of this country fully realize that such developments bear directly upon the vital problems of our national security."[24] Numerous newspapers ran columns and editorials emphasizing the danger to U.S. raw material lifelines posed by Japan's military encroachments.[25]

That afternoon, Roosevelt informed Ambassador Nomura that "this new move by Japan in Indochina created an exceedingly serious problem for the United States." Addressing Japan's propaganda claims that its security was at stake in Indochina, the president proposed to neutralize the colony if Japan would withdraw its troops. He would get China, Great Britain, and the Netherlands to promise not to disturb the status quo in Indochina, so no power would threaten it or Japan. Roosevelt also assured Nomura that Japan would have ready access to vital raw materials if it accepted those conditions and stopped menacing Southeast Asia. Roosevelt had nothing to lose: If Japan agreed, the pressure would be off U.S. interests in the region; if not, the refusal would expose the bankruptcy of Japan's position.[26] However, Nomura failed to report the offer to Tokyo until it was too late,[27] and Japan continued to consolidate its position in Indochina. Grew angrily condemned this escalation,[28] but Japan's troops kept moving.

In near desperation, Roosevelt finally played the economic card. On July 25, he announced the freezing of all Japanese assets within the United States and the licensing of all U.S. trade with Japan. The *New York Times* interpreted the action as "virtually severing trade ties with the empire" and said it dealt Japan "the most drastic blow short of actual war." On July 26 Roosevelt signed Executive Order No. 8832, actually implementing this decision. Roosevelt had declared economic war in the face of an almost certain decision by Japan to pursue its course of southward expansion.[29]

The governments of Great Britain and the Commonwealth countries followed suit almost immediately by instituting similar freeze orders against Japanese funds. The Dutch reacted more hesitantly, but on July 28 they extended export controls over all goods shipped to Japan from the Indies and threatened to impose a total embargo unless Japan showed more restraint.[30] Thus did the Western powers counter the military threat with severe, potentially crippling economic sanctions against Japan's own sources of raw materials.

The U.S. freeze order did not automatically cut off all shipments of oil to Japan. The State and Treasury departments theoretically could still approve such exports, and Roosevelt perhaps envisioned that they would do so on occasion. The practical effect of Roosevelt's sweeping order, however, was to completely disrupt all trade between the two countries. On August 1 the administration announced that all fuel exports would be subjected to a rigid licensing system, a move widely interpreted as a simple embargo. Indeed, as the days went by and lower-level bureaucrats issued no licenses, U.S. policy became abundantly clear—no oil for Japan. Neither Roosevelt nor Hull stepped in to reopen the door to trade.[31]

The Decision to Embargo Japan

The embargo, so long in coming, was not so much a gamble as an act of desperation. Without oil, government officials knew, Japan might accelerate its military timetable and seize the oil-rich Netherlands East Indies. By late July, however, the administration believed an attack was coming sooner or later anyway. Tough sanctions might make Japan think twice; if not, they still could weaken Japan enough to give the United States a military edge.

The agonizing debate over sanctions contrasted the consensus over national interests with the sharp division over how best to safeguard them. The State Department's official diplomatic history of the period observes that from 1938 to 1940, the United States government actively considered but finally held back from imposing any serious economic sanctions on Japan, lest it provoke "retaliatory action of a character likely to lead to this country's becoming involved in war."[32] The administration envisioned the war as starting with an attack not on Pearl Harbor, nor even necessarily on the Philippines, but on the rich European colonies of Southeast Asia.

The supreme importance of keeping Japan out of the region led officials to resist a powerful groundswell of public opinion that opposed on moral grounds the sale of war-related goods to Japan. On August 29, 1939, for example, 82 percent of people with an opinion favored a total U.S. embargo on war materials, a category that would have included oil and gasoline.[33]

On April 15, 1940, the day Japanese Foreign Minister Arita delivered his implied threat to the Netherlands East Indies, Secretary Hull and Assistant Secretary Long examined the various alternatives open to the United States to prevent Japan from entering the Indies. They considered, but rejected as foolhardy, the idea of sending the U.S. fleet to Singapore or to Java. The other major possibility was a general embargo on Japan. This, too, they rejected as carrying the risk of unacceptable retaliation against the Netherlands East Indies. "If we put an embargo on Japan and they occupied those islands," both men agreed, "they could place an embargo on tin and rubber against us."[34] The key issue, as always, was Southeast Asia and its resources, not China and its plight.

In the summer of 1940, with Japan inching southward, the issue of an embargo arose again. Hard-liners such as Stimson, Knox, and Morgenthau urged the president to block all war materials normally shipped to Japan. They hoped such vigorous action would stop Japan dead in its tracks, giving the United States more political leverage in the Far East. The State Department, represented at the time by Acting Secretary Welles, fiercely opposed the suggestion on the grounds that it might provoke Japan to accelerate its southward thrust, pushing the United States into a war it was not ready to fight. Roosevelt listened to the voices of caution and withheld his economic weapon.[35] Shortly after the signing of the Tripartite Pact, Roosevelt again faced pleas from Stimson, Morgenthau, and Ickes for an embargo, and again he declined to "force [Japan] into a military expedition against the Dutch East Indies."[36]

Hull and Long again brought up the subject of embargoing Japan on November 7, 1940; as before, both agreed that extreme economic sanctions were infeasible. "If we shut off oil from Japan it would force her to go to the Dutch East Indies, because she had to have oil," Long wrote. "Consequently, it becomes a matter of policy for us to continue to sell oil to Japan and to sell her other things."[37] Roosevelt continued to follow the State Department on this issue. He received flack not only from Morgenthau and Ickes but from his wife as well. After the administration tightened its trade restrictions against Japan following the Tripartite Pact, Eleanor wrote her husband asking why it was necessary to continue appeasing Japan by allowing it to buy U.S. petroleum products. He replied to her on November 13: "The real answer which you *cannot* use is that if we forbid oil shipments to Japan, Japan . . . may be driven by actual necessity to a descent on the Dutch East Indies. At this writing, we all regard such action on our part as an encouragement to the spread of war in the Far East."[38]

The issue became hot again in June 1941, when a serious oil shortage began developing on the East Coast. The public could not understand why the United States continued to ship oil to Japan while Americans ran short. Within the administration, Harold Ickes mounted an offensive to win from Roosevelt a pledge to embargo all petroleum exports to Japan. Time and again the president refused to budge. On July 1, for example, Roosevelt informed Ickes that Japanese leaders were locked in an internal struggle over whether to advance to the north, advance to the south, or wait it out and "be more friendly with us." No one knew what the decision would be, Roosevelt continued, "but, as you know, it is terribly important for the control of the Atlantic for us to help to keep peace in the Pacific. I simply have not got enough Navy to go round—and every little episode in the Pacific means fewer ships in the Atlantic." Roosevelt assumed the United States would eventually have to fight if Japan seized Singapore and the Netherlands East Indies.[39]

The intelligence that Japan was planning new expansion to the south forced the administration to reappraise its stand on the embargo. On July 10, Sumner Welles, with instructions from Roosevelt, informed British Ambassador Halifax that if Japan moved further to "conquer or to acquire alien territories in the Far East, the government of the United States would immediately impose various embargoes, both economic and financial, which measures have been under consideration for some time past."[40]

Hornbeck, usually the hard-liner, still opposed a total embargo, however. He proposed that the Navy display its ships more prominently and that trade restrictions be imposed—but not on petroleum and iron ore, the two most important items. "Action with regard to either or both of the commodities, if taken now, would have a tendency to prejudice Japan's choice between moving, if and when, northward or southward," he explained. "We certainly do not want to encourage Japan to choose, as between the two, to go southward rather than northward."[41]

Military officials aired similar concerns. In a letter sent to Roosevelt by Stark on July 19, Admiral Turner wrote: "An embargo would probably result in a fairly early attack by Japan on Malaya and the Netherlands East Indies and possibly would involve the United States in early war in the Pacific. If war in the Pacific is to be accepted by the United States, actions leading up to it should, if practicable, be postponed until Japan is engaged in war in Siberia."[42] But Hull, hearing the same argument from Far Eastern division chief Hamilton, said the chances of influencing Japan to go north were remote. He believed Japan's attention "was centered southward and that any action Japan might take against Siberia would be only after the collapse of Soviet resistance, should that occur, when Japan would simply pick up the pieces preparatory to embarking on a southward movement."[43] In order to "deter Japan and to place obstacles in the way of Japan's program of conquest," he proposed giving large credits to China and France to aid their resistance to the Japanese and urged the imposition of "economic, financial and other restrictions upon Japan"—in other words, all measures short of war.[44]

The gravity of the crisis prompted Roosevelt himself to warn Nomura that relations between the United States and Japan were unraveling fast. As he told the ambassador on July 24:

> The average American citizen could not understand why his Government was permitting Japan to be furnished with oil in order that such oil might be utilized by Japan in carrying on her purposes of aggression. The President said that if Japan attempted to seize oil supplies by force in the

Netherlands East Indies the Dutch would, without the shadow of a doubt, resist, the British would immediately come to their assistance, war would then result between Japan, the British and the Dutch, and, in view of our own policy of assisting Great Britain an exceedingly serious situation would immediately result. It was with all of these facts in mind, the President said, that notwithstanding the bitter criticism . . . the President up to now had permitted oil to be shipped by Japan from the United States.[45]

The two nations were now on collision course, as if playing a game of chicken. Colonel Iwakuro, the influential Japanese Army officer, warned against a freeze of Japanese assets during a conversation with Joseph Ballantine on July 25. If such measures were invoked, he declared flatly, "Japan would have no alternative but sooner or later to go south to Malaya and the Dutch East Indies in order to obtain essential supplies."[46]

The time had come for the administration to take its case to the public. Roosevelt first broached it in a series of "informal remarks" on July 24 to the Volunteer Participation Committee, which he hoped would "enlighten the average citizen." To all those Americans puzzled and angry that the United States continued to ship petroleum to Japan while curtailing consumption at home, Roosevelt explained in his condescending tone:

All right. Now the answer is a very simple one. There is a world war going on, and has been for some time—nearly two years. One of our efforts, from the very beginning, was to prevent the spread of that world war in certain areas where it hadn't started. One of those areas is a place called the Pacific Ocean—one of the largest areas of the earth. There happened to be a place in the South Pacific where we had to get a lot of things—rubber, tin, and so forth and so on—down in the Dutch East Indies, the Straits Settlements, and Indochina. . . .

And now here is a nation called Japan. Whether they had at that time aggressive purposes to enlarge their empire southward, they didn't have any oil of their own up in the north. Now, if we cut the oil off, they probably would have gone down to the Dutch East Indies a year ago, and you would have had war.

Therefore, there was—you might call—a method in letting this oil go to Japan, with the hope—and it has worked for two years—of keeping war out of the South Pacific for our own good, for the good of the defense of Great Britain, and the freedom of the seas.[47]

The logic of Roosevelt's explanation made clear that he would not have ordered the freeze the next day except for the fact that Japan's preparations for a southward thrust were by now considered a fait accompli. The southward advance was underway, even without the instigation of U.S. economic pressure; the logic of caution now gave way to the logic of sanctions.[48]

The White House's fears that the severing of economic ties might prompt Tokyo simply to accelerate its aggression were soon realized, however. On July 31, Nomura received from Tokyo a telegram, deciphered by the United States, that defined the Japanese position. With economic relations between Japan and the Anglo-American bloc of nations "gradually becoming so horribly strained that we cannot endure it much longer," the Japanese Empire "to save its very life, must take measures to secure the raw materials of the South Seas." This in turn meant breaking "asunder this ever-strengthening chain of encirclement, which is being woven under the guidance of and with the participation of England and the United States, acting like a cunning dragon seemingly asleep."[49]

The implications of the crisis were as clear to policymakers as they were deadly. From his vantage point in Tokyo, Grew best captured the frightening sense of fatalism that now gripped the two countries: "We and the British, who also seem to have done with so-called appeasement, immediately met the move into Indochina with retaliatory steps, and Japan responded in kind. The vicious circle of reprisals and counter-reprisals is on.... Unless radical surprises occur in the world, it is difficult to see how the momentum of this downgrade movement in our relation can be arrested nor how far it will go. The obvious conclusion is eventual war."[50]

The Strategy of Delay

The tragic events of July 1941 all but sealed the fate of the United States and Japan, setting the stage for Pearl Harbor. Yet for more than four months after Japan's seizure of southern Indochina the two nations remained at peace. They resumed their negotiations, seemingly searching for an alternative to war. But the talks brought only stalemate and despair rather than reconciliation of their incompatible interests. As both adversaries talked, their armies and navies used the last days of peace to prepare for war.

On the Japanese side, the prospect of bringing the "China Incident" to an unfavorable conclusion, after so many years of struggle and national sacrifice, was intolerable even to civilian leaders. Ultimately there was no budging, either, from the goal of dragging Southeast Asia into Japan's Greater East Asia Co-Prosperity Sphere.

Nothing, meanwhile, led the Roosevelt administration to question its fundamental proposition that the United States and Britain could not afford to lose the raw material wealth and sea lanes of Southeast Asia—not even the knowledge that defense of those interests was leading rapidly to war. After the events in July, and with their secret intelligence gleaned from MAGIC, U.S. policymakers and diplomats were not about to accept any Japanese promises of peaceful intent or willingness to respect the status quo in the South Seas. Hull later claimed that as early as 1933 he adopted the guiding axiom that "Japan had no intention whatever of abiding by treaties but would regulate her conduct by the opportunities of the moment." Certainly nothing that happened in the fall of 1941 caused him to doubt that principle.[51]

Military intelligence estimates in the final months before Pearl Harbor painted a grim picture of continuing Japanese preparations for further conquests to the south, especially against Thailand, whose loss would undermine the position of British Malaya.[52] Armed with these reports and his own experience, Hull, as Stimson put it, "made up his mind that we have reached the end of any possible appeasement with Japan and that there is nothing further that can be done with that country except by a firm policy and, he expected, force itself." A few days later the secretary of state was "asking searching questions ... of the Navy what they'll do next in case any of these issues that he has been handling brings up an impasse and the necessity of force."[53] In conversation with Welles, Hull suggested the question was not if but when. "Nothing will stop them except force," he declared on August 2.[54]

The administration's conviction that a Japanese attack on Southeast Asia was only a matter of time would alone have made any serious and lasting agreement between the two countries nearly impossible, given Tokyo's territorial ambitions. But as if to clinch the matter, China began looming as an insurmountable obstacle to a settlement. Far from acting out of a sentimental attachment to China, as some historians have claimed, the administration refused to compromise over China precisely because more fundamental interests in Southeast Asia would be jeopardized if China's collapse freed a million Japanese troops for aggression elsewhere.

Washington's strategy of aiding China hinged on the hope that Japan's military strength would be dissipated on Asia's vast mainland rather than set loose on Southeast Asia. Had sentiment for China's plight, regard for principle, or even concern over the "Open Door" in China dominated the administration's perception of the national interest, it would never have fought public opinion and delayed the embargo against Japan so long. Instead, U.S. leaders used China cynically as a web in which to tangle Japanese forces and keep them from more vital regions.

This policy, however, ultimately backed the United States into a corner. To guarantee Washington's support, all the Chiang regime had to do was threaten to collapse. Chiang Kai-shek had built up a well-placed lobby within the United States to plead for more aid and resist any compromise over China's future.

Through friends in the Treasury Department and through Owen Lattimore and Lauchlin Currie, Chiang passed along his pleas for material assistance and political support, suggesting always that China's morale and military resistance were near collapse.[55] And should anyone in Washington forget China's part in the grand strategy, Hornbeck was always on hand to remind them that "far and away the least expensive" insurance against having to fight Japan was "giving aid of the right sort in adequate amounts and with effective promptness to China. . . . If we fail in this and do have to fight Japan, we will have ourselves to blame."[56]

With so little to negotiate about and so thick an atmosphere of distrust in Washington, why did Hull agree to a whole new round of negotiations with the Japanese ambassador? Ever the diplomat, he could not rule out the possibility that the U.S. embargo would make Japan come to its senses. More realistically, the secretary hoped to delay war until rearmament at home and in the Philippines could be completed. "The point is how long we can maneuver the situation until the military matter in Europe is brought to a conclusion" he told Welles. "I just don't want us to take for granted a single word they say, but appear to do so, to whatever extent it may satisfy our purpose to delay further action by them."[57] Japan also needed time to complete its military buildup. By August 5 it had stationed 40,000 troops in Indochina.[58] However, further consolidation of its position would take time, so Tokyo returned to the negotiations.

To reopen the conversations with Hull, Japan seized the opportunity opened by Roosevelt's proposal for neutralizing Indochina. On August 6, Nomura returned with the Japanese government's long-awaited response. But rather than addressing the proposal directly—which would risk laying bare the expansive aims of Japan's foreign and military policy—Nomura presented a counterproposal providing for a removal of Japanese troops from Indochina only after a satisfactory settlement of the "China Incident," a recognition by the United States of the "special status of Japan in French Indo-China even after the withdrawal of Japanese troops from that area," the suspension of all U.S. military activity in the Southwestern Pacific (including the Philippines), and an implied requirement that the United States cease aiding China if it refused to negotiate with Japan. Finally, the United States would have to remove trade restrictions against Japan.[59]

Individually and collectively, these points were nonstarters, and Hull told Nomura so. In effect, Japan was asking the United States to reverse the freeze order but otherwise accept the status quo, including the threatening Japanese military presence in Indochina. As Hull noted immediately, "from Indochina [Japan] could menace the Philippines and the British and Dutch Far Eastern possessions," whereas the United States could do nothing to stop them.[60]

Welles informed the British undersecretary of state for foreign affairs, Lord Cadogan (who was lobbying the administration to warn Japan that further advances southward could lead to war with the United States), that the White House found Japan's latest offer totally unacceptable. If Japan continued to try and dominate the Pacific, war with the United States would be inevitable. Nevertheless, the administration would continue the diplomatic charade because "it was wiser, if only to obtain delay, to utilize this counter proposal as a means of prolonging the conversations between the two Governments of Japan and the United States in order to put off a show-down (if such was inevitable) until the time that such a show-down was from our standpoint more propitious." Welles said he hoped the British government, rather than issuing an ultimatum to Japan or provoking war, would follow the policy of the United States, "namely, the dragging out of conversations on this latest Japanese proposal to the utmost without the slightest relaxation of the military or economic measures which had been taken."[61]

So the United States carried on with the conversations. Secretary Hull met with Nomura on August 8 to deliver the official U.S. response to the new Japanese initiative. He told the ambassador that the proposal was clearly unacceptable and "lacking in responsiveness to the suggestion made by the President." Hull objected to Japan's unwillingness to "neutralize" Indochina and told Nomura that serious peace negotiations could begin only if "the Japanese Government would refrain from occupying Indochina or establishing bases there with its military and naval forces or, in case such steps had already actually been begun, would withdraw such forces."[62]

Meeting Hull again on August 16, Nomura this time argued that Japan needed to control Indochina in order to obtain necessary foodstuffs. Hull countered by pointing out that Japan could obtain all the rice it needed in the world market. The secretary declared that Japan's feverish building of military bases in southern Indochina, far from helping to secure adequate supplies of rice, "would mean about the last step prior to a serious invasion of the South Sea area." Without spelling out the consequences, he said, "this Government could not for a moment remain silent in the face of such a threat, especially if it should be carried forward to any further extent."[63]

Only this last point, not the basic assessment of U.S. interests in the region, aroused debate. Roosevelt had just returned from the Atlantic Conference, where Churchill had impressed upon him the need to gain time to complete the complex preparations for defense against Japan in the Southeast Asia. The president decided to continue delaying Japan with negotiations rather than prematurely issuing threats.[64]

On August 17, with Hull attending, Roosevelt met with Nomura to discuss the ambassador's request that negotiations be resumed on a formal basis. The president opened by deploring Japan's policy of expansion. Nomura then announced some startling news: Prince Konoe, Japan's premier, so sincerely desired a peace settlement with the United States that he would meet with Roosevelt personally to discuss and if possible resolve the differences pushing Japan and the United States toward war. Roosevelt, clearly taken by surprise, did not bite. The offer would take time to digest. Instead, he simply continued on his theme, expressing his administration's unalterable opposition to Japan's foreign policy. The United States would resume normal discussions if Japan indicated its desire to follow a more peaceful policy, Roosevelt promised. But if Japan continued on its current course, his administration would be "compelled to take immediately any and all steps which it may deem necessary toward safeguarding the legitimate rights and interests of the United States."[65]

On the morning of August 28, Hull took Nomura in to see the president. The ambassador delivered two messages from his government. The first was a direct communication from Konoe urging that the two leaders meet for a summit conference as soon as possible so that the two countries could reach a settlement. This time Roosevelt expressed immediate interest in the proposal and suggested a three- or four-day meeting with the Japanese premier. The second message Nomura carried seemed less hopeful, however. Although the Japanese government announced its peaceful intentions regarding the Pacific, it would withdraw troops from Indochina only when "the China Incident is settled or a just peace is established in East Asia." Japan further offered not to use military force against any neighboring country "without provocation," a slippery phrase that could only irritate the State Department.[66]

Although Roosevelt seemed genuinely interested in Konoe's proposal for a face-to-face summit, which Grew called "unprecedented in Japanese history," Hull examined the plan with a suspicious eye. No doubt he saw some merit in Hornbeck's suggestion that the proposal be given favorable consideration "only if the Japanese authorities give evidence, by suspension of offensive military operations, of a desire to have and to maintain peace."[67] His attitude was probably stiffened even more by an intelligence summary sent by Stimson of Japan's furious military preparations. "It was another example of Japanese duplicity," Stimson observed in his diary. "They are trying now to get up a conference between the Japanese Prime Minister Konoye and President Roosevelt on a most engaging program of peace while at the same time they are carrying on negotiations with their Ambassadors throughout the world showing that on its face this is a pure blind and that they have already made up their minds to a policy of going south through Indo-China and Thailand. The invitation to the President is merely a blind to try to keep us from taking definite action."[68]

Hull was in no hurry to accept Konoe's offer. He believed that if the two governments did not decide beforehand on certain basic principles, the conference would end in failure. That in turn might exacerbate tensions, frustrate further negotiations, and lead all the faster to war. During a meeting with Nomura on the evening of August 28, Hull suggested that the basic differences separating the countries be explored and an agreement in principle be worked out before the meeting began.[69]

Nomura replied that only the issue of Japanese troops would present a problem. He suggested that the United States bend its efforts toward bringing the Chinese and Japanese governments together for peace negotiations. But even this point stirred Hull's objections, lest China sense a sellout and quit resisting. "We should be involved in this matter through Japan's requesting us to exercise our good offices," he replied. "In order to exercise such good offices we need to have the confidence and friendship of the Chinese Government before and after. We can't propose that the Chinese negotiate with Japan until we know what Japan's basic terms are. You can imagine what a difficult situation would arise if, after a meeting between Prince Konoye and the President, an explosion should occur in China over dissatisfaction with the results of the meeting."

Hull leveled with the ambassador. "We can't afford to have the Chinese think we are ignoring their interests in going ahead with any arrangements," he said truthfully. "It is our idea to help the Japanese establish friendship on a *solid* basis."[70]

As State Department experts reviewed the proposal for a Roosevelt-Konoe summit meeting, their objections mounted. First, Hull and others believed that if Japan failed to agree to basic points before the conference, no explicit settlement would result, only general statements of each side's peaceful intents, which Japan would bend to its own purposes. "Moreover," the secretary argued, "she could then say she had the President's endorsement of her actions."[71]

Hull believed further that the militaristic ruling groups in Japan could stifle any residual hope that Konoe might accept a settlement agreeable to the United States. His suspicions came to the fore again. "We knew that Japanese leaders were unreliable and treacherous," he recalled later. "We asked ourselves whether the military element in Japan would permit the civilian element, even if so disposed, to stop Japan's course of expansion by force and to revert to peaceful courses." These views were not just made up for the benefit of postwar audiences. In early October, Stimson recorded Hull's agreement that "no promises of the Japs based on words would be worth anything."[72]

An even more telling point within the State Department was Konoe's own record. Under his premiership Japan had invaded China in 1937, bombed the U.S. ship *Panay*, and signed the Tripartite Pact in 1940.[73] If allowed to meet with Roosevelt, Konoe would gain prestige, strengthening the militarists. "If we seek merely to gain time," came the inevitable Hornbeck analysis, "we should, presumably, not wish at the same time to enhance unnecessarily the prestige of Konoye and that group."[74]

Finally, the State Department worried that "the very holding of the meeting between the President and Konoe, following so soon after the Atlantic Conference, would cause China grave uneasiness, unless an agreement had already been reached that would protect China's sovereignty."[75] Such a meeting, Hornbeck agreed, "would unquestionably have a decidedly adverse effect on Chinese morale which is China's greatest weapon." For similar reasons, "an agreement would weaken Dutch morale in the Netherlands East Indies and would thus facilitate Japan's other major aim—penetration and eventual domination of those vastly wealthy islands." Other members of the Division of Far Eastern Affairs agreed with Hornbeck's analysis.[76]

So did Stimson. Armed with a military intelligence estimate proposing that the United States obtain major concessions from Japan before holding a summit conference, he wrote: "Quite independently I have reached similar conclusions and hold them strongly. I believe, however, that during the next three months while we are re-arming the Philippines great care must be exercised to avoid an explosion by the Japanese army. Put concretely this means that while I approve of stringing out negotiations during that period, they should not be allowed to ripen into a personal conference between the President and [the Japanese Prime Minister]. I greatly fear that such a conference if actually held would produce concessions which would be highly dangerous to our vitally important relations with China."[77]

To forestall any weakening of China's morale, Hull took pains to reassure the Chiang regime. He met with Ambassador Hu Shih on September 4 to discuss briefly the state of Japanese-U.S. negotiations, and through Clarence Gauss, the U.S. ambassador, Hull informed the Chinese government that in the administration's talks with Japan, "no consideration had been or would be given to any arrangement permitting the continuance of aggression in China."[78]

The State Department methodically recorded all of its objections to a summit without some prior agreement on principles, but Japan pressed on in the hope of keeping the United States out of war. Already feeling the pinch of the embargo, Japanese leaders agreed at a September 3 conference to pursue their negotiations until late October and then prepare for war if no agreement were reached.[79]

The Japanese ambassador, reflecting Tokyo's hope that Roosevelt and Konoe might yet meet, submitted to Hull a new set of proposals on September 6. Among other points, Japan promised not to undertake "any military advancement from French Indochina against any of its adjoining areas, and likewise will not, without any justifiable reason, resort to military action against any regions lying south of Japan." The United States, for its part, would be required to suspend its defensive preparations in the South Pacific and to cut off aid to British and Dutch positions in the area. Both Japan and the United States would suspend their freeze orders, and the United States would have to cut off its aid to China.[80] These were, in fact, Japan's minimum demands.[81]

But they were no more acceptable to Washington than ever. The State Department took particular note of the qualification in Japan's terms, "without any justifiable reason." It also noted that Japan "still evaded the President's suggestion that she withdraw her troops from Indo-China in exchange for neutralization of that colony."[82] Hull's "primary consideration," he told the British chargé, was still "delaying the possible expansion movements of Japan—which I have had in my mind since last spring."[83] This policy of delay, however frustrating, was giving the U.S. military time to fortify its positions in the South Seas.[84]

But China, the linchpin of this strategy, was still shaky. English-language radio broadcasts from China, transcribed and distributed within the State Department, warned against a sellout of China or a relaxation of the embargo and expressed alarm over the outcome of U.S.-Japanese negotiations.[85] On September 10 the Chinese minister of foreign affairs, Dr. Quo Tai-chi, called upon Ambassador Gauss to report that news of the negotiations had "given rise to considerable uneasiness on the part of the general Chinese public." Although they appreciated U.S. aid, "they were apt to be easily discouraged by suggestions that they are not receiving wholehearted support from the United States." Any agreement reached behind China's back, he warned, would inevitably work to China's disadvantage.[86]

Lauchlin Currie went straight to President Roosevelt to protest any accord with Japan that would allow it to remain in China. Unless the United States could guarantee the territorial integrity of China, Currie argued, the result "would do irreparable damage to the good will we have built up in China . . . and would largely nullify the effect of lend-lease aid to China."[87]

Gauss reinforced this message with his nightmarish report of "a strong undercurrent, even in [Chinese] Government circles, tending toward the view that continued resistance to Japan might not be in the best interests of China, that China might not now fare so badly in negotiations with a Japan anxious to be rid of the 'China Incident' in order to engage in adventures elsewhere, and that ultimately, in any circumstances, China and Japan must arrive at some common understanding in the Far East." Any U.S.-Japan detente that addressed only

Southeast Asia would lead to a strengthening of the peace camp in China, he warned.[88]

State Department officials took this suggestion of blackmail seriously.[89] The cumulative effect off all of these warnings from China was to reinforce the tactical linkage of China to Southeast Asia. China's interests could not be shrugged off. Joseph Ballantine summed up the consensus in the State Department that if a summit conference merely discussed the two nations' differences without reaching an accord, the appearance would remain "that some kind of secret agreement or understanding [had] been reached." The psychological blow would have "a far-reaching and immediate effect in China detrimental to the interests of the forces opposing aggression."[90] Only Grew, who saw hope of at least temporarily preventing a Japanese assault on Anglo-American interests in Southeast Asia and whose vantage point made him less receptive to Chinese concerns, still saw merit in a meeting with Konoe.

Evidence of further Japanese military preparations and demands for bases in southern Indochina was accumulating almost daily throughout late September and October, giving U.S. diplomats even more reason to believe that negotiations were unlikely to prevent a conflict.[91] With such concerns in mind, Hull delivered on October 2 the first substantive U.S. response to the Japanese peace offer of September 6. His reply to Nomura reflected weariness as well as pessimism and disappointment over the toughening of Japan's peace terms. Though not ruling out a future meeting between Konoe and Roosevelt, the secretary now rejected a fundamental Japanese demand to station troops in China indefinitely. He asked for "a clear-cut manifestation of Japan's intention in regard to the withdrawal of Japanese troops from China and French Indochina" to make known "Japan's peaceful intentions and Japan's desire to follow courses calculated to establish a sound basis for future stability and progress in the Pacific area."[92] As Nomura later cabled his government, the negotiations had reached a "deadlock."[93]

Indeed they had. Japanese leaders were beginning to suspect that they had merely been strung along for weeks by a U.S. administration eager to buy time.[94] The State Department, for its part, remained uncompromising in its hostility to Japanese aspirations on the Asian continent and in Southeast Asia.[95]

The hardening of the U.S. negotiating position, specifically Roosevelt's refusal to meet Konoe on Japan's terms, contributed to the downfall of the Konoe government on October 16 and its replacement the next day with the even more militant cabinet of War Minister Tōjō Hideki. Japanese newspapers said the country would expect the new premier "to pursue the Chinese War to victory and to establish Japan's Greater East Asia co-prosperity sphere."[96] Although most U.S. leaders did not believe Tōjō would break off the negotiations immediately, they could not fail to recognize the growing militancy of the Japanese leadership. Some officials argued that nothing fundamental had really changed, but they were as pessimistic as the rest. An October 17 War Department analysis, which went to Harry Hopkins in the White House, downplayed the significance of Japanese cabinet changes and asserted, "Whether or not a policy of peace or a policy of further military adventuring is pursued is determined by the military based on their estimate as to whether the time is opportune and what they are able to do, not by what cabinet is in power or on diplomatic maneuvering, diplomatic notes or diplomatic treaties."[97] Stimson was so sure that war was only a short matter of time that he began considering how to blame it on Japan by maneuvering her into making "the first bad move."[98]

As expected, the new Tōjō cabinet was no more inclined than the last to seek peace on terms amenable to the United States. "Our country has said practically all she can say in the way of expressing of opinions and setting forth our stands," the Tokyo government wired Nomura, in a dispatch read by the State Department through MAGIC. "We feel that we have now reached a point where no further positive action can be taken by us except to urge the United States to reconsider her views."[99]

The honorable Nomura knew the United States would not reconsider. He could see no end in sight but war. He understood that his final days as ambassador would be used for deception and not for peace and begged to be relieved of his post: "I am sure that I, too, should go out with the former cabinet.... There are some Americans who trust this poor novice and who say that things will get better for me, but, alas, their encouragement is not enough. Among my confreres here in the United States there are also some who feel the same way, but, alas, they are all poor deluded souls.... I don't want to be the bones of a dead horse. I don't want to continue this hypocritical existence, deceiving other people. No, don't think I am trying to flee from the field of battle, but as a man of honor this is the only way that is open for me to tread. Please send me your permission to return to Japan."[100]

Administration officials read this pitiful plea to the Tōjō government on October 23, the day after it was sent; the impression Nomura's cable made was powerful. But Tokyo refused Nomura's request the next day.[101]

The Final Negotiations

Japanese leaders had previously agreed to fight by late October if all peace efforts with the United States failed. But a last-minute intervention by the emperor forced Tōjō to delay plans for war and extend the negotiations. Japan's militant rulers resolved firmly to give the United States only a brief respite, however, lest Washington drag its feet at the expense of Japan's imperial ambitions.[102] On November 2, Tokyo explained to Nomura that it would reach a final policy decision on November 5. "This will be our Government's last effort to improve diplomatic relations. The situation is very grave."[103]

Another message from Foreign Minister Tōgō Shigenori to Nomura two days later sounded even more desperate: "[Th]is is our last effort. Both in name and spirit this counter-proposal of ours is, indeed, the last. I want you to know that. If through it we do not reach a quick accord I am sorry to say the talks will certainly be ruptured. Then, indeed, will relations between our two nations be on the brink of chaos. I mean that the success or failure of the pending discussions will have an immense effect on the destiny of the Empire of Japan. In fact, we gambled the fate of our land on the throw of this die."[104]

Grew confirmed, in a cable of November 3, that Japanese leaders were willing to plunge their nation into "a suicidal struggle with the United States" if they found no other way to achieve their objectives. "Action by Japan which might render unavoidable an armed conflict with the United States," he concluded gravely, "may come with dangerous and dramatic suddenness."[105]

Japanese leaders held an Imperial Conference on November 5 to formally approve a final negotiating program. The Tōjō cabinet decided to present the Roosevelt administration with its last two proposals—Plans A and B. Plan A's provisions differed little from previous Japanese drafts, but Plan B was a modus vivendi to be offered in the hope that the United States and Japan might yet step back from the brink of war. "Proposal B is not an excuse for war," Premier Tōjō told one official. "I am praying to the Gods that somehow we will be able to get an agreement with the United States with this proposal."[106]

Through MAGIC, U.S. leaders read the terms of the drafts as they were sent out to Nomura. The United States learned not only of Japan's negotiating position but of its "absolutely immovable" deadline for peace as well: November 25. Japan would fight if this date passed without a peace agreement, U.S. officials had every reason to believe.[107] Faced with this threat of war, the nation's leaders scrutinized the new proposals in the hope of finding some basis for delay, even if not common ground for a lasting agreement.

The major terms of Plan A included the principle of commercial equality in the Pacific (provided it were adopted in all other parts of the world), retention of the Tripartite Pact with slight modifications, and Japanese agreements to withdraw from China two years after the establishment of peace in that country. Japan would keep troops in Indochina until peace reigned in East Asia and would not evacuate troops from northern China and Mongolia for twenty-five years. The United States, for its part, would be bound to persuade Chiang Kai-shek to negotiate with Japan or cut off his aid.[108]

Plan A, like earlier Japanese proposals, persuaded no one in the administration. With Japanese troops massing in southern Indochina and on the border of Thailand, the plan's lack of guarantees stood out in bold relief. Hornbeck had recently prepared yet another exhaustive recitation of the evidence of Japan's total unreliability. "In the light of the foregoing record of the continual expansion of stated policies and of assurances withdrawn or contradicted by subsequent statements and actions," read one such memorandum, "any expectation by the Japanese Government that the United States should rely upon further assurances is somewhat surprising."[109] If Japan wanted peace, it would first have to prove its intentions not with words but by withdrawing from Indochina.

The problem of China posed almost as much difficulty. Japan's demand that the United States stop "interfering" with its efforts to bring about peace with China amounted to a demand that it suspend all military aid.[110] The administration could not agree without risking the collapse of its major Asian ally. Since late October Chiang had stepped up his urgent pleas for help, predicting an imminent Japanese attack on Yunnan and Kunming through Indochina, cutting off China's line of communication with the United States and Britain. In a telegram to Roosevelt on November 2 the generalissimo warned: "Once Kunming is taken, the Japanese would be rid of all fear of attack in the rear. You will, I feel sure, be the first to see that its capture is not merely one objective of Japan's war of aggression on China but is a first and necessary step to free herself for fresh enterprises. And you will appreciate how vitally the coming battle will bear upon the safety of all countries on the Pacific, upon yourselves and ourselves alike." If Japan succeeded in this new military venture, Chiang continued, "the morale of the Chinese army and the Chinese people will be shaken to its foundation," and "for the first time in this long war a real collapse of resistance would be possible."[111] If China were knocked out of the war, no area of the Pacific would be safe from Japan's armies—least of all Southeast Asia.[112]

On the evening of November 7, Ambassador Nomura handed Hull the penultimate Japanese peace offer, Plan A. Hull barely looked at the document, having seen its basic text before with the aid of MAGIC. He managed only a distracting remark to the effect that Japan could gain the moral leadership of Asia by voluntarily withdrawing its troops from occupied territories. Nomura promised to think about it.[113]

The ambassador next met with Roosevelt as well as Hull on November 10, still promoting his government's first offer. He read a long explanation of Plan A, obviously much impressed by the deadline imposed upon him by Tōjō. Roosevelt said little, displaying no great sense of urgency. He emphasized once again his wish that Japan would "pursue peaceful courses instead of opposite courses."[114] Plan A truly was "dead before its was delivered."[115]

Only one hope for peace remained—Plan B. Nomura was caught now between an intransigent U.S. administration and equally intransigent superiors in Tokyo who were demanding that he hasten the talks. "You see how short the time is," they told the ambassador; "therefore do not allow the United States to sidetrack us and delay the negotiations any further."[116] To make sure that nothing would go wrong, the Japanese government sent Kurusu Saburo, an experienced diplomat, to the United States to help Nomura present the plan. Kurusu hardly helped win the administration's confidence, however; he had been Japan's ambassador to Germany when the Tripartite Pact was signed. "Kurusu seemed to me the antithesis of Nomura," Hull wrote later. "Neither his appearance nor his attitude commanded confidence or respect. I felt from the start that he was deceitful."[117]

Bound by his orders, Nomura presented his government's final proposal to Secretary Hull on November 20. Its terms read:

1. Both the Government of Japan and the United States undertake not to make any armed advancement into any of the regions in the South-eastern Asia and the Southern Pacific area excepting the part of French Indo-China where the Japanese troops are stationed at present.
2. The Japanese Government undertakes to withdraw its troops now stationed in French Indo-China upon either the restoration of peace between Japan and China

or the establishment of an equitable peace in the Pacific area. In the meantime the Government of Japan declares that it is prepared to remove its troops now stationed in the southern part of French Indo-China to the northern part of the said territory upon the conclusion of the present arrangement which shall later be embodied in the final agreement.

3. The Government of Japan and the United States shall cooperate with a view to securing the acquisition of those goods and commodities which the two countries need in Netherlands East Indies.
4. The Government of Japan and the United States mutually undertake to restore their commercial relations to those prevailing prior to the freezing of the assets. The Government of the United States shall supply Japan a required quantity of oil.
5. The Government of the United States undertakes to refrain from such measures and actions as will be prejudicial to the endeavors for the restoration of general peace between Japan and China.[118]

The last point, of course, meant the United States would have to cease aiding Chiang. When Hull objected, Kurusu immediately asked how the United States could reconcile its public stand in favor of peace "with continued assistance to Chiang Kai-shek, which actually hinders peace."[119] Instructions from Tokyo a few days later reaffirmed this stance: "[O]ur demand for a cessation of aid to CHIANG . . . is a most essential condition."[120] Not even a return to the pre-July status quo would satisfy Tokyo.[121] Japan's offer to withdraw from southern Indochina was a false enticement, therefore. Hull could not let Japan completely off the hook in China and lift the embargo without jeopardizing the whole strategy of tying Japan down on the Asian mainland.

Hull was also inclined to assume the worst even about Japan's proposal to evacuate southern Indochina. He termed it "meaningless" because "they could have brought those troops back to southern Indochina within a day or two, and furthermore they placed no limit on the number of troops they might continue to send there." As a result, Japan would still have "threatened the security of the countries to the south and menaced vital trade routes."[122]

Hull explained these problems to Nomura and Kurusu on November 22. He told the diplomats that he had been discussing with various other governments the possibility of relaxing the freeze order against Japan if Tokyo would present concrete evidence of its peaceful intentions. He said everyone he talked to shared the same misgivings about Japan's southward plans, especially in light of the chauvinistic statements aired daily in the semiofficial Japanese press. Kurusu asked what sort of steps Japan would have to take to satisfy the United States. Japan, replied the secretary, must withdraw all its troops from Indochina, not just those from the southern half of the colony. Any forces left in Indochina could be moved south overnight—"therefore this would not relieve the apprehensions of neighboring countries. The British, for example, would not be able to move one warship away from Singapore."

Ambassador Nomura protested that Japan's real interest was simply to bring the China Incident to a satisfactory conclusion, after which it would move troops out of the French colony. Hull emphasized again that he could not consider this, that if Japan really wanted a peaceful settlement it "should get out of Indochina." Hull mentioned China only to say the United States would continue to aid the Chiang regime but that he did not want to block progress by "injecting the China matter in the proposal."[123] Plan B, like Plan A before it, died in the secretary's hands. It died above all over the question of Southeast Asia.[124]

By rejecting the Tōjō government's last offer, the United States knew it would almost certainly have to fight in the Pacific. Japan now went ahead at full speed to prepare for war. But administration officials still hoped for a few more months of peace to complete defensive preparations in the Philippines and the European colonies. Stimson had come up with a plan to defend the South China Sea with B-26 bombers based in the Philippines, but preparations would take time—of which there was now precious little.[125]

152 *Japan Moves South*

To delay Japan, Roosevelt came up with a draft modus vivendi of his own, with which the United States could live better than Japan's Plan B.[126] It offered no solution to the China Incident but focused rather on preventing a Japanese attack on Southeast Asia. It read:

Six Months

1). U. S. to resume economic relations—some oil and rice now—more later.
2). Japan to send no more troops to Indo-China or Manchuria border or any other place south (Dutch, Brit. or Siam).
3). Japan to agree not to invoke tripartite pact if U. S. gets into European war.
4). U. S. to *introduce* Japs to Chinese to talk things over but U. S. take no part in their conversations.

Later on Pacific agreements.[127]

The State and Treasury departments also worked on truce plans that could temporarily stabilize conditions in the Far East while fortification of the Philippines continued apace. Even if Japan rejected such a new offer, Hull reasoned, it might be encouraged to continue with the negotiations.[128]

Roosevelt's modus vivendi went through several drafts. The final version was completed on November 25. In return for an end to the full U.S. embargo on Japan, the proposal would require Japan to remove all troops from southern Indochina and all but a token force of 25,000 from the north. With respect to China, the proposal said only that the United States "would not look with disfavor upon the inauguration of conversations" between China and Japan to bring about a peace settlement.[129] The State Department also attached to the plan a ten-point, long-term peace proposal. It called for a multilateral nonaggression pact among Japan, the European powers and their colonies in Southeast Asia, Thailand, China, and the United States; required those governments and colonies to respect the territorial integrity of Indochina and help guarantee the Open

Door to the colony; and demanded that Japan withdraw all military forces from Indochina and China.[130] In effect, this document asked Japan to surrender all of its gains since 1931 throughout Asia.

The ten-point plan was needlessly, almost provocatively harsh and probably not meant for negotiation as much as it was a statement of policy for the record. But the modus vivendi showed promise. U.S. military leaders, who sought any excuse to delay a conflict they were not yet ready for, embraced it. Said Brig. Gen. L. T. Gerow: "The adoption of its provisions would attain one of our present major objectives—the avoidance of war with Japan. Even a temporary peace in the Pacific would permit us to complete defensive preparations in the Philippines and at the same time insure continuance of material assistance to the British—both of which are highly important."[131]

On November 22, Hull gave copies of Plan B and a preliminary draft of the U.S. proposal to representatives of Britain, Australia, China, and the Netherlands. "Each of the gentlemen present seemed to be well pleased with this preliminary report to them, except the Chinese Ambassador," Hull noted. The latter complained that U.S. draft plan contained no provision preventing further Japanese attacks on China.[132]

The U.S. modus vivendi, unlike Japan's various proposals, at least did not make matters worse for China. But the Chiang regime was not about to ease up on the administration now. It rounded up its lobbyists to shoot down the proposal before the Japanese ever laid eyes on it. First Chiang contacted Ambassador Hu Shih to express his fierce objections "to any measure which may have the effect of increasing China's difficulty in her war of resistance, or of strengthening Japan's power in her aggression against China."[133] The next day, November 25, Hu Shih called on Secretary Hull to discuss the U.S. modus vivendi. The secretary said the United States' intent was not to dump China but rather to keep Japan interested in negotiating by trying a new avenue to peace. China would benefit from a reduction of troop levels in Indochina. Furthermore, Hull pointed out, Chiang missed the significance of the U.S. proposal, "the fact that our proposal would relieve the menace of Japan in Indochina to the whole South Pacific area, including Singapore, the Netherlands East Indies, Australia, and also the United States, with the Philippines and the rubber and tin trade routes."[134] The generalissimo, however, had not overlooked those facts; his last-minute intervention was calculated precisely to prevent those interests from distracting Washington's attention from China's plight.

Pleas from China continued to pour into the State Department and White House. Chiang telegrammed T. V. Soong on November 25 asking him to approach Stimson and Knox immediately to play China's trump card—the threat of collapse:

> Please explain to them the gravity of the situation. If America should relax the economic blockade and the freezing of Japanese assets, or even if reports that the United States is considering this should gain currency, the morale of our troops will be sorely shaken. During the past two months the Japanese propagandists have spread the belief that in November an agreement will be successfully reached with the United States. They have even come to a silent but nonetheless definite understanding with the doubtful elements in our country. If, therefore, there is any relaxation of the embargo or freezing regulations, or if a belief of that gains ground, then the Chinese people would consider that China has been completely sacrificed by the United States. The morale of the entire people will collapse and every Asiatic nation will lose faith, and indeed suffer such a shock in their faith in democracy that a most tragic epoch in the world will be opened. The Chinese army will collapse, and the Japanese will be enabled to carry through their plans, so that even if in the future America would come to our rescue the situation would be hopeless. Such a loss would not be to China alone.
>
> We could therefore only request the United States Government to be uncompromising, and announce that if the withdrawal of Japanese armies from China is not settled, the question of relaxing of the embargo or freezing order could not be considered.[135]

As if this barrage from China were not enough, Britain began expressing reservations about the final U.S. draft. On November 25 the British embassy proposed that the United States require the withdrawal from Indochina of all Japanese land, sea, and air forces, "in addition to satisfactory assurances regarding other areas in South East Asia, the Southern Pacific and Russia." The British also felt the modus vivendi should require Japan to halt temporarily further military campaigns in China in order to ease the psychological blow to China of an agreement between the United States and Japan. Of course, Japan would never agree to such terms, but the Australian and Netherlands governments sided with the British in insisting that the plan be modified.

The coup de grace came in a telegram directly from Churchill, received at the White House early in the morning of November 26, stressing the importance of looking after China's interests. Britain had no special interest in China per se, but like the United States it counted on China's continued resistance as a drag on further Japanese aggression. Churchill said he certainly did not want an additional war but could not ignore China. "If they collapse our joint dangers would enormously increase," he wrote. "We are sure that the regard of the United States for the Chinese will govern your action."[136]

Hull was worn down by the steady barrage of "objections, arguments and pleas" from China and "especially impressed" by the last-minute communication from the British prime minister.[137] "The slight prospect of Japan's agreeing to the *modus vivendi* therefore did not warrant the risks involved in proceeding with it," Hull recalled later, "especially the risk of collapse of Chinese morale and resistance, and even of disintegration in China."[138] In despair, Hull talked to President Roosevelt on November 26. Although he deplored the "utter lack of an understanding of the vast importance and value otherwise of the *modus vivendi*" on the part of the other governments, Hull suggested that it be dropped in the face of such opposition. He recommended instead that the administration present Japan only

156 *Japan Moves South*

with the harsh ten-point note, formerly intended only as a supplement to the truce plan.[139]

Roosevelt quickly agreed to scrap the modus vivendi he had originated. Only that morning Stimson had informed him of new Japanese troop movements from Shanghai to Indochina. Roosevelt "fairly blew up—jumped up into the air, so to speak, and said he hadn't seen [the news] and that that changed the whole situation because it was an evidence of bad faith on the part of the Japanese that while they were negotiating for an entire truce—an entire withdrawal (from China)—they would be sending this expedition down there to Indo-China."[140]

Without any practical proposals to explore and with Japan on the move, Hull simply handed Nomura the ten-point note on November 26. The document was marked "Strictly Confidential, Tentative and Without Commitment." Its demand for the total capitulation of Japan reflected rather than caused the breakdown of negotiations. Hull himself had no illusions that the Japanese would accept, for they had seen and rejected milder proposals before. Rather, he offered it for the historical record.[141] For all intents and purposes, the two countries' efforts for a lasting peace had long since ended. As reports of an imminent Japanese thrust against Thailand, the Philippines, or the Netherlands East Indies began to stream in, Secretary Hull told Stimson, "I have washed my hands of it, and the situation is now in the hands of you and Knox—the Army and the Navy."[142]

The United States was going to war.

6

Roosevelt Plans for War

> I give to you and to the people of this country this most solemn assurance: there is no secret treaty, no secret obligation, no secret commitment; no secret understanding in any shape or form, direct or indirect, with any other government, or any other nation in any part of the world, to involve—no such secrecy that might or could, in any shape, involve this nation in any war or for any other purpose. Is that clear?
>
> We are arming ourselves not for any purpose of conquest or intervention in foreign disputes. I repeat again that I stand on the platform of our party: "We will not participate in foreign wars and will not send our Army, naval or air forces to fight in foreign lands outside of the Americas except in case of attack."
>
> Franklin Roosevelt,
October 23, 1940

The collapse of negotiations in late November 1941 left Roosevelt with a critical problem. Japan was almost certain to strike a blow against vital U.S. and British economic interests in Southeast Asia. But if Japan avoided a direct attack on U.S. territory, could the administration convince Congress to commit forces for the defense of that region?

Roosevelt did not wait for the last few days of peace to consider the question. All through 1941, the beleaguered British government had begged Roosevelt for some commitment that the United States would enter the war (in both theaters) if

Japan attacked the rich European colonies in Southeast Asia. Time and again, however, the president refused to enter into any binding agreements. When Secretary of Commerce Hopkins traveled to London in December 1940 to consult with the British government, Foreign Secretary Eden took him aside to determine what U.S. intentions were in the case of such an attack. "Of course," the presidential adviser told Eden, "it was perfectly clear that neither the President nor Hull could give an adequate answer to the British on that point because the declaration of war is up to Congress, and the isolationists and, indeed, a great part of the American people, would not be interested in a war in the Far East merely because Japan attacked the Dutch."[1]

Although Roosevelt declined to enter any formal agreements with the British, he went as far in support of their cause as he could given constitutional and domestic political constraints. Above all, he encouraged joint British-U.S. naval planning and the nonbinding ABC-1 accord, which provided for U.S. naval support of Britain in the Pacific should war break out with Japan in Southeast Asia. As if to emphasize the United States' commitment to the agreement, the U.S. Navy, at the request of the State Department, sent a temporary detachment of ships to Australia in late March 1941, when all parties signed the accord. Admiral Turner, war plans officer and chief adviser to Chief of Naval Operations Stark, explained the reason for this maneuver:

> The detachment went to Australia for the purpose of indicating to Japan solidarity between the United States and the British Commonwealth, and to indicate to Japan that if British interests were attacked that the United States would enter the war on the side of the British. Admiral Stark kept the commanders-in-chief informed, to the best of his ability, as to the international political situation and the probabilities of the future. While the Government could not guarantee that we would enter the war if Japan attacked Great Britain, they fully believed that we would do so.... Conversations were held in the Far East with

the Dutch and the British authorities, and joint plans, not too definite in nature, were drawn up, but we never could be sure that if the Netherlands East Indies or the British were attacked the United States would surely come into the war.[2]

The British were nonetheless eager for every possible reassurance that in the event of a Japanese attack on Singapore, Roosevelt would expend all his political capital to bring the United States into war. On August 4, Lord Halifax, the British ambassador, sounded out Welles by reporting an assessment from the British embassy in Tokyo that nothing now would stop Japan's militarists from trying to take over Southeast Asia. Welles cautiously replied that if Singapore or the Netherlands East Indies were actually threatened, "a situation would be created . . . which could not possibly be tolerated either by the United States, by Great Britain, by the Netherlands, by China, or by any other peace-minded and civilized nations." Welles added that "such a situation as that in my opinion would sooner or later inevitably result in war with Japan." That was welcome news to British ears. But Welles then cautioned that given the limitations of the United States' constitutional system, "no definite commitments or threats to this effect could officially be made."[3]

On August 11, at the Atlantic Conference, Churchill and Roosevelt met to discuss British-American cooperation. Churchill made no secret of his intense desire for the United States to declare war on the Axis and thus relieve pressure on Britain. He told some of Roosevelt's advisers that he "would rather have an American declaration of war now and no supplies for six months than double the supplies and no declaration." But Roosevelt was still chafing under constitutional restrictions. "He may take action as Chief Executive, but only Congress can declare war," Churchill understood. As Roosevelt watched the threat to Britain grow, however, his resolve hardened to bring the United States into war on its side. "I may never declare war," the president reportedly told Churchill in private. "I may make war. If I were to ask Congress to declare war, they might argue about it for three months."4

Short of an actual declaration of war, the British prime minister suggested issuing a joint warning to Japan to terminate its program of military expansion. Roosevelt, as usual, could not agree to such a formal declaration without the approval of Congress. But he promised to contact Nomura when he returned to Washington and lay matters on the line. The message would be simple: No more stationing of troops in Indochina or elsewhere in Southeast Asia if Japan wanted peace. If Japan refused, Roosevelt promised to say, "various steps would have to be taken by the United States notwithstanding the President's realization that the taking of such further measures might result in war between the United States and Japan."5 The president did indeed deliver such a warning to Nomura on August 17.6 Upon hearing of this threat, Stimson asked Hull to research whether "the executive power of the United States could in the absence of action by Congress take forcible action of reprisal against Japan, citing the precedents of the use of the Navy by President Adams against the French in 1798 and the action against the Barbary pirates."7

London took heart from these moral commitments. When in late August the Australian government proposed issuing a joint warning against Japan, the British turned the idea down, knowing that without support from the United States such a warning would be meaningless and even provocative. But their reply to the Australian government had encouraging words regarding Washington's intentions. From the Atlantic meeting, London had concluded there was "no doubt that in practice we could count on United States support if, as a result of Japanese aggression, we became involved in war with Japan."8

By November the Roosevelt administration knew of Japan's strict negotiating deadline. With so little time left, it stepped up its preparations for war. On November 3, L. T. Gerow, assistant chief of staff, wrote his superior, General Marshall, on behalf of the War Plans Division to suggest contingencies. He argued that the United States should fight in case of an attack on the

British or Dutch possessions but not if Japan merely stepped up its offensives in China. "It is desirable that large Japanese forces be kept involved in China," he wrote. "However, from the larger viewpoint, prospective Chinese defeat would not warrant involvement of the United States at this time in war with Japan."[9]

At a meeting the same day, Stark, Marshall and a dozen other top-level military officers considered these and other recommendations. The consensus, which also reflected priorities in the State Department and White House, was that the United States should continue aiding China, especially as a Japanese attack on China through Yunnan seemed imminent; however, Washington should only declare war if Japan attacked the European colonies or the Philippines, as opposed to China, Siberia, or Thailand. Admiral Stark presented the view of the Navy Department that, following the ABC-1 accord, the United States should undertake a limited naval offensive in the Pacific, if need be, to defend the British. Finally, all agreed that the administration should negotiate as long as possible until the Philippines could be adequately defended—perhaps by the middle of December. "Until powerful United States forces had been built up in the Far East," General Marshall noted laconically, "it would take some very clever diplomacy to save the situation."[10]

These discussions culminated in a military contingency plan jointly recommended by Admiral Stark and General Marshall. They agreed that only extreme conditions should distract the United States from its primary interest in Europe. In their opinion, China's plight did not endanger U.S. interests enough to warrant military intervention. Faced with the prospect of a two-front war, the United States should fight only for the vastly important territories of Southeast Asia:

> War between the United States and Japan should be avoided while building up defensive forces in the Far East, until such time as Japan attacks or directly threatens territories whose security to the United States is of very great importance. Military action against Japan should be undertaken only in one or more of the follow-

ing contingencies: (1) A direct act of war by Japanese armed forces against the territory or mandated territory of the United States, the British Commonwealth, or the Netherlands East Indies; (2) The movement of Japanese armed forces into Thailand to the West of 100° East, or South of 10° North; or into Portuguese Timor, New Caledonia, or the Loyalty Islands. Considering world strategy, a Japanese advance against Kunming, into Thailand except as previously indicated, or an attack on Russia, would not justify intervention by the United States against Japan. Specifically, they recommend:

That the dispatch of United States armed forces for intervention against Japan in China be disapproved.

That material aid to China be accelerated consonant with the needs of Russia, Great Britain, and our own forces.

That aid to the American Volunteer Group [in China] be continued and accelerated to the maximum practicable extent.

That no ultimatum be delivered to Japan.

Both Roosevelt and Hull "agreed thoroughly" with the recommendations.[11]

At a Cabinet meeting two days later, Roosevelt opened by polling those present as to whether they believed the American people would back up the administration if it chose to fight for the Western position in Asia. All members agreed that the public would support such a move.[12] Hull warned that the state of Japanese-American relations was becoming "extremely critical" and that the United States "should be on the lookout for a military attack by Japan anywhere at any time."[13] With Hull's words in mind, the cabinet agreed that officials should tour the country giving speeches to prepare the public for war.[14]

Defensive preparations in the Philippines were stepped up in anticipation of a southward thrust by Japan after the anticipated breakdown of negotiations in late November. Gen. Douglas MacArthur worked feverishly to turn the Philippine Army into a fighting force; the War Department sent bombers to reinforce the islands' air defenses. Stimson had even grander designs in mind. On November 21 he discussed with Roosevelt "the question (danger) of poison gas in the Philippines." The War secretary believed the Japanese were using gas in China and wanted to turn their own weapon against them. Stimson raised the matter privately, and Roosevelt agreed with him. Stimson then ordered General Gerow to prepare the shipments and avoid any leak to the press. The administration was not taking any chances, with Japan or with the American public.[15]

A MAGIC intercept on November 22 underscored how little time the administration had to complete its preparations. The Japanese government wired Nomura and Kurusu that the negotiating deadline would be extended—but only until November 29. If no agreement were achieved by then, Japan would strike. "This time we mean it, that the deadline absolutely cannot be changed," the message read. "After that, things are automatically going to happen."[16]

In this tense atmosphere, Roosevelt, Hull, Knox, Stimson, Marshall, and Stark met on November 25 at noon to plot their next moves. Roosevelt had no false hopes. He immediately pointed out that "we were likely to be attacked perhaps [as soon as] next Monday, for the Japanese are notorious for making an attack without warning, and the question was what we should do." The United States, all agreed, had no choice but to defend its interests in Southeast Asia with force. They "brought out the fact that any such expedition to the South as the Japanese were likely to take would be an encirclement of our interests in the Philippines and cutting into our vital supplies of rubber from Malaysia."

By the next day, Hull had given up on talks and turned the future of U.S.-Japan relations over to the military. Stimson, Knox, Stark, and Gerow (acting for General Marshall) scrambled to devise ways of meeting the threat. The top military leaders still pleaded for more time to erect proper defenses. A memorandum to Roosevelt prepared by Marshall and Stark emphasized this point: "The most essential thing now, from the United States viewpoint, is to gain time. Considerable Navy and Army reinforcements have been rushed to the Philippines but the desirable strength has not yet been reached. The process of reinforcement is being continued.... The longer the delay, the more positive becomes the assurance of retention of these Islands as a naval and air base. Japanese action to the south of Formosa will be hindered and perhaps seriously blocked as long as we hold the Philippine Islands." The memo proposed going to war "only if Japan attacks or directly threatens United States, British, or Dutch territory" and warning Japan of the line beyond which it could not go.[17]

Stimson and Knox accepted these recommendations, although the war secretary said he was not willing to buy time "at any cost of humility on the part of the United States or of reopening the [negotiations] which would show a weakness on our part."[18]

The administration knew by this time that a large Japanese expeditionary force was moving south from Shanghai to points unknown, "but probably ... into Thailand and to hold a position from which they can attack Singapore when the moment arrives."[19] Policymakers were unanimous in the belief that, as Welles put it, "The gravity of the situation ... could not be exaggerated."[20] On the morning of November 27, Roosevelt followed Stimson's suggestion and ordered a final alert sent to the top Army and Navy commanders in the Far East. Stark issued a war warning from the Navy Department that day to Adm. Husband Kimmel at Pearl Harbor and Admiral Hart in the Far East. The message spotlighted the expected Japanese attack on Southeast Asia: "Negotiations with Japan looking toward stabilization of conditions in the Pacific have ceased and an aggressive move by Japan is expected within the next few days. The number and equipment of Japanese troops and the organization of naval task forces indicates an amphibious expedition against either the Philippines Thai or Kra peninsula or possibly Borneo. Execute an appropriate defensive deployment."[21]

Stimson helped draft a similar message for the War Department, which went to MacArthur in the Philippines and Lt. Gen. Walter Short in Hawaii: "Negotiations with Japan appear to be terminated to all practical purposes with only the barest possibilities that the Japanese Government might come back and offer to continue. If hostilities cannot, repeat cannot, be avoided the United States desires that Japan commit the first overt act. This policy should not, repeat not, be construed as restricting you to a course of action that might jeopardize your defense."[22]

Early the next morning, newly arrived intelligence on Japanese naval operations along the Asiatic coast prompted Stimson to speak to Roosevelt. They agreed there were only two alternatives for action: Either issue an ultimatum or begin offensive operations against Japan immediately. Stimson favored the latter course, arguing, "It is axiomatic that the best defense is offense." The war secretary believed Japan had already been given plenty of warning regarding U.S. interests and intentions. However, he "realized that the situation could be made more cleancut from the point of view of public opinion if a further warning were given."[23]

Roosevelt brought up the issues at a meeting of the war cabinet later that day. Stimson recorded the consensus of the cabinet that an attack on Southeast Asia would be "a terrific blow" to the United States, Great Britain, and the Netherlands and "must not be allowed." If the Japanese expedition went as far as the Kra Isthmus, the British would fight, and "if the British fought, we would have to fight," and a "whole chain of disastrous events" would ensue.[24] Roosevelt himself was convinced that an attack on the Netherlands East Indies "should result in war" with Japan, but the question remained how to overcome the resistance of isolationists in Congress and the public.[25] The cabinet hit on the most straightforward approach: Roosevelt would speak to Congress, laying out his case for action. Roosevelt directed Stimson, Knox, and Hull to begin preparing his speech.[26] In making the case for war, it would have to spell out the stakes and define the nation's interests in definitive terms.

Stimson began drafting his version that day. It emphasized the "danger to our vital interests which now confronts the United States on the failure of these negotiations." Japan had destroyed the United States' "peaceful and profitable commercial relations" with China and now threatened to do the same in the Philippines. But a Japanese attack on Southeast Asia would be the biggest blow of all. It would "cut off and destroy our commerce with the Netherlands East Indies and the Malayan Settlements," and the United States' imports from them would be "interrupted and destroyed. These imports, principally rubber, are vital to our welfare both in time of peace and war." In wartime, he concluded, "such an interruption of our trade with the Netherlands East Indies and the Malaya States would be catastrophic."[27]

Secretary Knox completed his own draft by November 29. Like Stimson, he highlighted the strategic importance of Southeast Asian raw materials. "The successful defense of the United States, in a military sense, is dependent upon supplies of vital materials which we import in large quantities from this region of the world," Knox maintained. "To permit Japanese domination and control of the major sources of world supplies of tin and rubber is a menace to our safety which cannot be tolerated."[28]

The State Department did not begin work on its draft until November 29. Hull, who called his subordinates' attention that day to a long editorial in the *Baltimore Sun* on the United States' "vital material interests" in Southeast Asia, turned the job over to his political adviser.[29] But an exhausted Hornbeck groused that he "couldn't draft a message unless he knew what was going into it: was it peace, war, or what?" With copious notes from Hornbeck, Stimson, and Knox, Assistant Secretary Adolf Berle composed the department's draft, which Hull gave to Roosevelt.[30]

The State Department's draft contained a long and characteristically academic summary of the United States' relations with the Far East, stressing the U.S. doctrine of "fair and equal treatment among nations" and Japan's mistreatment of China. It maintained that Japan's expansionism threatened not only a proper and peaceful world order but also U.S. commerce "between the Pacific and the Indian Ocean." More specifically, echoing both Stimson and Knox, the draft stated, "To permit Japanese domination and control of the major sources of world supplies of tin and rubber and tungsten would jeopardize our safety in a manner and to an extent that cannot be tolerated." If Japan sent its forces into the southwestern Pacific, "our commerce with the Netherlands East Indies and Malaya would be at their mercy and probably be cut off. Our imports from those regions are of vital importance to us. We need those imports in time of peace. With the spirit of exploitation and destruction of commerce which prevails among the partners in the Axis Alliance, and with our needs what they are now in this period of emergency, an interruption of our trade with that area would be catastrophic."[31]

The speech was never read, although as late as December 2 Roosevelt intended to send such a message to Congress.[32] Japan's attack on Pearl Harbor lifted the need for a specific explanation of the crucial nature of U.S. interests in the region and thus left no definitive, public, official statement of the real stakes.[33]

Until December 7, Roosevelt was far from sure that even his exceptional rhetorical skills could incite an ambivalent public to support what inevitably would become a two-front war. Nor could he count on the Japanese to be so foolish as to unite the American public by attacking U.S. possessions such as the Philippines. Yet the peril to the broader region was mounting daily. Army and Navy intelligence experts originally predicted a strike by Japan on November 30; later they revised it to the weekend of December 7. Officials in the War and Navy departments compiled lists of possible targets in Malaya, the Netherlands East Indies, and the Philippines.[34]

On December 1, Ambassador Halifax met Roosevelt and Hopkins to say his government expected an attack on Thailand and the Kra Isthmus imminently, preparatory for a move on Singapore. He said further that his government was contemplating a series of countermoves—but would the United States give its unqualified support? Roosevelt satisfied the ambassador's greatest hopes. If Japan attacked British, Dutch, or U.S. territory, he said, "we should obviously all be together." The problem would arise if Japan chose a more ambiguous strategy by moving only to gain more concessions in Thailand instead of attacking the isthmus itself. Halifax concluded from Roosevelt's tone that the United States would still come to Britain's aid in resisting such a less-than-overt move by Japan.[35] Two days later Roosevelt reaffirmed his promise to send armed support to aid the British in the South Seas, and Churchill ordered Halifax to express his government's "very deep appreciation of the President's response."[36]

On December 5, the British Chiefs of Staff informed Sir Robert Brooke-Popham, commander of the Royal Air Force in Malaya, that the United States had committed military support if Japan attacked British territory or the Netherlands East Indies; the same commitment applied should the British implement contingency plan MATADOR. The latter plan provided for a preemptive British attack to seize the Kra Isthmus in case Japan moved against *any* part of Thailand.[37] The next day Capt. John Creighton, the U.S. naval attaché at Singapore, cabled Admiral Hart, commander-in-chief of the U.S. Asiatic Fleet, to inform him of this news:

> Brooke-Popham received Saturday from War Department London Quote We have now received assurance of American armed support in cases as follows: a) we are obliged execute our plans to forestall Japs landing Isthmus of Kra or take action in reply to Nips invasion any other part of Siam XX b) if Dutch Indies are attacked and we go to their defense XX c) if Japs attack us the British XX Therefore without reference to London put plan in action if first you have good info Jap expedition advancing with the apparent intention of landing in Kra second if the Nips violate any part of Thailand Para If NEI are attacked put into operation plans agreed upon between British and Dutch. Unquote.[38]

Hart received the dispatch from Singapore and relayed it in turn to Stark and to Admiral Kimmel, commander of the U.S. fleet at Pearl Harbor. Thus did Roosevelt's guarantee to the British government make its rounds throughout the Pacific. But by the time Admiral Kimmel received Hart's query, it was no longer relevant; Japanese planes had already laid waste to Pearl Harbor.[39]

Roosevelt's assurance to the British was bold and gutsy in view of his limited constitutional authority. One can only speculate how he imagined he could make it stick. Perhaps he thought his persuasive powers were strong enough to squeeze a declaration of war out of Congress. Perhaps he considered presenting the country with a fait accompli as commander-in-chief, staking his career on the hope that the public would rally around him. But a third possibility exists—that Roosevelt was prepared to engineer an incident to ensure that Japan committed the first "overt act" to bring the country into war. In Roosevelt's war cabinet meeting of November 25, the discussion had turned to just that issue. As Stimson summed up the group's thinking, "The question was how we should maneuver them into the position of firing the first shot without allowing too much danger to ourselves. It was a difficult proposition."[40]

On December 2, Admiral Stark received directly from the president a strange and disturbing order. Superficially insignificant, it conjured up a whole series of possible ramifications. Stark cabled Hart that day:

> President directs that the following be done as soon as possible and within two days if possible after receipt this despatch. Charter 3 small vessels to form a "defensive information patrol." Minimum requirements to establish identity as U.S. men-of-war are command by a naval officer and to mount a small gun and 1 machine gun would suffice. Filipino crews may be employed with minimum number naval ratings to accomplish purpose which is to observe and report by radio Japanese movements in west China Sea and Gulf of Siam. One vessel to be stationed between Hainan and Hue one vessel off the Indo-China Coast between Camranh Bay and Cape St. Jacques and one vessel off Pointe de Camau.... Report measures taken to carry out president's views.[41]

Stark, himself mystified by this order, then added to it his own request: "At the same time inform me as to what reconnaissance measures are being regularly performed at sea by both army and navy whether by air surface vessels or submarines and your opinion as to the effectiveness of these latter measures."[42]

The Asiatic Fleet obediently ordered one small boat, the *Isabel*—little more than a large yacht with four 3-inch guns—toward Indochina and prepared another lightly armed schooner, the *Lanikai*, to sail in its wake. However, Admiral Hart already had extensive air reconnaissance underway from the Philippines. No expert in the Navy Department believed more effort should be expended on this phase of the operations. Adm. Stuart Ingersoll, who helped Stark draft the order to Hart, remarked later, "I am sure Admiral Stark would not have done this unless he had been told."[43] Why, then, did Roosevelt personally order a minor reconnaissance mission, one his own theater commanders considered unnecessary?

Roosevelt must have known he was risking a serious incident by placing U.S. warships—albeit ones of insignificant value—directly in the path of the Japanese fleet. Aircraft could cover more range, were harder to spot, and could leave the scene more quickly to avoid an armed clash. As Admiral Ingersoll put it, "the chances of an overt incident occurring in the case of a plane search are very much less than that of a small ship trying to trail a force."[44] As a former assistant secretary of the Navy, Roosevelt knew this. It is hard to avoid the conclusion that here he hoped to find his casus belli for war.

The executive officer on the *Isabel*, Lt. J. G. Marion Buaas, had no doubt as to why he was sent sailing so close to danger. "The true nature of our mission was to endeavor to locate Japanese ships and as such it was expected that our reporting would result in an incident in which the ship would probably be sunk," he said later. Fortunately for the crews, the attack on Pearl Harbor led to the *Isabel*'s recall and cancellation of the *Lanikai*'s voyage.[45]

Roosevelt issued one final ultimatum to Japan in the form of a futile message to the emperor. Sent on December 6, the message threatened war if Japan followed through with its military plans. Assuring the emperor that the United States would not invade Indochina if Japan withdrew, he said that none of the peoples of Southeast Asia "can sit either indefinitely or permanently on a keg of dynamite." The president concluded with an urgent plea for peace.[46]

But Japan's war plans were fast nearing fruition. The administration learned that Tokyo had ordered its Washington embassy to destroy all secret cipher systems in advance of hostilities. Nomura also began receiving the text of a final reply from the Japanese government concerning the collapse of diplomatic relations. When Roosevelt was handed the first thirteen of fourteen parts of this message, he said simply, "This means war."[47] The conflicting interests of leaders in Tokyo and Washington made coexistence of the great Pacific powers an impossibility. Tōjō chose to break the peace in search of a new balance of power in Asia, and Roosevelt meant to stop him.

By the time President Roosevelt finished reading the intercepted dispatch from Tokyo, the Japanese naval strike force under Admiral Nagumo had almost reached the U.S. base at Pearl Harbor. Japan's preemptive surprise attack on the U.S. fleet, coordinated with an invasion of Southeast Asia, launched the Japanese nation on its suicidal mission and sealed the fate of the two giants in the Pacific.

The Pearl Harbor attack was a military disaster but an unexpected political gift for the administration. Roosevelt reacted with shock but also "great relief" when he heard the news; the United States, he now knew for certain, would enter the war on the side of Britain. Harry Hopkins recalled

> talking to the President many times in the past year [1941] and it always disturbed him because he really thought that the tactics of the Japanese would be to avoid a conflict with us; that they would not attack either the Philippines or Hawaii but would move on Thailand, French Indo-China, make further inroads on China itself and possibly attack the Malay Straits. . . . This would have left the President with the very difficult problem of protecting our interests.

... Hence his great relief at the method that Japan used. In spite of the disaster at Pearl Harbor and the blitz warfare with the Japanese during the first few weeks, it completely solidified the American people and made the war upon Japan inevitable.[48]

7

Defining the National Interest

> [A]s you know, I am more skeptical than most about the extent to which action of national governments is determined by considerations of principle. They almost always can find some principle—like some extract from scripture—to uphold the morality of what they do or want to do. And more particularly, I don't think I am willing to elevate the principle of national security to the same special peak that you do. For so often what seems to one country an act justified in behalf of national security seems to another a threat to its national security.
> *Letter from Herbert Feis to Stanley Hornbeck, November 26, 1962*

Pacifist and acute social critic A. J. Muste described World War II as a struggle between the "have" nations and the "have-nots" for "survival and domination":

> One set of powers, which includes Britain and the United States, and perhaps "free" France, controls some 70% of the earth's resources and thirty million square miles of territory. The imperialistic status quo thus to their advantage was achieved by a series of wars including the last one. All they ask now is to be left at peace, and if so they are disposed to make their rule mild though firm. . . . On the other hand stands a group of powers, such as Germany, Italy, Hungary, Japan, controlling about 15% of the

earth's resources and one million square miles of territory, equally determined to alter the situation in their own favor, to impose their ideas of "order", and armed to the teeth to do that even if it means plunging the whole world into war.[1]

The war was about much more than resources, of course; the fact that the "have" nations represented a generally liberal order and the "have-not" nations a militarist or totalitarian challenge gave this conflict a deeply ideological cast. But Muste was onto something; along with the Manichean contest of political philosophies there was a baser clash of power and interests, a struggle for economic hegemony over vast stretches of the world.

Political scientist Robert Keohane has defined economic hegemony as command of a "preponderance of material resources," including access to and "control over raw materials."[2] By any test, the Anglo-American condominium enjoyed that position in the prewar period. "The two national groups, which account for over 60 percent of the world's industrial output and exercise financial or sovereign control over 75 percent of the mineral resources, hold the balance of power in so far as the essential commodities of peace and war are concerned," Harvard political scientist Brooks Emeny declared in 1934.[3]

With economic hegemony came political and military superiority as well, as power ultimately rested in great degree on industrial prowess. Japan's challenge to vital U.S. economic interests was thus a challenge to the United States' very national security. In much the same way, Japan's national security was challenged by Washington's imposition of a trade embargo in July 1941. Out of those challenges came an awesome war for the highest of stakes, nothing less than dominance of the Pacific.

There was no Leninist inevitability about the struggle between the haves and the have-nots, no force intrinsic to capitalism that pitted the United States against Japan in a war to the finish. As Raymond Vernon noted in 1983, the United States and Japan today dominate the world's raw material markets without engaging in military competition or direct colonial control over supplies. "The common dependence of these two giant economies on a set of vitally important raw materials suggests rich possibilities—for both conflict and cooperation," he observed. " . . . On the whole, however, bearing in mind the critical importance of industrial raw materials, the postwar relations of the two countries on that delicate subject have appeared remarkably unruffled."[4]

In the 1930s and culminating on December 7, 1941, the possibilities for conflict in the U.S.-Japan relationship tragically came to dominate the possibilities for cooperation. The economic stress of the Great Depression germinated seeds of rivalry. The growing political gulf between Japan's strange blend of modernism, militarism, and feudalism, on the one hand, and the Roosevelt administration's Wilsonian liberalism, on the other, was put into sharp focus by the China Incident, Japan's brutal attempt at conquest on the Asian mainland. In this poisoned atmosphere, policymakers on both sides of the Pacific viewed economic competition as a form of economic attack and economic attack in turn as a threat to national security.

Yet both the Roosevelt administration and the American public could have lived with a degree of unwanted rivalry. China's plight stimulated the public's sympathies but not serious demands for military intervention. In 1938, historian and influential Far Eastern expert A. Whitney Griswold summed up the country's mood toward the conflict:

> While the sympathies of the average citizen are obviously with China, all the auguries of public opinion indicate that the American people are more vitally concerned with the progress of social reform and economic recovery at home than with political issues abroad. Such concern for political issues abroad as does exist is motivated chiefly by the desire to prevent alien political ideologies from infecting our own body politic. The premise that the preservation of democratic institutions at home requires active opposition to other forms of government abroad is hardly a consideration in the Far Eastern war. While Japan is an

absolute monarchy with both fascist and feudal elements, China is a military dictatorship resting on shifting elements of communism, fascism, personal ambition, factional strife, and sheer anarchy. The victory of either belligerent should carry no greater menace to the safety of democratic government within the United States than did Japan's victories over China in 1895 and Russia in 1905. The menace would be far less serious than the failure of President Roosevelt to solve such domestic problems as recovery, unemployment, or, to mention a more important issue in foreign affairs, the security of the American continent from European intervention.

The Administration has, therefore, acted wisely in putting first things first. It has not allowed a natural sympathy for China to translate itself into official government policies in the Far East that would endanger more vital popular aspirations both at home and in other parts of the world.[5]

Washington had indeed "put first things first." When Japan invaded Manchuria in 1931, fully ten years before Pearl Harbor, the United States merely withheld recognition of the Japanese puppet state. Japan launched a massive invasion of southern China in late 1937, but U.S. leaders did no more than denounce the aggression. On some issues, indeed, the administration stayed a few steps behind public opinion. Americans overwhelmingly opposed abetting Japan's aggression in China through sales of oil, scrap metal, and other war materials. "The average American," wrote Owen Lattimore in 1940, "has an uneasy conscience about the amount of help that America has been giving Japan by supplying the raw materials of war. He would like to see that stopped. He is vague about the actual figures, but he is uncomfortably aware that China has been holding out not against Japan alone but against a virtual Japanese-American alliance."[6]

Despite this groundswell of public opinion the Roosevelt administration adamantly refused, until July 1941, to impose severe economic sanctions against Japan. As late as April 1941, an official in the State Department's Division of Controls could write: "Since the imposition on July 26, 1940 of restrictions on the export of certain petroleum products, the Department has licensed about 9,200,000 barrels of gasoline for export to Japan and has applications for 2 million additional barrels now pending. The amount already licensed represents more than twice the normal annual pre-war imports of Japan from all sources and is nearly three times the quantity of gasoline which the United States exported to Japan in 1940, a most abnormal year. . . . In fact a large proportion of the license applications state quite frankly that the gasoline is intended for aviation use by the Japanese Army or Navy."[7]

Roosevelt and his advisers were not about to cut off trade with Japan on China's behalf. Even less did they ever imagine going to war for China. "It may be regarded as axiomatic," Stanley Hornbeck declared, "that the United States is not going to fight in defense of China or for the maintenance of American investments in or even existing American trade with China."[8] Another expert in the Far Eastern division, noting that China was not much friendlier than Japan toward the United States' treaty rights, confirmed Hornbeck's assessment: "It is generally understood that our material interests (commercial, educational, and eleemosynary) are of too slight monetary value to defend with a policy which involves risk of war. Our intangible interests in China, that is, our treaty rights, are also scarcely worth the risk of war for the reason that treaty rights in other parts of the world are being too frequently impaired to make it reasonable to defend those rights in any one part of the world by a policy involving a risk of war."[9]

The onset of war in Europe only stiffened the administration's interest in avoiding an armed conflict with Japan. The United States simply could not afford a two-front war. The U.S. Navy could not simultaneously patrol two oceans, the Caribbean, and the American coasts with the number of ships at its disposal. Thus, the Roosevelt administration worked hard to prevent a conflict in the Pacific.

However, if the United States had no choice but to write off its stake in China, Southeast Asia was another matter. As Grew put it in 1940, "We need not aim to drive Japan out of China now. . . . We can tolerate her occupation of China for the time being, just as we have tolerated it for the past three years. I doubt if we should tolerate any great extension of the southward advance."[10] Top Washington officials viewed an attack on the European colonies of Southeast Asia as a direct economic attack on the United States, as well as its embattled British ally. Numerous studies of the United States' raw material position in the prewar years had debunked the myth of national self-sufficiency. They found the country to be dangerously dependent on foreign sources of rubber, tin, and over a dozen other strategic commodities. The failure of the United States to secure adequate supplies of those materials in time to meet the sudden Japanese threat posed a virtually unprecedented problem. By a seeming accident of history, control of a few colonies in the southeastern corner of Asia became a vital concern of those who watched Japan march south.

Roosevelt and his advisers had reason to fear that a sudden shortage of certain important raw materials would further disrupt the nation's depressed economy, lowering living standards, provoking social unrest, slowing the pace of rearmament, and adding pressure for further government regimentation of the economy. Until substitutes or alternate sources of supply could be found, they believed, the nation could not stand idly by while Japan delivered such a blow.

The same blow would also jeopardize British interests by cutting off its lifelines to the region. The loss of Singapore, in Stimson's words, "would be an almost vital blow to the British Empire as well as to our own future commercial interests in the Pacific."[11] Indirectly, Britain would also suffer fallout from the economic damage to its chief ally, the United States. "[W]e cannot under existing conditions give effective assistance to Britain and get along without rubber and tin, etc., from the Singapore area," Hornbeck had warned.

As the military's definition of "strategic" materials suggested, loss of them would directly impair the United States' ability to defend itself. Without tungsten to harden the armor of tanks or high-quality natural rubber for the tires of trucks, the United States could not fight a war or, in the longer perspective, use force to guarantee a world friendly to Anglo-American institutions and principles. The administration had to choose whether to maintain an armed peace with Japan while its stockpiles dwindled or fight Japan for mastery of the Pacific Basin.

The State Department therefore devised a careful strategy of delay to keep Japan out of Southeast Asia as long as possible. The first prong of this strategy involved negotiations. Although Hull and his subordinates sincerely hoped that talks would achieve some settlement, they were far too pessimistic to bank on any breakthroughs. As early as 1935, Hornbeck had concluded that "no conceivable concessions on the part of the Government and people of the United States would have any conclusive effect" on the *"politik* of force . . . upon which Japan relies."[12] Hull claimed later that he distrusted Japan as early as 1933. Even before Japan signed the Tripartite Pact, Hull angrily declared that he had "come to the end of the road and that nothing would be understood by the Japanese except a show of force."[13] But Hull kept Japan talking while the United States rearmed. As he explained to Stimson and Knox in 1940, negotiations were aimed at "slowing Japan up, so to speak, as much as we could by fighting a rear guard diplomatic action, without doing it so stringently as to drive her to get her supplies by making an attack on the Netherlands [East Indies]."[14]

The second prong in the strategy of delay was to keep Japan occupied in an endless land war on the Asian continent. By granting China just enough aid to keep its armies in the field and its soldiers in fighting spirits, the administration hoped to keep Japanese troops "bogged down," in Stimson's words. Trapped in the quagmire, Japan would be "less likely to make further excursions south and to attack Australia, or even the East Indies, or Singapore."[15] Grants of military and economic aid to China would counter the ill effects of continued U.S. trade with Japan. *Fortune* magazine explained this subtle strategy in 1941:

It is perfectly true that U. S. businessmen were permitted to sell $488 million of oil, steel scrap, machine tools, and other materials to Japan in 1939 and 1940. But during the same period the U. S. Government lent $170 million to New China to back the Chinese currency and to keep Chiang Kai-shek's armies fighting the Japanese expansion. Do the two policies, the trade policy and the loan policy, add up to moral obliquity? The purist might say so, but the purist would fail to reckon with the State Department's very evident desire to keep Japan from making its final push to the south. The argument for Mr. Hull's policy has run this way: "Check Japan by aiding China, yes. But beware of cutting off her purchases of oil and other materials in this country lest, out of desperation, she be forced to make a grab for the oil and materials of the Dutch East Indies, which are protected by Singapore.[16]

If anyone imagined that Washington was aiding China for its own sake, Joseph Grew put that notion to rest: "Japan's advance to the south . . . constituted for us a real danger, and it was definitely in our national interest that it be stopped, by peaceful means if possible, by force of arms if necessary. American aid to China should have been regarded, as we believe it was regarded by our Government, as an indirect means to this end, and not from a sentimental viewpoint. The President . . . sensed the important issues in the Far East, and . . . he did not include China, purely for China's sake, among them."[17] China's leaders understood this strategy as well as anybody, and to squeeze more aid and diplomatic concessions out of Washington they had to threaten to collapse altogether, opening the door to further Japanese advances.[18]

The third prong in the strategy was a gradual closing of the economic noose on Japan as a deterrent against any attack on Southeast Asia. Until Japan actually began its march in that direction, Roosevelt was careful not to give Tokyo any economic excuse to head south. But Japan's insatiable appetite for territory and resources forced his hand. As Hornbeck's assistant Alger Hiss noted, U.S. economic sanctions were "imposed to restrain Japan's southward appetite or for urgent reasons of domestic rearmament rather than to 'impede' Japan in China."[19]

The embargo on war materials became complete only after Japan occupied southern Indochina, convincing Roosevelt that a full-blown invasion of Southeast Asia was simply a matter of time. Sumner Welles later described the significance of this crisis: "The entrance of Japan into French Indo-China . . . was the last overt danger signal. Obviously, the occupation of Indo-China was not really, as the Japanese claimed, for strategic operations against China. It could only be regarded as an immediate threat to the British position in Burma and Malaya, and a thrust at the highly vulnerable position of the United States in the Philippines. The time which passed between that move and the actual outbreak of war between Japan and the United States was so much time saved for military preparations by this country."[20]

On the day of the Pearl Harbor attack, President Roosevelt himself explained to a group of congressional leaders why Japan's occupation of southern Indochina had triggered such a powerful reaction from his administration:

> [T]he importance of [southern Indochina] lies in the fact that geographically Indo-China was at a hub, from which any attack can be made in a number of directions. It is only a very short distance from there to the Philippines in the east. It is a relatively short distance from there down to the Dutch East Indies, which is the most industrial part—southwest there is Singapore—fortified. To the west there is the Malay Peninsula, parts of Thailand, parts of the Malay Straits. . . . Only a short distance from there, of course, lies Burma, and the entry—the bottleneck to the Burma Road, a short distance from Siam. We are getting a very large proportion of our supplies—rubber, tin, etc.—from that whole area of southwestern Pacific, and we are getting out over the Burma Road—the two way road—we are getting a large amount of very important material, such as tungsten and some [wood] oil—for the manufacture of paint.[21]

The administration's embargo against Japan forced Tokyo to decide between capitulation or war. Washington was caught in a similar bind that made compromise difficult. Roosevelt could not afford to reach a settlement with Japan over Southeast Asia without also getting guarantees for China; the blow to Chinese morale if he failed might take China out of the war and leave Japan unchallenged everywhere in Asia. Nor could the administration afford to relax its economic sanctions without some concrete act of reconciliation by Japan, such as withdrawal from Indochina, because no one in the U.S. government believed Tokyo's verbal assurances. As the talks continued, officials in Washington kept their eyes on the calendar while the Army and Navy scrambled to prepare. When Japan's self-imposed negotiating deadline passed, the question for administration policymakers became one of "selling the anticipated war with Japan to the American people" by convincing them that "an attack on non-American soil—on Thailand, Malaya, Singapore or the Netherlands East Indies—constituted an attack on the United States."[22] The Pearl Harbor disaster, although an unwanted and unexpected tragedy, relieved the administration of its terrible dilemma.

The Roosevelt administration's position was consistent and plausible but not always well articulated to the American people, who would have to sacrifice mightily in the next four years. "Realistic public opinion in Japan and the United States can still avert war if America is not bent on defending China or the Dutch East Indies," columnist David Lawrence argued shortly after the Tripartite Pact was signed. "But if American youth is to be asked to go to war to defend interests 5,000 miles away, on the grounds that important raw materials are at stake, then it may be said in criticism of the Administration that it has not prepared the way for its policy."[23]

Nor was the administration's case beyond challenge. There was nothing sacrosanct about its conception of the national interest or its consequent policy toward Japan. Material factors never decide debates; they simply set their parameters, in conjunction with a host of other individual and institutional preferences, ideologies, and interests. The 1940–1941 period was no different.

More open debate would have raised important questions about the likely fate of the U.S. economy and national defense if Japan were not challenged in Southeast Asia. Would its autarkic policies drive world prices of rubber and tin higher than British producer cartels had already managed? Would Japan really cut the United States off altogether, thus denying itself the largest market for those products? Those were legitimate fears, especially given Japan's alliance with Nazi Germany. Even so, the American people, if given the choice, might have preferred privation to war.

Those questions had other possible answers, moreover. Some experts pointed out, for example, that Japanese companies in Manchukuo were eager to trade with the United States.[24] Gen. Robert Wood, head of the America First Committee, claimed that a peaceful United States would have little trouble maintaining commercial relations even with a Greater East Asia Co-Prosperity Sphere encompassing Southeast Asia: "Japan needs us far more than we need her. Our trade with Japan incidentally runs between five and six times the trade of China, whom we are making such great efforts to help. Even if Japan gets control of the Dutch East Indies—and that is not assured—she is going to be more anxious to sell us rubber and tin to obtain dollar exchange than we are to buy the products. And if war with Japan comes, we can get Bolivian tin and develop our synthetic rubber. We are certainly as resourceful as the Germans who are filling 90 percent of their rubber requirements with the synthetic article."[25]

Wood's views enjoyed at least temporary support from some U.S. defense planners. Faced with the daunting prospect of engaging enemy powers on two fronts, they understandably resisted any commitment to fight Japan. In discussions with British military representatives in Washington, the U.S. Staff Committee stated on February 19, 1941:

The denial to the United States and Britain of strategic war materials now obtained from Malaysia would be detrimental to the war effort of both countries, but would no more be a vital blow to them then [sic] it has been to Germany. Means could doubtless be devised to overcome difficulties during war, and, during peace, these difficulties would disappear, since Japan necessarily would be obliged to carry on trade in order to support her own economic position.... There is no question that the loss of Malaysia to Japan would be unfortunate from moral, economic and strategic viewpoints. Nevertheless the United States Staff Committee holds the view that this loss need not have a decisive effect upon the issue of the war.[26]

The United States' political leadership was not so sanguine, however. And in later months, U.S. war planners changed their stance and endorsed the need to draw a line beyond which Japan could not go unchallenged in Southeast Asia.[27]

A retrospective analysis offers a mixed assessment of the administration's decision to fight for Southeast Asia. On the one hand, the United States survived four years of war without rubber, tin, and other materials from the region by developing substitutes and synthetics to replace them. Surely the country's economy could have fared even better unburdened by the military demands of fighting Japan. Technologically advanced market economies, when unconstrained by price controls and other government regulations, have an enormous (if usually underappreciated) capacity to respond to shortages by discovering substitutes, new supply sources, and new technologies.[28]

Roosevelt-era planners, however, had not looked with much faith to the free market to overcome the Depression and were hardly inclined to put their faith in its ability to protect U.S. industry from the trauma of losing vital raw material supplies.[29] Moreover, evidence supporting the alarmist camp's view was plentiful once the United States went to war.[30] Within days of the Pearl Harbor attack, the U.S. chemical industry was in an uproar over the loss of tung and coconut oils from the Far East.[31] Citing the shutoff of vital chromite, manganese, tin, and other supplies from Southeast Asia, *Fortune* magazine warned in March 1942 that "war and losses in the Far East have dangerously upset the geopolitical balance of the U.S. economy." Substitutes such as synthetic rubber proved extremely costly and difficult to bring on line, in part because a maze of cartel agreements tied up critical patents.[32] In mid-1942, Roosevelt appealed to the nation to conserve scrap rubber, noting that shortages were a serious problem "from one end of the country to the other" and "a challenge to the sound judgment of the government and to the ingenuity of the American people." The Army and Navy, he declared, had "already been forced to cut their use of rubber by 25 percent."[33] Even when developed, synthetic rubber could not fully replace what Japan now denied the United States. Roosevelt's top expert informed him in 1944 that despite "the remarkable progress made in the production of synthetic rubber, a substantial proportion of natural crude rubber is required . . . in heavy duty and combat tires and for certain other essential purposes. Natural rubber is, therefore, still one of the most critical of all the strategic materials needed by the United Nations for the prosecution of the war."[34]

As late as the spring of 1945, Acting Secretary of State Joseph Grew was complaining that "Japan has her tentacles firmly embedded in the richest sources of many of the world's raw materials—materials which became necessary to the normal economies of the rest of the world. . . . As long as these vital materials are denied to the rest of the world, as long as access to them and to the trade routes of the east are hers to dominate and exploit for selfish and aggressive purposes, neither we nor our allies can hope for any return of peace, normal trade, or a decent standard of living for mankind."[35]

With the benefit of hindsight, moreover, a postwar study of raw materials declared that

> World War II highlighted dramatically the value of assured access to raw material sources as contrasted with the hardships suffered by an economy suddenly cut off from its usual sources of a vital material. The United

States, for example, was among the most self-sufficient of nations as regards raw materials, yet when a swift military stroke by Japan in 1942 shut off the flow of crude rubber from the Netherlands East Indies, the United States found its much-vaunted self-sufficiency to be a myth. Its needs for rubber at that time amounted to some 400,000 long tons per year, yet it had no domestic rubber-producing industry. Even though untold money and effort were spent to develop substitute production, to exploit new resources, and to conserve existing supplies, not until mid-1944 was it possible to avoid dipping further into our dwindling stockpile of natural rubber. The lack of abaca (manila fiber), quartz crystals, tantalite, and a host of other materials made an empty boast of the assertion that the United States was self-sufficient in raw materials.[36]

The trauma of that experience exercised powerful influence over postwar U.S. policy in Asia. Even as World War II brought the United States to a new position of preeminence in the region, it unleashed forces of revolutionary change, triggering responses from Washington toward communism and nationalism reminiscent of the Roosevelt administration's response to Imperial Japan. In May 1947, for example, Secretary of State George Marshall warned of the "danger that nationalist movements" could upset an area "of greatest economic importance," thus giving the United States "special concern" for the future of Southeast Asia.[37] In July 1949, the National Security Council concluded that in pursuing control of Southeast Asia, "the Kremlin is, of course, motivated in part by a desire to acquire SEA's resources and communications lines, but its immediate and perhaps even greater desire is to deny them to us."[38] The State Department warned in 1951 that the fall of Indochina to communism "would also pave the way for aggression against Indochina's neighbors," who supplied "80 percent of the free world's supply of natural rubber and half of its tin. The loss of these resources would be serious to the free world and would enormously increase the military capabilities of the Communist bloc."[39] That year, replaying the experience of a decade earlier, but this time with the Korean War underway, the Truman administration undertook a crash program "directed toward the purchase of all the rubber and other materials . . . originating in Indonesia, Malaya, Thailand and French Indochina . . . at the highest rate of speed possible."[40] At the same time, Truman personally directed the formation of a Materials Policy Commission under William Paley to report on the "broader and longer range aspects of the nation's materials problem." Truman termed it "one of the crucial problems facing the nation," as shortages threatened to "jeopardize our national security" and "become a bottleneck to our economic expansion."[41]

Although a myriad of other motives entered into the United States' disastrous involvement in Vietnam, the legacy of its showdown with Japan over Southeast Asia certainly played a part. This clash over raw materials thus continued to haunt U.S. policy in the region for decades to come. The millions of lives lost in that part of the world since 1941 are reason enough to continue the quest to understand the real motives and interests that propelled the United States on the road to the Pacific War.

Notes

Preface

1. Richard Barnet, *The Lean Years: Politics in the Age of Scarcity* (New York: Simon and Schuster, 1980), 17, 19. The Club of Rome study was published as Donella Meadows, et al., *The Limits to Growth* (New York: University Books, 1974).

2. A classic in this genre is Nazli Choucri and Robert North, *Nations in Conflict: National Growth and International Violence* (San Francisco: W. H. Freeman, 1975); see also Nazli Choucri, Michael Laird, and Dennis Meadows, *Resource Scarcity and Foreign Policy: A Simulation Model of International Conflict* (Cambridge: Massachusetts Institute of Technology, 1972). For a wide-ranging and critical analysis of the literature and its application to twentieth-century history, see Ronnie Lipschutz, *When Nations Clash: Raw Materials, Ideology and Foreign Policy* (Cambridge: Ballinger, 1989).

3. Lenin described the struggle for raw materials as a product of late capitalism, which drove nations toward imperialism and war. Serious examination of raw materials issues and U.S. policy has thus often been left to Marxist scholars. See, for example, Gabriel Kolko, *The Roots of American Foreign Policy* (Boston: Beacon Press, 1969) and Harry Magdoff, *The Age of Imperialism* (New York: Monthly Review Press, 1969).

4. Donald Sherk, *The United States and the Pacific Trade Basin* (San Francisco: The Federal Reserve Bank of San Francisco, 1972), 41.

5. Ibid., 12, 42; Department of Commerce, *Foreign Commerce and Navigation of the United States, 1940* (Washington: U.S. Government Printing Office, 1941), Table I.

6. Ethel Dietrich, *Far Eastern Trade of the United States* (New York: Institute of Pacific Relations, 1940), 16. Much of the tin shipped

from Malaya was actually mined in the Dutch East Indies or Thailand and only smelted in British Malaya.

7. Rupert Emerson, "Dutch East Indies Adrift," *Foreign Affairs* 18 (July 1940), 736–737; "Mineral Resources of the South Sea Countries," *Far Eastern Review* 46 (January 1940), 38–41.

8. Hiriam Farley, "America's Stake in the Far East: Trade," *Far Eastern Survey* V (July 29, 1936), 149.

9. E. Janeway, "The Americans and the New Pacific," *Asia* 39 (February 1939), 109–113.

10. Stanley Hornbeck memorandum, "Economic and Strategic Importance of the Far Eastern Area," June 14, 1940, in box 414, Stanley Hornbeck papers, Hoover Institution. For more on this memorandum, which was a reprint of an article by Robert Burnett Hall from *Geographical Review*, see Chapter 3.

11. For discussions of mercantilism and international relations, see Richard Ashley, *The Political Economy of War and Peace* (New York: Nichols Publishing Co., 1980); Robert Gilpin, *War and Change in World Politics* (New York: Cambridge University Press, 1981); and Stephen Krasner, *Defending the National Interest: Raw Materials Investments and US Foreign Policy* (Princeton: Princeton University Press, 1978).

12. A few relatively obscure studies—particularly those written soon after the events themselves—are exceptions to this rule. The conservative Asian specialist George Taylor declared in 1942, "There has never been any question but that the United States would fight when its vital interests were at stake. Free access to the raw materials of Southeast Asia has always been a vital interest. When Japan was ready, therefore, to seize Southeast Asia and monopolize for war purposes the strategic products of that area, it went without saying that the United States had to block her, by force if necessary. The very fact that Japan struck the first blow shows that she know America could not be indifferent to the fate of Southeast Asia." See Taylor, *America in the New Pacific* (New York: Macmillan, 1942), 36. For a more complete statement of this theme, see his appendix in G. F. Hudson and Marthe Rajchman, *An Atlas of Far Eastern Politics* (New York: John Day Co., 1942). For less explicit suggestions of the same argument, see T. A. Bisson, *America's Far Eastern Policy* (New York: Institute of Pacific Relations, 1945), and Arthur Schlesinger Jr., *The Bitter Heritage* (New York: Fawcett World Library, 1967), 22. More recently, Rogers Spotswood argued, "When the importance of Great Britain's survival as a bulwark against the Axis suddenly was realized in Washington, the economic value of Southeast Asia quickly assumed a new importance in the thinking of American leaders." Unfortunately, he was also

convinced that "American economic interests in Southeast Asia were minimal" and thus made no effort to examine the vast literature on raw materials from that period. See Rogers Spotswood, "Japan's Southward Advance as an Issue in Japanese-American Relations, 1940–1941" (unpublished Ph.D. thesis, University of Washington, 1974), 16–17.

13. Paul Schroeder, *The Axis Alliance and Japanese-American Relations, 1941* (Ithaca: Cornell University Press, 1958), 200.

14. Proceedings of the Lake Kawaguchi Conference on Japanese-American Relations, 1931–1941 (July 1969), mimeograph.

15. Frederick Marks III, *Wind Over Sand: The Diplomacy of Franklin Roosevelt* (Athens: University of Georgia Press, 1988), 10–11, 47–49, 52, 76. Marks also sees a general desire to protect British interests in Asia (93–94).

16. Norman Graebner, "Hoover, Roosevelt, and the Japanese," in Dorothy Borg and Shumpei Okamoto (eds.), *Pearl Harbor as History* (New York: Columbia University Press, 1973), 51; also "Nomura in Washington: Conversations in Lieu of Diplomacy," in Hilary Conroy and Harry Wray (eds.), *Pearl Harbor Reexamined* (Honolulu: University of Hawaii Press, 1990), 108.

17. David Reynolds, *The Creation of the Anglo-American Alliance, 1937–1941* (Chapel Hill: University of North Carolina Press, 1982), 59.

18. Reynolds, *Anglo-American Alliance*, 248; Akira Iriye, *Power and Culture: The Japanese-American War, 1941–1945* (Cambridge: Harvard University Press, 1981), 29–30, is representative of Iriye's argument in several books. Michael Barnhart sees "a strong economic component" to the "clash of visions for East Asia" that set Washington and Tokyo at odds. Citing Utley and Iriye as the best guides to U.S. motives, he sees the "principle of 'international cooperation' and the Open Door" as the core of the Roosevelt administration's interests. Michael Barnhart, *Japan Prepares for War* (Ithaca: Cornell University Press, 1981), 272. Waldo Heinrichs avoids any direct analysis of U.S. interests but points to a "Wilsonian faith in collective security and the appeal to principle in successive American protests against Japan's unlawful action." He also grants in passing that Roosevelt "was anxious to deter an attack on Malaya and the Dutch East Indies, which he regarded as vital because of their resources and British supply in the Middle East." Waldo Heinrichs, *Threshhold of War: Franklin D. Roosevelt and American Entry into World War II* (New York: Oxford University Press, 1988), 37, 134.

19. William Appleman Williams, *The Tragedy of American Diplomacy* (New York: Dell Publishing Co., Inc., 1962); Lloyd Gardner, *Economic Aspects of New Deal Diplomacy* (Boston: Beacon Press, 1971).

See also Robert Freeman Smith, "American Foreign Relations, 1920–1942," in Barton Bernstein ed., *Towards a New Past* (New York: Random House, 1968), 232–262, and the essays by Williams and Gardner in David Horowitz ed., *Corporations and the Cold War* (New York: Monthly Review, 1969), 71–104, 105–142.

20. Jonathan Utley, *Going to War with Japan, 1937–1941* (Knoxville: University of Tennessee Press, 1985), xii, 5, 68, 85–87, 178, 181. Although deficient in its examination of U.S. motives, Utley's book is an excellent and valuable analysis of bureaucratic decisionmaking.

21. Deborah Miner, "United States Policy Toward Japan 1941: The Assumption that Southeast Asia was Vital to the British War Effort," (Ph. D. thesis, Columbia University, 1976). She rightly notes, however, that when other scholars acknowledge the importance of Southeast Asia, they "do not probe into the rationale behind the assumption" (10).

22. Robert Dallek, *Franklin D. Roosevelt and American Foreign Policy, 1932–1945* (New York: Oxford University Press, 1979), 531: "In short, to gain a national consensus for fighting fascism overseas, Roosevelt could not discriminate between Germany and Japan; both had to be opposed at the same time." Among other problem with this line of argument, as we shall see, is that far from yielding to public pressure, the administration was desperately searching in December 1941 for ways to convince the public to support military action against Japan in Southeast Asia.

23. Abraham Ben-Zvi, *The Illusion of Deterrence: The Roosevelt Presidency and the Origins of the Pacific War* (Boulder: Westview Press, 1987), 94, 32.

24. Ben-Zvi's work is one of the more systematic attempts to look at the interests and worldview of competing cliques of policymakers; the Williams school also keeps fundamental interests at the focus of its attention.

25. John Toland, *Infamy: Pearl Harbor and Its Aftermath* (Doubleday, Garden City, 1982), xv.

26. Some readers may note the substantial weight put on the views of one secondary official, Stanley Hornbeck, who was Secretary of State Cordell Hull's chief adviser on the Far East. Hornbeck's irritating style should not be confused with lack of bureaucratic clout. For evidence of his influence, see footnote 72 in Chapter 3. Of course, my thesis rests on the expressed views of many policymakers other than Hornbeck.

1. Raw Materials and National Power

1. For a contemporary discussion of the significance of these trends, see Arthur Upgren, "Geographical Directions of United States

Foreign Trade: A Study in National Interests," Council on Foreign Relations Memorandum E-B15, June 28, 1940. See also the section later in this chapter on the Council's role in postwar planning.

2. Jacob Viner, "National Monopolies of Raw Materials," *Foreign Affairs* 4 (July 1926), 595–600.

3. I. F. Stone, *Business as Usual* (New York: Modern Age, 1941), 28.

4. Quoted in Magdoff, *Age of Imperialism*, 49–50. For a similar assessment, see Percy Bidwell, *Raw Materials: A Study of American Policy*, (New York: Council on Foreign Relations, 1958), 1–2.

5. Quoted in Laurence Shoup and William Minter, *Imperial Brain Trust: The United States Foreign Policy* (New York: Monthly Review Press, 1977), 24.

6. *Fortune* 20 (September 1939), 82.

7. After U.S. marines occupied the Philippines in 1898, President McKinley decided to retain the islands as a colony in part on the basis of investigations of their mineral wealth. See Benjamin Williams, *Economic Foreign Policy of the United States* (New York: McGraw Hill, 1929), 373. Also note the State Department's exertions to oppose a German monopoly on the world's available potash, a material needed for fertilizers and other chemicals. Joseph Brandes, *Herbert Hoover and Economic Diplomacy* (Pittsburgh: University of Pittsburgh Press, 1962), 108–109.

8. H. Foster Bain, *Ores and Industry in the Far East* (New York: Council on Foreign Relations, 1927).

9. *Congressional Record* 84 (April 25, 1939), 4747–4748.

10. William C. Redfield, *Dependent America* (New York: Houghton Mifflin, 1926), 17.

11. Bryan to Ambassador Page, November 12, 1914, in Special Committee Investigating the Munitions Industry, hearings, *Munitions Industry* (Washington: U.S. Government Printing Office, 1936), 8258–8262.

12. Associates in International Relations, Department of Social Sciences, *Raw Materials in War and Peace* (West Point: U.S. Military Academy, 1947), 86–87.

13. U.S. Army, *Strategic and Critical Raw Materials*. Service Forces Manual M104. (Washington: U.S. Government Printing Office, 1944), 10; Associates in International Relations, *Raw Materials*, 86–87.

14. Redfield, *Dependent America*, 18. Cf. Address of Dr. George Smith, director of U.S. Geological Survey, at January 6, 1922, conference of Council on Foreign Relations, "Mineral Resources and Their Distribution as Affecting International Relations."

15. James Gould, *Americans in Sumatra* (The Hague: Martinus Nijhoff, 1961), 97–99; Oliver Lawrence, "The International Control of Rubber," in W. L. Holland, ed., *Commodity Control in the Pacific Area*

(Stanford: Stanford University Press, 1935), 402–408, 412; Royal Institute of International Affairs, *Notes on Raw Materials in the Far East and Pacific Dependencies* (London: Royal Institute of International Affairs, 1933), 15–18; K. E. Knorr, *World Rubber and its Regulation* (Stanford: Stanford University Press, 1945); B. Wallace and L. Edminster, *International Control of Raw Materials* (Washington: Brookings Institution, 1930), Ch. VI; Brandes, *Hoover*, 85–86.

16. Quoted in Brandes, *Hoover*, 71.

17. Cited in Gould, *Sumatra*, 98. For more on his position, see Herbert Hoover, "America Solemnly Warns Foreign Monopolists of Raw Materials," *Current History* 23 (December 1925), 307–311.

18. Lawrence, "Control of Rubber," 413.

19. According to one study of international cartels, the "great political and economic repercussions aroused [by] the Stevenson scheme . . . [were] still mentioned even in 1945 . . . as a reason why the United States public should resist all kinds of international marketing controls." Ervin Hexter, *International Cartels* (Chapel Hill: University of North Carolina, 1945), 284.

20. Harry Whitford, "The Crude Rubber Supply," *Foreign Affairs* 1 (June 15, 1924), 613–621. For more on the concern over U.S. dependence during this period, see Bain, *Ores and Industry*, 21–22; C. K. Leith, "The Political Control of Mineral Resources," *Foreign Affairs* 3 (July 1925), 541–555; C. K. Leith, "Mineral Resources of the Far East," *Foreign Affairs* 4 (April 1926), 433–442; Josiah Spurr, "Steel-Making Minerals," *Foreign Affairs* 4 (July 1926), 601–612; Viner, "National Monopolies," 595–600.

21. Eugene Staley, *Raw Materials in Peace and War* (New York: Council of Foreign Relations, 1937) 38, 87.

22. Ibid., 38. Coconut shells were important because they produced the highest-quality charcoal used in gas-mask filters. For other important evaluations of U.S. dependency during the early 1930s, see C. K. Leith, *World Minerals and World Politics* (New York: McGraw Hill, 1931); Mineral Inquiry, *Elements of a National Mineral Policy* (New York: Council on Foreign Relations, 1933). This study, conducted by various members of the Council on Foreign Relations, seems to have been an outgrowth of the famous Inquiry following World War I, many of whose leaders later founded the CFR. See also Brooks Emeny, *The Strategy of Raw Materials* (New York: Macmillan, 1934).

23. House Committee on Foreign Affairs, hearings and report, *The Tin Investigation* (Washington: U.S. Government Printing Office, 1935).

24. Staley, *Raw Materials*, 118.

25. C. K. Leith, "Mineral Resources and Peace," *Foreign Affairs* 16 (April 1938), 522–523.

26. C. K. Leith, "Role of Minerals in the Present War," *Mining Congress Journal* 26 (November 1940), 34–38.

27. C. K. Leith, "Strategic Minerals in War and Peace," *Science* 93 (March 14, 1941), 244–246.

28. Stark to FDR, November 12, 1940, President's Secretary's File (hereafter "PSF"): Plan Dog, Roosevelt papers, Franklin Roosevelt Library, Hyde Park.

29. House Committee on Military Affairs, hearings, *Strategic and Critical Raw Materials* (Washington: U.S. Government Printing Office, 1939), 109, 110, 115.

30. Ibid., 212–213. The Committee on Military Affairs, in its final report to Congress, concluded no less forcefully that the United States lacked "certain raw materials essential to the needs of the armed forces of the Nation and to the well-being of the civilian population in event of war" and would "find itself at a grave disadvantage in the event that war or other emergency should close the sea lanes or block the normal sources of supply." *Congressional Record* 84 (April 25, 1939), 4749.

31. Army and Navy Munitions Board, *The Strategic and Critical Materials* (Washington: Army and Navy Munitions Board, 1940).

32. G. A. Roush, *Strategic Mineral Supplies* (New York: McGraw Hill, 1939), viii–ix. He wrote further, "On the whole, the total United States imports of mineral origin in 1937 constituted about one-sixth of the total value of all imports; but of this one-sixth more than 40 percent was in the strategic group, and more than 20 percent in the one metal tin. This illustrates rather pointedly the exaggerated importance of this small group of a dozen materials, and explains to some extent their indispensable character in our present-day industrial life." Roush worked in the Commodity Division of the Office of the Assistant Secretary of War and was a major in the Staff Specialist Reserve, U.S. Army. His book won an award from the Society of American Military Engineers.

33. Munitions Board, *Strategic Materials*, 6; Office of Emergency Management, *Materials for Defense* (Washington: Government Printing Office, 1941). See also "The Facts About Chromium," *Far Eastern Review* 37 (April 1941), 140, 143. Chromium was considered at one time the highest-priority material. See memorandum of conversation between Feis, Clayton, et al., 811.20 Defense (M)/865 1/2, Records of the Department of State, Record Group 59, National Archives. Hereafter cited by decimal file and record group.

34. Alvin Barber, "Philippine Chromite Now a Factor in World Market," *Far Eastern Survey* 8 (March 1, 1939), 58–59; Department of Commerce, *Foreign Commerce and Navigation of the United States*,

1940, 168. On the Philippines chromium potential, see U.S. Tariff Commission, *United States-Philippine Trade*, Report no. 118, 2nd series (Washington: U.S. Government Printing Office, 1937).

35. Munitions Board, *Strategic Materials*, 8. See also "Manganese and Preparedness," *Mining and Metallurgy* 21 (October 1940), 453–455.

36. Department of Commerce, *Foreign Commerce*, 167.

37. Munitions Board, *Strategic Materials*, 11.

38. Ibid., 9. On the great significance of abaca, see also H. J. Trueblood (EA) to Hornbeck (PA), March 4, 1941, 811.20 Defense (M)/2218, RG 59, National Archives.

39. Robinson Newcomb, "The United States and Southeast Asia's Strategic Products," *Far Eastern Survey* 8 (April 12, 1939), 88.

40. M. Kerbosh, "Some Notes on Cinchona Culture and World Consumption of Quinine," *Far Eastern Review* 36 (April 1940), 156–160.

41. Lt. Col. Herman Beukema and Lt. Arnold Sommer, "Dependence of U.S. Economy on Raw Materials from the Far East," *Amerasia* 3 (May 1939), 108.

42. Munitions Board, *Strategic Materials*, 19; Sir Lewis Fermer, "Burma's Mineral Resources and the War," *Far Eastern Review* 36 (April 1941), 124–127. See also Jonathan Marshall, "Opium, Tungsten and the Search for National Security, 1940–1952," in William O. Walker III ed., *Drug Control Policy: Essays in Historical Perspective* (University Park: Pennsylvania State University Press, 1992), 89–116.

43. Munitions Board, *Strategic Materials*, 18.

44. Newcomb, "Strategic Products," 89.

45. Munitions Board, *Strategic Materials*, 18. See also December 2, 1941, memorandum from the Division of Far Eastern Affairs in Leo Pasvolsky office file, box 2, RG 59, National Archives; Adolph Bregman, "Tin," *Iron Age* 146 (July 4, 1940), 29–31; "Tin and Preparedness," *Mining & Metallurgy* 21 (September 1940), 412–413.

46. Colonel Rutherford testimony, House Committee on Military Affairs, hearings, *Strategic and Critical Raw Materials*, 129; William Fox, *Tin: The Working of a Commodity Agreement* (London: Mining Journal Books Ltd., 1974), 57–61; Norman Gall, *Bolivia: The Price of Tin, Part I: Patino Mines and Enterprises* (New York: American University Field Staff, 1974), 12–13. Sidney Ball observed, "The optimist might hope that Latin America, in the future, will furnish us with ore for from a quarter to a third of our consumption, provided we had smelters to treat it. For the rest, we must look elsewhere. The tin situation is critical." *Engineering & Mining Journal* 141 (September 1940), 39–41.

47. Army and Navy Munitions Board, memorandum to Industrial Materials Department, Advisory Commission to Council of National Defense, September 13, 1940, in entry 8, package 3, Rubber Survey Committee papers, Franklin D. Roosevelt Library.

48. George B. Emeny to W. W. Knight, Jr., July 16, 1941, 345.13413 C, RG 179, Records of the War Production Board, National Archives.

49. Indeed, the United States imported as much as 60 percent of the entire world output of rubber. Munitions Board, *Critical Materials*, 15.

50. William Christians and Otis Starkey, "The Far East as a Source of Vital Raw Materials," *Annals* 215 (May 1941), 84–85.

51. Munitions Board, *Strategic Materials*, 15–16.

52. Besides those already cited, see J. C. de Wilde and George Monson, "Defense Economy of the United States, An Inventory of Raw Materials," *Foreign Policy Reports* 16 (November 15, 1940), 202–212; Adolph Bregman, "Non-Ferrous Materials and Strategic Position," *Iron Age* 145 (January 4, 1940), 98–100; G. A. Roush, "Strategic Mineral Supplies," *Military Engineer* 30 (September-October 1938), 370–374; August Maffry, "Strategic Materials in United States Import Trade," *Survey of Current Business* 20 (December 1940), 10–15; "Strategic Materials: 14 Items Essential to National Defense Must Be Imported in Whole or in Part," *Barron's* 20 (May 20, 1940), 6; "Essential Defense Materials," *Barron's* 20 (June 3, 1940), 6; Robert Burnett Hall, "American Raw Material Deficiencies, and Regional Dependence," *The Geographical Review* 30 (April 1940), 1977–186, "America's Material Interests in the Far East Are Vital," *Baltimore Sun*, November 29, 1941. This latter article was particularly noted by Secretary of State Hull; see Leo Pasvolsky office file, box 2, in RG 59, National Archives. More optimistic accounts include "U.S. Dependence on Far East Discounted," *Baltimore Evening Sun*, July 20, 1940, and "Experts Say This Hemisphere Can Produce Defense Materials," *Baltimore Evening Sun*, July 4, 1940.

53. Senate Committee on Naval Affairs, hearings, *Construction of Certain Naval Vessels* (Washington: U.S. Government Printing Office, 1940), 23. Other Navy officials discussed these issues even more bluntly. Rear Admiral Woodward wrote a column for the *New York Journal American* on February 23, 1941, entitled, "Philippines and U. S. Trade Routes Doomed if Japs Take Singapore."

54. Senate Naval Affairs Committee, hearings, *Nomination of William Franklin Knox* (Washington: U.S. Government Printing Office, 1940), 9.

55. Japanese plans for a New Order have been widely analyzed and described. For a good summary of Japan's position, see the articles of

Akira Iriye reprinted in Esmonde Robertson, ed., *The Origins of the Second World War* (London: Macmillan, 1971), especially 254–261, 269–271.

56. Andrew Roth, *Japan Strikes South* (Institute of Pacific Relations, 1941), 47–48, 2–3.

57. Address by Raymond Geist, May 21, 1941, *Department of State Bulletin*, May 24, 1941.

58. Stanley Hornbeck, "Japan Versus the United States," September 16, 1941, box 145, Stanley Hornbeck papers, Hoover Institution.

59. For evidence of the administration's deep concern, see 1940 *Department of State Bulletin*, 29–42, 63–81, 97–109, 176–186, 206–214, 25–245, 390–397, 461–464, 473–479, 506–510.

60. League of Nations, *The Network of World Trade* (Geneva: League of Nations, 1942), 87–88.

61. Dietrich, *Far Eastern Trade*, 11.

62. League of Nations, *World Trade*, 126.

63. Ibid., 80.

64. Department of Commerce, *Foreign Commerce*, Table I.

65. Kate Mitchell and W. L. Holland eds., *Problems of the Pacific, 1939* (New York: Institute of Pacific Relations, 1940), 16.

66. Address by Grady to the National Foreign Trade Council, July 31, 1940, *Department of State Bulletin*, August 3, 1940, 84–85.

67. Address by Raymond Geist, May 2, 1941, *Vital Speeches* 7 (August 1, 1941), 632.

68. *Department of State Bulletin*, April 6, 1940, 364; Franklin Roosevelt, message to the National Foreign Trade Convention, July 25, 1940, in *Report of the Twenty-Seventh National Foreign Trade Convention* (New York: NFTC), 346–347.

69. Speech by Will Clayton, "The World Cotton Situation," reprinted in Frederick Dobney, ed., *Selected Papers of Will Clayton* (Baltimore: Johns Hopkins University Press, 1971), 53–54. Clayton prefaced these remarks by saying, "This much seems certain: If the dictators win this war, the United States must embark on a preparedness program of colossal proportions. That means, among other things, an economic, and to some extent, a political revolution in the United States."

70. Edgar Smith, "Foreign Trade and the Free Enterprise System," speech of July 31, 1940 to Second General Session of the 27th Convention of the NFTC, in box 306, Hornbeck papers.

71. Emeny, *Strategy of Raw Materials*, 17.

72. Miner, "United States Policy," 61–62. First on the British War Department's list of "Far Eastern interests which we must do our utmost to defend in the event of war with Japan" were "essential sea

communications" (Chiefs of Staff Committee, "The Situation in the Far East in the Event of Japanese Intervention Against Us," July 31, 1940, PREM3 156/2, Public Records Office, London).

73. "General Strategy Review," July 31, 1941, cited in Miner, "United States Policy," 272; cf. Memorandum from First Sea Lord, "Essential Imports from the Far East," August 8, 1941, cited in ibid., 277. For more on British view of Singapore's importance, see minutes, memoranda, and cables in "Admiral Ghormley" folders of ComNavEu file, Operational Archives, Navy Yard, Washington D.C.

74. Churchill to Roosevelt, February 15, 1941, in Joint Committee on the Investigation of the Pearl Harbor Attack, *Hearings and Exhibits* XIV, 3452–3453. (Hereafter PHA Hearings or PHA Exhibits.)

75. For example, Churchill authorized a buildup of troops and aircraft in Malaya after the August 8, 1940, War Cabinet meeting. See War Cabinet, Chiefs of Staff Committee, COS(40)676, F4144/193/61, Public Records Office.

76. Kate Mitchell, "Japan's Southern Drive Faces Obstacles, *Amerasia* 5 (June 1941), 139–140. See also Michael Greenberg, "Malaya—Britain's Dollar Arsenal," *Amerasia* 5 (June 1941), 144–151; Ernest Hauser, "Britain's Economic Stake in Southeast Asia," *Far Eastern Survey*, 6 (December 22, 1937, 283–288; Denis Weaver, *The Battle of Supplies* (London: Hodder & Stoughton Ltd., n.d.).

77. Alexander Kiralfy, "American Pacific Strategy," *Asia* 39 (November 1940), 567–569.

78. "Navy Reaches Out in Pacific With Eyes on Aid to Britain," *Newsweek*, January 13, 1941, 33–34.

79. Stark to FDR, November 12, 1940, PSF:Plan Dog, Roosevelt papers.

80. James Herzog, *Closing the Open Door* (Annapolis: Naval Institute Press, 1973), 116. British representatives explained these considerations in more detail at an unofficial, private conference on "Anglo-American Cooperation in the Pacific" held on December 7–8, 1940 and attended by representatives of the U.K., Canada, Australia, the Netherlands East Indies, and the United States. In response to a question as to why the British wanted more aid in the Pacific instead of the Atlantic, they gave two answers: "Admittedly the situation in Europe is precarious. Britain requires full American aid. But it is essential to Britain's success in Europe that the war be prevented from spreading to the Pacific. The Far East is vital to the British war effort, particularly in the Near East. Australian manpower and materials are immediately important in the Mediterranean; in a long war the contribution of the Pacific Dominions, the Far Eastern colonies, and India may be decisive. Strategically the function of Singapore is to block Japan from

the Indian Ocean. Once British communications are disrupted by the Japanese Navy, the British may be lost in the Near East for lack of supplies. If this happens, the blockade of Europe is broken. American aid in the Pacific is essential, therefore, to prevent Germany and Italy from joining hands in the Near East with Japan in the Far East to break the back of British resistance." E. C. Carter, of the Institute of Pacific Relations, sent a copy of the transcript to Hornbeck, to be distributed through the Department. See box 460, Hornbeck papers.

Hull, in a discussion with Halifax, speculated about the possibility of a vast domino effect: "I myself have visualized the problem and issue in a broader way and that issue is presented by the plan of the Japanese to invade by force the whole of the Indian Ocean and the islands and continents adjacent thereto, isolating China, sailing across probably to the mouth of the Suez Canal, to the Persian Gulf oil area, to the Cape of Good Hope area, thereby blocking by a military despotism the trade routes and the supply sources to the British. I added that this broad military occupation would perhaps be more damaging to British defense in Europe than any other step short of the German crossing of the Channel." See Hull's memorandum of conversation in Department of State, *Peace and War* (Washington: U.S. Government Printing Office, 1943), 710–711.

Note that some administration officials also feared the consequences to Britain if Japan sent its surplus raw materials to Nazi Germany, reinforcing the Axis war effort. See Department of State, *Foreign Relations of the United States: The Far East, 1940* (Washington: U.S. Government Printing Office, 1955), Volume IV, 232–233. (Hereafter these volumes are cited as *FR*.)

81. Many experts both at the time and subsequently believed the public awoke too late to the magnitude of the crisis. Commenting on the persistently widespread belief that the United States was invulnerable to blockades owing to its self-sufficiency, the U.S. Military Academy's *Raw Materials in War and Peace* observed: "The folly of such views, revealed in the train of events down to VJ-Day, was clear at least to American experts who were concerned with the problem of our raw materials resources in World War I. Unfortunately, the fallacy of our self-sufficiency persisted in popular opinion so strongly and for so long as to hamper seriously our preparation for the emergency precipitated by World War II. The heavy and needless cost of atonement for such errors of judgment and forethought has ushered in a more realistic examination of the nation's materials resources present and future" (80). The Armed Service Forces manual *Strategic and Critical Raw Materials*, similarly lamented that "It is a common form of misinformation long employed by propagandists, publicists, and wishful

thinkers to assure the American public that we have no vital needs which cannot be supplied within our own borders. Such misinformation is not only potentially harmful to our highly industrialized economic system, but it is a menace to the institution of an adequate program for war" (11). See also the discussion in the section on stockpiling.

82. Cyrus Peake, editorial, *Amerasia* 1 (May 1937), 100.

83. Statement of Senator Walsh, *Congressional Record* 83 (April 1938), 5518.

84. *Naval Expansion Program*, Senate report 1611, 75th Congress, 3rd session, April 18, 1938, 3–4. In hearings before the Senate Naval Affairs Committee in 1938, Navy Secretary Claude Swanson enumerated the many raw materials for which the United States was dependent on foreign sources and said, "It is necessary that we be able to defend the trade routes ... for American ships to go in order to bring back the necessary raw materials." Senate Naval Affairs Committee, hearings, *Naval Expansion Program* (Washington: U.S. Government Printing Office, 1938), 384.

85. *Vital Speeches* 7 (November 15, 1940), 75–76. See also his News Reel Address in New York City, September 18, 1940, in box 449, Hornbeck papers. In a letter to Hull on July 25, 1939, Hornbeck noted, "Admiral Yarnell has made for himself during this his last detail, in the Far East, a magnificent record. Our own [Foreign Service] officers, American and foreign civilians in the Far East, the 'foreign' press, and even the Japanese Navy, have given repeated testimony to the respect in which he is held and the admiration with which those near him have viewed his upholding of the traditions and the prestige of the United States in connection with the performance of the functions which have appropriately been his." Box 449, Hornbeck papers. See also the praise given Yarnell in Evans Carlson to Miss LeHand, January 23, 1941, PHA Exhibits, XX, 4282–4283.

86. *Fortune* 21 (January 1940), 79.

87. *Fortune* 21 (April 1940), 92.

88. Ibid., emphasis in the original. One businessman at the conference was moved to argue, "I believe that our foreign-trade policy should be based almost entirely upon our need for materials that we do not produce in this country, such as rubber, coffee, tea, silk, and other items. Our desire for these products rather than the pressure to sell our products abroad should be controlling" (104).

89. "America's Raw Material Needs: The Potential Availability of Strategic Supplies," *The Index* 20 (Winter 1940), 86–87.

90. Watson address, July 30, 1940, in box 306, Hornbeck papers. Watson used tin as an example of a vital import. "Tin is very impor-

tant in our manufacturing," he said, "because, in our great canning industry we have to import all of the tin we use. We import 34% of the world's production of tin." See also *Report of the 27th National Foreign Trade Convention*, 352.

91. *Business Week*, August 1940, 52.
92. *Fortune* 22 (April 1941), 90.
93. *Fortune* 24 (July 1941), 75.
94. *Time*, September 16, 1940, 45. See also Capt. Po-shen Yen, "The Economic Factor of American Far Eastern Policy," *China Monthly* II (April 1941), 15–17, 19; "Man in the Street Drives U.S. Stake in N.E.I.," *China Weekly Review*, October 26, 1940, 259–260. For a more elaborate popular discussion of the strategic resources of Southeast Asia, see Wilbur Burton, "The Dutch East Indies: Vital Resources," *The Living Age* CCCLIX (November 1940), 263–267. Daily newspapers also followed up the story of U.S. dependence on Far Eastern raw materials. The *Washington Evening Star*, for example, published a five-part series on U.S. dependence in May 1940 based on the Munitions Board study. (Copies of these articles may be found in the Hornbeck papers, box 403.) Other editorials and articles from major newspapers are cited later in the text. The Europe-oriented Committee to Defend America by Aiding the Allies also turned its propaganda efforts toward the Far East question. In a pamphlet by Livingston Hartley, the committee argued that Japan could greatly damage the British war effort by cutting off supplies of raw materials and men (from Australia and New Zealand) if it seized the strategic port. As the pamphlet pointed out, Japan could also weaken the United States by cutting off its supplies of rubber and tin and ultimately become a military threat to the United States. See Livingston Hartley, "Singapore," Hornbeck papers, box 389.

95. On the views of these public opinion leaders and regional elites, see Council On Foreign Relations, *Some Regional Views on our Foreign Policy, 1941*, especially 30–31, 119, 137, 162, 178. It shows that elites generally recognized Japan's threat to vital raw material sources in Southeast Asia and favored a more militant foreign policy. The regional viewpoints expressed in this CFR study are those of members of the Committees on Foreign Relations located in strategic metropolitan centers throughout the country, such as Los Angeles, San Francisco, Cleveland, St. Louis, Detroit and Chicago. The membership of these organizations reflected an upper-class and professional bias; top businessmen were most heavily represented. Other examples of statements by internationalist opinion makers include Mark Ethridge, "The Economic Consequences of a Hitler Victory," address before the Retail Merchants Association of Louisville, January 21, 1941, in *Inter-*

national Conciliation 370 (May 1941), 558–559; Charles Woolsey Cole, "International Economic Dependence," monograph for Commission to Study the Organization of Peace, in *International Conciliation* 369 (April 1941), 242; John Oakie, "Today We Need Access to Eastern War Materials," and John Condliffe, "We Must Keep China and the Indies Within the World's Free Trade Area," both in *San Francisco Chronicle*, June 30, 1941.

96. Miriam Farley, "America's Stake in the Far East Trade," *Far Eastern Survey* 5 (July 29, 1936), 169–170. See also her pamphlet, *America's Stake in the Far East* (New York: Institute of Pacific Relations, American Council, 1936).

97. Robert Barnett, *America Holds the Balance in the Far East* (New York: Institute of Pacific Relations, American Council, 1940), 21.

98. Henry Douglas, "Japan's Expansion," *China Today*, March 1940.

99. Robert Aura Smith, *Our Future in Asia* (New York: Viking Press, 1940). Smith worked with the *New York Times* through 1941. The theme of his book might be summed up in his sentence, "The South China Sea is the battle-ground for our future in Asia." He dealt at great length with Southeast Asia's raw materials reserves and with U.S. needs and concluded that the United States must fight to protect its lifelines to Southeast Asia. Also see his "Japan Forces America's Hand," *China Monthly* 1 (December 1940). Trade expert Ethel Dietrich observed that the loss of trade from the Far East would burden U.S. consumers in a host of ways that went well beyond the loss of militarily strategic materials: "Other commodities vitally important to American industries, if not themselves war necessities, include bristles, coconut oil and copra, jute and kapok, shellac, perilla oil, pyrethrum, soya beans, tapioca and tung oil, over 75 percent of which come from these countries. Among the food imports, tea, pepper and spices come almost wholly from Southeastern Asia. Medical supplies include, in addition to quinine, camphor, menthol, agar-agar and nux vomica" (Dietrich, *Far Eastern Trade*, 170.) Other books include Claude Buss, *War and Diplomacy in Eastern Asia* (New York: Macmillan, 1941): "The United States would be in an industrial predicament if a war should cut off the stream of imports from the land of the setting sun" (510), and Mark Gayn, *The Fight for the Pacific* (New York: William Morrow & Co, 1941), ch. 18, "Treasure Box of Asia."

100. A number of these are quoted in later chapters on diplomacy.

101. Stone, *Business as Usual*, 29.

102. Hanson W. Baldwin, *United We Stand* (New York: Whittlesey House, 1941), 87. For a sample refutation of this line of argument, see R. Veatch, "South America as a Source of United States Strategic Materials," March 21, 1940, in box 56, Feis papers.

103. Justus Doenecke, ed., *In Danger Undaunted: The Anti-Interventionist Movement of 1940–1941 as Revealed in the Papers of the America First Committee* (Stanford: Hoover Institution Press, 1990), 169–170.

104. "Did you know that the Western Hemisphere by itself possesses all the materials necessary for American industry in war or peace?" in Doenecke, *In Danger Undaunted*, 169 (no. 17, August 8, 1941). In another document, issued as Japan was seizing southern Indochina, the committee repeated, "A threat to the rubber and tin supply line is not the emergency that the President and General Marshall are talking about. American boys need not die for old Dong Dang." ("Did you know that Congress is being asked to declare a national emergency whose nature is unknown?" no. 12, July 24, 1941, in Ibid., 365.)

105. Ibid., 172.

106. On the early history, see Whitney Shepardson, "The Early History of the Council on Foreign Relations," privately printed, in Shepardson papers, Roosevelt Library; "Report of the Committee appointed by an informal meeting of persons attached to the British and American peace delegations at the Hotel Majestic on May 30th, 1919," in box 329, Hornbeck papers.

107. Hamilton Fish Armstrong speech, quoted in CFR, "Proceedings at the Opening of the Harold Pratt House," April 6, 1945.

108. The most substantial published work on its influence is Laurence Shoup and William Minter, *Imperial Brain Trust: The Council on Foreign Relations & United States Foreign Policy* (New York: Monthly Review Press, 1977). Its chapter 4 deals cogently with the issues raised here.

109. Lester Milbraith, "Interest Groups and Foreign Policy," in James Rosenau, ed., *Domestic Sources of Foreign Policy* (New York: The Free Press, 1967), 247.

110. Joseph Kraft, "School for Statesmen," *Harper's Magazine*, July 1958, 64.

111. Quoted in Kraft, "Statesmen," 67. Feis and Stimson both published books through the council. Roosevelt was not himself a member, but many of his close friends were, including council president Norman Davis, one of his most trusted advisers. Roosevelt founded the Woodrow Wilson Foundation, which helped finance the council. (See grants list in box 58, Arthur Sweetser papers, Roosevelt Library.) *Foreign Affairs* editor Hamilton Fish Armstrong later became president of the foundation. Roosevelt even lived next door to the council's headquarters in New York. See Hamilton Fish Armstrong, *Peace and Counterpeace: From Wilson to Hitler* (New York: Harper & Row, 1971), 439.

112. In a single year, the journal published C. K. Leith, "The Political Control of Mineral Resources," *Foreign Affairs* 3 (July 1925), 541–555; C. K. Leith, "Mineral Resources of the Far East," *Foreign Affairs* 4 (April 1926,) 433–442; Josiah Spurr, "Steel-Making Minerals," *Foreign Affairs* 4 (July 1926), 601–612; Jacob Viner, "National Monopolies of Raw Materials," *Foreign Affairs* 4 (July 1926), 595–600. Among its books were Council on Foreign Relations, *Mineral Resources and Their Distribution As Affecting International Relations* (New York: Council on Foreign Relations, 1922); H. Foster Bain, *Ores and Industry in the Far East* (New York: Council on Foreign Relations, 1927); Mineral Inquiry, *Elements of a National Mineral Policy* (New York: Council on Foreign Relations, 1933); and Staley, *Raw Materials*. See also Eckes, *Global Struggle*, 38, 53.

113. Council on Foreign Relations, *The War and Peace Studies of the Council on Foreign Relations, 1939–1945* (New York: Council on Foreign Relations, 1946), 2–3; Harley Notter, *Postwar Foreign Policy Preparation, 1939–1945* (Washington: U.S. Government Printing Office, 1949), 19–22; Kraft, "Statesmen," 67. Breckinridge Long recorded in his diary for January 4, 1940, "It is all to be be secret, and if anything is known about it, it is to be given the color of economic activity in support of the Trade Agreements program" (Fred Israel, ed., *The War Diary of Breckinridge Long* [Lincoln: University of Nebraska Press, 1966], 51). The head of the council's postwar planning group was Norman Davis, Roosevelt's close friend and foreign policy adviser. Other key figures included Johns Hopkins University president and geographer Isaiah Bowman, a former member of President Wilson's team in Paris; Allen Dulles, then an attorney with Sullivan and Cromwell; and Harvard economist Alvin Hansen.

114. Mallory letter to Eugene Staley, September 18, 1945, CFR file, box 2, Bay Region IPR papers, Hoover Institution.

115. See minutes of May 2, 1942, meeting of the Division of Special Research in box 85, Hull papers, Library of Congress; Hull's letters to Hamilton Fish Armstrong and Isaiah Bowman, July 30, 1945, in box 54, Hull papers; and Hull memo to Gray, April 14, 1944, box 85, Hull papers.

116. Winfield Riefler, quoted in council discussion paper T-A14, June 17, 1941.

117. E-B27, "Economic Trading Blocs and Their Importance for the United States," February 15, 1941.

118. E-B34, "Methods of Economic Collaboration: Introductory. The Role of the Grand Area in American Economic Policy, July 24, 1941.

119. E-B31, "Intra-Bloc Preferential Tariff and Other Devices for Encouraging Economic Integration," March 7, 1941.

120. E-B12, "A Pan-American Trade Bloc," June 7, 1940; P-A12, discussion re effects of Russia's entry into the war, June 25, 1940; E-B17, "The Resources of Germany and the United States," June 28, 1940; E-B18, Supplement II, "The Future Position of Germany and the United States in World Trade: A Western Hemisphere-Pacific Area Economic Bloc," September 6, 1940; E-B27, "Economic Trading Blocs."

121. E-B34, "Methods of Economic Collaboration."

122. William Diebold Jr. comment, in T-A14, June 17, 1941.

123. E-B31, "Intra-Bloc Preferential Tariff."

124. T-B8, "Political Regions of Eastern Asia," May 20, 1940 [prepared by Owen Lattimore]. For Roosevelt's glowing praise, see his letter to Chiang Kai-shek, June 23, 1941, in PSF:China, FDR papers.

125. E-B26, "American Far Eastern Policy," January 15, 1941. See Pasvolsky note to Hull, January 28, 1941, in box 75, Hull papers.

126. Ibid. This strategy of confining the conflict to China was foreshadowed by study group reports from late 1940, which envisioned the country as serving as "fly paper" for Japan's Imperial Army: "If Japan is to be deterred from a southward thrust (without a very remote and difficult naval war by the United States), it must, therefore, be forced to devote greater resources of manpower, material, and shipping to its struggle against Nationalist China. By assisting the Chinese to intensify their resistance to Japanese conquest the United States might help so burden Japan that its reserves of shipping, material, and manpower would not be adequate to embark on the conquest of the Netherlands East Indies and of Singapore" (T-B20, "Aid to China," October 11, 1940). For the "fly paper" analogy, see T-B22, "Alternatives of American Policy Toward Russia," December 9, 1940.

127. T-A14, June 17, 1941, discussion of Lattimore's memo, Coordination of American Policy in the Far East. Many CFR studies and discussions were quite sympathetic to Japan, seeing it as a preeminent organizing power in the postwar Asian economy, an ally in supplanting European influence and a worthy trading partner. See CFR Study Group, "Do Bases for a Real Peace Exist Between the United States and Japan?" November 3, 1941; E-B33, "The Economic Organization of Peace in the Far East," June 20, 1941. Riefler pointed out that "from a strategic point of view it would be wise to bring Japan into the Grand Area by making her dependent on our market rather than building up the Far East as an autonomous region" (E-A16, May 17, 1941). Another study assumed that "Japan will play a leading role in that peace because of her position in the Far East and in the world. . . . Basically, Japan must secure a commercial role commensurate with her importance as an economic power" (E-B33).

2. The Rush to Stockpile

1. Staley, *Raw Materials*, 89.
2. Joint Board No. 324, letter to Franklin Roosevelt from Secretary of the Navy Swanson and Secretary of War Dern, May 29, 1934, box 56, Feis papers; memorandum by Claude Swanson, November 24, 1934, 811.24/1021 RG 59, National Archives; Feis memo to William Phillips, June 4, 1934, F.W. 811.24/1027, RG 59, National Archives.
3. Cordell Hull, *The Memoirs of Cordell Hull* (New York: Macmillan, 1948), Volume I, 457–458; Herbert Feis, *Seen from E. A.* (New York: Alfred A. Knopf, 1947), 9–11. The failure of the British to comply proved a sore point in U.S.-British relations and in American public opinion. Because the tin producers were operating far below capacity during the Depression, and because the British could not afford to pay back the debts directly in scarce foreign exchange, the State Department felt its own solution was best. The British, of course, preferred not to pay anything at all and realized that large U.S. stockpiles would undercut any future producers cartel.
4. Proposals for stockpiling had come as early as the mid-1920s from a group organized by C. K. Leith and the Mining and Metallurgical Society of America. It declared that "a wise national policy should in general favor the free use of foreign sources of supply of minerals which we do not have in adequate quantities, in order to conserve our own resources," because "if we long continue on our present policy of exploiting our resources to the utmost, regardless of their limitations, some of them will be soon exhausted, making the United States entirely dependent upon other countries for these materials in times of peace—and dangerously dependent in times of war." Quoted in Alfred E. Eckes, Jr., *The United States and the Global Struggle for Minerals* (Austin: University of Texas Press, 1979), 40.
5. Henry Wallace, "Science and the Military," *New Republic*, February 3, 1947, 27.
6. Hull, *Memoirs*, I, 624; Herbert Feis, "The State Department's Activity for the Purpose of Safeguarding the United States Against the Rubber Shortage in the Event of an Emergency," May 22, 1942, in box 85, Hull papers; and in papers of Herbert Feis, Library of Congress (hereafter called Feis report).
7. Feis, *Seen from E. A.*, 7–8. Of all State Department officials, Feis spent the most time dealing with raw materials questions. See Dean Acheson, *Present at the Creation* (New York: Norton & Co., 1969), 170.
8. Hull to Roosevelt, May 29, 1935, 811.24/1034, RG 59, National Archives.

9. The list of members is in container 115, Henry Hopkins papers, FDR Library.
10. Feis, *Seen from E. A.*, 6.
11. U.S. Army, *Strategic and Critical Raw Materials*, 17.
12. Ibid.; Associates in International Relations, *Raw Materials*, 89.
13. Ibid. Small additional funds were appropriated in later years to add to the Navy's stockpiling program. See U.S. Army, *Strategic and Raw Materials*, 17.
14. *Congressional Record*, March 28, 1939, 3401.
15. Quoted by William O'Neil, president of General Tire & Rubber, in *Houston Post*, November 14, 1944. At least some executives shared Hull's concerns. See J. J. Blandin's letters to Charles Cooke, November 2, 1938 and April 11, 1939, in box 4, Charles Cooke papers, Hoover Library.
16. Department of State, *Peace and War* (Washington: U.S. Government Printing Office, 1943), 431–432.
17. Feis memorandum, October 21, 1938, box 5, Feis papers.
18. 811.24 Raw Materials/11, RG 59, National Archives; cf. Feis, *Seen from E. A.*, 8n. Many other reports are quoted in Feis report, 4–8 and enclosures.
19. Quoted in Department of State, *Peace and War*, 63.
20. Ibid. Bernard Baruch claims to have originated the idea; see Baruch, *Baruch: The Public Years* (New York: Holt, Rinehart & Winston, 1960), 301. Hull had earlier opposed such barter arrangements because they directly contradicted the principles of multilateral trade embodied in his Trade Agreements program. See Hull's letter to Senator Harrison on June 6, 1939, in which he expressed grave concern over the inadequacy of U.S. supplies but refused to condone state barter arrangements. See Department of State, *FR, 1939*, I, 852–853. Hull finally changed his mind because "the amount of money Congress was willing to appropriate was far from sufficient to assure us an adequate reserve of strategic materials" (Hull, *Memoirs*, I, 625). On all of these questions, see Feis, *Seen from E. A.*, 38–43. On the negotiations, see also *FR, 1939*, II, 234–266.
21. Rubber Reserve Company, *Report on the Rubber Program 1940–1945* (Washington: Government Printing Office, 1945), 14; Office of War Mobilization, *Rubber, First and Second Reports of the Inter-Agency Committee on Rubber* (Washington: Government Printing Office, 1946).
22. "The President Urges Immediate Appropriations for the Purchase of Strategic War Materials," in Franklin D. Roosevelt, *Public Papers and Addresses of Franklin D. Roosevelt, 1940* (New York: Macmillan Co., 1941), 94–95.

23. For Hull's expression of concern, see his memo in *FR, 1940*, II, 250. On Morgenthau's views, see ibid., 257.

24. Feis, *Seen from E. A.*, 55–58; Bascom Timmons, *Jesse Jones: The Man and the Statesman* (New York: Henry Holt and Co., 1956), 301–302.

25. Welles to Roosevelt, May 1, 1940, cited in *FR*, 1940, II, 253–255. Welles was apparently inspired by a memorandum by Roy Veach, "United States Position in Rubber, Tin and Quinine," April 26, 1940, which emphasized the urgency of stockpiling in light of the unstable conditions in the Far East. Copy in box 85, Hull papers.

26. "Scramble for Strategics," *Engineering and Mining Journal* 141 (June 1940), 32; "A Billion for Strategics," ibid., 70.

27. Adolf Berle to Admiral Land, May 20, 1940, *FR, 1940*, II, 259–60. Berle was requesting that Land, Chairman of the U. S. Maritime Commission, expedite the shipping of rubber and tin from the Far East.

28. Transcript of conversation, May 16, 1940, in Senate Committee on the Judiciary, *Morgenthau Diary (China)*, Volume I (Washington: Government Printing Office, 1965), 151; *FR, 1940*, II, 253–255; Feis, *Seen from E. A.*, 56–80. Feis notes that Roosevelt sent back his approval to Welles and instructed the acting secretary to inform the director of the budget, the federal loan administrator, and the secretary of the treasury of plans to use the RFC as a purchasing agency.

29. Jones, *Fifty Billion Dollars*, 436–445. President Roosevelt sent Henry Grady, president of American President Lines and assistant secretary of state for economic affairs from 1939–1941, to Southeast Asia to organize the purchase of minerals for the Metals Reserve Company. See Henry Francis Grady, "Adventures in Diplomacy," 1953, typescript, in Grady papers, Hoover Library.

30. Jesse Jones, *Fifty Billion Dollars* (New York: Macmillan Co., 1951), 396–397; Timmons, *Jesse Jones*, 301–302; Rubber Reserve Company, *Report*, 14; Office of War Mobilization, *Rubber*; U.S. Army, *Strategic and Raw Materials*, 17.

31. Russell McBride, "Strategic Buying Planned," *Engineering & Mining Journal* 141 (July 1940), 33–34.

32. Timmons, *Jesse Jones*, 303; Feis, *Seen from E. A.*, 64–65.

33. Jones, *Fifty Billion Dollars*, 402–406; Timmons, *Jesse Jones*, 304–306. Bernard Baruch claims that "Jones demonstrated no great sense of urgency, either in stockpiling natural rubber or in pushing the development of the synthetic rubber industry." But it seems likely that Baruch, an even greater empire builder than Jones, simply felt jealous of his rival's position (Baruch, *Baruch: The Public Years*, 301). For Stettinius's point of view, see his letter to Roosevelt, September 12, 1940

in OF [Office File] 3, Roosevelt papers, and his letter to Jones, November 25, 1940, in box 327, Hopkins papers. For a good history of rubber programs, see *A History of the U.S. Government's Natural and Synthetic Rubber Programs, 1941-1955*, manuscript prepared by Reconstruction Finance Corporation, 1948-1955, in box 204, Jesse Jones papers, Library of Congress; also Civilian Production Administration, Bureau of Demobilization, "Rubber Policies of the National Defense Advisory Commission and the Office of Production Management, May 1940 to December 1941," *Historical Reports of the WPB*, no. 28, April 25, 1945, 570.2 R, Records of the War Production Board, RG 179, National Archives.

34. For more information on this subject, see John Blum, *From the Morgenthau Diaries: Years of Urgency, 1938-1941* (Boston: Houghton Mifflin, 1965), 122-129. Another useful source, revealing the true purpose of the China loans, is Robert Barnett, "Opening El Dorado With a Loan," *Amerasia* 4 (April 1940), 72-75.

35. Federal Loan Agency press release FLA-48, September 25, 1940, in box 52, Hornbeck papers.

36. *Washington Star*, December 22, 1938.

37. Memorandum, November 20, 1939, in Senate Judiciary Committee, *Morgenthau Diary (China)*, I, 52-53. See also "Tung Oil," *Far Eastern Review* 36 (February 1940), 76-77.

38. Memorandum from Harry Dexter White to Henry Morgenthau on the "Tin Loan, " November 22, 1939, in Senate Judiciary Committee, *Morgenthau Diary, (China)*, I, 54.

39. Memorandum of November 20, 1939, in ibid.

40. Ibid.

41. Federal Loan Agency Press Release FLA-48, box 52, Hornbeck papers; Jesse Jones to Roosevelt, November 30, 1940, in OF 150, Roosevelt papers; Comments of Franklin Roosevelt, in Roosevelt, *Public Papers and Addresses, 1940*, 587-595.

42. Jones, *Fifty Billion Dollars*, 439, 444-450; Stone, *Business as Usual*, 26-27. Another example of such "enlightened self-interest" was Roosevelt's suggestion to the Departments of State and the Treasury that the United States buy large quantities of strategic materials, such as manganese, chromite, mercury, platinum, and asbestos, from the Soviet Union, in return for which the USSR would grant military loans to China. The sum Roosevelt had in mind was $200 million for this three-cornered deal. Ultimately the plan fell through because State opposed cooperation with the Soviet Union. Blum, *Years of Urgency*, 347; Senate Judiciary Committee *Morgenthau Diary (China)*, I, 181-2, 191-2 208-216, 225-231, 233-235; Israel, *War Diary of Breckinridge Long*, September 25 and 28, 1940, 132.

43. Emerson, "Dutch East Indies Adrift," 740.

44. Testimony before Senate Military Affairs Committee, *Strategic and Critical Materials*, 52–53. For a comparison of stockpile objectives to actual deliveries, see memo of Gordon Arneson, Bureau of Research and Statistics, War Production Board, to C. K. Leith, January 27, 1941, WPB 112.01 R, RG 179, National Archives.

45. K. E. Knorr, *Tin Under Control* (Stanford: Food Research Institute, 1945), 183.

46. Rubber Reserve Company, *Report*, 14–15.

47. Eckes, Jr., *Global Struggle*, 101.

48. Israel, *War Diary of Breckinridge Long*, January 3, 1940, 240.

49. *The Rubber Situation* (report of the Baruch Committee), House Document No. 836, 1942. See also Office of Emergency Management, *Materials for Defense* (Washington: U.S. Government Printing Office, 1941): "We could, by a heroic effort, build more huge factories for the manufacture of synthetic rubber, but it is doubtful if that could be done rapidly enough to compensate us for the lack of crude rubber in case our supply was suddenly stopped. Rubber men . . . point out that synthetic rubber produced in, say, 1944 would be of little use to our defense production effort in 1942." Copy in WPB 111B, RG 179, National Archives.

50. Jesse Jones to William Knudson (OPM), June 25, 1941, WPB 112.1C, RG 179, National Archives.

51. See notes in box 56, Feis papers.

52. Henry Kanee memo to Stephen Early, March 8, 1939; Kanee, "Memo for the files," March 9, 1939; Kanee memo to Louis Johnson, March 15, 1939; Johnson memo to Franklin Roosevelt, June 14, 1939, in OF 25, Roosevelt library; also D. W. Bell (Bureau of the Budget) to Hull, March 13, 1939, 811.24 Raw Materials/54, RG 59, National Archives.

53. Eliot Janeway, *Struggle for Survival* (New York: Weybright and Talley, 1968), 26.

54. Roosevelt press conference, 645-A, May 23, 1940; Eckes, Jr., *Global Struggle*, 76, 78.

55. Quote from Associates in International Relations, *Raw Materials*, 8; Beukema and Sommer, "Dependence of U.S. Economy," 102–103.

56. *Engineering and Mining Journal* 142 (July 1941), 32–33.

57. *Congressional Record* 87 (October 30, 1941), 8335.

58. The political pressures against excessive preparations for war were so strong in the United States that before the 1940 election, in the face of near unanimous opinion by his experts that economic defense measures were essential, Roosevelt downplayed all moves for

stockpiling. See William Langer and S. Gleason, *The Undeclared War 1940–1941* (New York: Harper & Bros., 1952), 195–212; Baruch, *Public Years*, 281; as an example of the way FDR had to promise never to fight in the Pacific, see "Informal, Extemporaneous Remarks at Buffalo, New York, November 2, 1940," in Roosevelt, *Public Papers and Addresses, 1940*, 541–543. For the State Department's similar fears in 1937, see Feis, *Seen from E. A.*, 38.

59. *Congressional Record* 84 (April 25, 1939), 4750.

60. Ibid., 4768.

61. "Strategics and Politics," *Engineering and Mining Journal* 141 (April 1940), 32. See also Janeway, *Struggle*, 26. As Feis put it, "It was the period of belief that the Government should scour the Dakota hills for tin before buying it from Malaya, and that our poor supplies of manganese should be used up before we brought it from elsewhere" (*Seen from E. A.*, 37).

62. *Congressional Record* 80 (August 2, 1939), 10859. In late 1941 he was still complaining: "Mr. Chairman, every time the matter of strategic materials comes before the House of Representatives we see this same old fight that is raging here today, the fight between the producers of low-grade materials in the United States and those who really wish to procure those materials in the interest of national defense. Every time the fight is made to prostitute national defense in the interest of sectional advantages." He continued, with reference to the manganese lobby, "It is a fact that during the days of the World War, when the price of manganese rose to unprecedented heights, we never were able to produce over 20 percent of what we need in this nation. The same thing applies to all of these strategic materials. The would-be producers, the promoters and representatives from mining sections, have made extravagant claims, but these claims have produced very little of these badly needed strategic materials. The same story applies to all of them.... It is essential that we get these materials and that we no longer get promises. We can no longer run mills making automobiles on promises; we can no longer operate on promises of rubber; and if we are to make high-grade tool steel, we must have tungsten to make it; and if we are to make certain grades of steel, we must have chromium; and we must have manganese if we are to turn out any steel at all." *Congressional Record* 87 (October 7, 1941), 7708. See also Senate Judiciary Committee, *Morgenthau Diary (China)*, I, 33–35, regarding the debate between elements in the administration and in Congress over whether to purchase manganese ore from domestic or foreign sources. Several pages of quotes from outraged senators and representatives appear in response to moves to purchase the ore from foreign mines—clear evidence of the power of the manganese interests.

63. *Oil, Paint and Drug Reporter* 140 (December 8, 1941), 5.
64. *Congressional Record* 87 (October 7, 1941), 8335–8336.
65. Quoted in *Refrigerator Engineering* 42 (September 1941), 159–160; cf. Langer and Gleason, *Challenge*, 181–182, 191.
66. Baruch, *Public Years*, 301–302.
67. On U.S. dealings with the rubber and tin restriction committees, see *FR, 1939*, I, 858–905, 928, 933 (rubber) and 867–868, 900, 906–947 (tin); *FR, 1940*, II, 261–288 (rubber) and 288–300 (tin); *FR, 1941*, I, 492–507 (rubber) and 507–530 (tin).
68. Oliver Lawrence, "International Tin Restriction," in William Holland, ed., *Commodity Control in the Pacific Area*, 380–385; James Gould, *Americans in Sumatra* (The Hague: Martinus Nijhoff, 1961).
69. Holland, *Commodity Control*, 386–387; Knorr, *Tin*, 137.
70. Holland, *Commodity Control*, 391.
71. Knorr, *Tin*, 146–148; Holland, *Commodity Control*, 398.
72. Knorr, *Tin*, 171–175.
73. Ibid., 177.
74. Ibid., 180–181.
75. Ibid., 179; Gould, *Sumatra*; Jones, *Fifty Billion Dollars*, 437.
76. Knorr, *Tin*, 183; "Tin Container Industry's Sales Show Big Increase on Heavier Army, Civilian Demand," *Wall Street Journal*, July 7, 1941.
77. K. E. Knorr, *World Rubber and its Regulation* (Stanford: Stanford University Press, 1945), 101, 105, 108; Gould, *Sumatra*, 102. Also see articles by E. G. Holt and Warren S. Lockwood, "How International Rubber Restrictions Came About," *Asia* 35 (June 1935), 327–331, and "The Rubber Control Scheme at Work," *Asia* 35 (July 1935), 422–427.
78. Knorr, *World Rubber*, 129; Feis, *Seen from E. A.*, 26–27.
79. Knorr, *World Rubber*, 130.
80. Feis, *Seen from E. A.*, 24, 28–29.
81. Rubber prices in New York shot up 16.7 cents a pound in August, reaching 24 cents in September. See Feis, *Seen from E. A.*, 48–49; Knorr, *World Rubber*, 135.
82. Feis, *Seen from E. A.*, 49–50. Knorr comments: "From what is known of the deliberations of the IRRC it appears that it was ever prone to underestimate future absorption and was afraid of a sudden turn of the market that might cause a drop in price while stocks were high.

"Thereafter, until Japan conquered the major rubber-growing areas of Malaysia, the rubber-supply situation was dominated by an unexampled increase in United States rubber consumption for civilian use and the endeavor of the United States government to build up a large stockpile of this strategic material in case the imminent war emergency materialized." (136)

83. Timmons, *Jesse Jones*, 303–304; Feis, *Seen from E. A.*, 73–75.
84. Timmons, *Jesse Jones*, 304–305.
85. Jones, *Fifty Billion Dollars*, 399.
86. Feis, *Seen from E. A.*, 84–85.
87. *Wall Street Journal*, July 22, 1941. Russia's stockpiles were depleted because Great Britain had tried to embargo sales of rubber to it while the Nazi-Soviet pact was in effect. See also Feis, *Seen from E. A.*, 80.
88. Stone, *Business as Usual*, 27.
89. Jones, *Fifty Billion Dollars*, 399–400; on the policy of sending Army transports to Singapore to load up with rubber, see Long's conversation with Feis, February 15, 1941, in Israel, *War Diary of Breckinridge Long*, 180. See also Clayton memorandum, April 24, 1941 in Dobney, *Papers of Will Clayton*, 60–61, for a discussion of the transportation crisis, and Berle to Land, May 20, 1940 in *FR, 1940*, II, 259–260, for an early discussion of the problem. Berle noted in May 1940: "The real reason why rubber is not moving eastward from the East Indies—we may need the rubber very badly if the Japanese cork the bottle there—is that our American ships, which are subsidized to the guller, would rather carry jute at a fifty cent rate than rubber at a thirty-six cent rate" (Beatrice Berle and Travis Jacobs, eds., *Navigating the Rapids 1918–1971: From the Papers of Adolf A. Berle* [New York: Harcourt Brace Jovanovich, 1973], 316–317). Clayton, the deputy federal loan administrator, was in charge of the importation of strategic and critical materials and ran the foreign buying operations of the Metals Reserve Corporation, the Rubber Reserve Company, and the Defense Supplies Corporation. He recounted the events of late 1941 to his daughter Ellen in 1947 in a recorded interview: "Before we got into the war I was buying, in August, 1941, all sorts of stuff from the Philippines, Malay Straits, Dutch East Indies, Australia, North Caledonia [sic]. We couldn't get enough ships and the stuff was piling up out there. Rubber and tin were two very critical things—coming over the Pacific, going through the Panama Canal, going up East Coast by ship. [Harvard Professor William Elliot] at the War Production Board was working with me in August to get all this stuff in. We were sure to get into war with Japan any time and we had to get all this material in before. To do this we decided to have them unload the ships on the Pacific Coast which would save a 30 day trip but cost more. We then had to ship the West Coast by rail—rubber to Akron, tin to Pittsburgh. Then those West Coast ports got blocked with these things, because the railroads couldn't take them away fast enough. The next 6 months this transportation cost 30 to 50 million dollars extra." Dobney, *Papers of Will Clayton*, 67.

90. Jones, *Fifty Billion Dollars*, 371–372.
91. *Congressional Record* 87 (October 7, 1941), 7692.
92. Associates in International Relations, *Raw Materials*, 93.
93. Feis, *Seen from E. A.*, 75–76.

3. The Emerging Threat

1. William Neumann, "How American Policy in the Pacific Contributed to War in the Pacific," in Harry Elmer Barnes (ed.), *Perpetual War for Perpetual Peace* (Caldwell, Idaho: The Caxton Printers, Ltd., 1953), 242–243.

2. Ienaga Saburo, *The Pacific War: World War II and the Japanese, 1931–1945* (New York: Pantheon Books, 1978), 37.

3. Henry Stimson and William Bundy, *On Active Service in Peace and War* (New York: Harpers, 1948), 234.

4. Ibid., 243–244. See also quote from Herbert Hoover in Walter Johnson, *The Battle Against Isolation* (Chicago: University of Chicago, 1944), 25.

5. Neumann, "American Policy," 248–249; A. Whitney Griswold, *The Far Eastern Policy of the United States* (New York: Harcourt, Brace, 1938), 446–448.

6. Ōhata Tokushirō, "The Anti-Comintern Pact," in James William Morley (ed.), *Deterrent Diplomacy: Japan, Germany and the USSR, 1935–1940* (New York: Columbia University Press, 1976).

7. Sumner Welles pulled together the group within the Far Eastern branch. Their December 5, 1938 memorandum, "Steps of a Positive Character Which the United States Might Take Against Japan in Retaliation for Japan's Injury to American Rights and Interests in China: Examination Thereof," is in box 1, Leo Pasvolsky office file, RG 59, National Archives. See also Laurence Salisbury (FE), "America's Economic Policy in the Far East," January 30, 1939, 793.94/14667 1/2, RG 59, National Archives.

8. George Gallup, "American Institute of Public Opinion Surveys, 1935–38," *Public Opinion Quarterly* 2 (July 1938), 389; Gallup, "American Institute of Public Opinion—Surveys, 1938–1939," *Public Opinion Quarterly* 3 (October 1939), 599. A propaganda piece by the California Committee on Pacific Friendship suggests why some residual admiration for Japan remained: "Japan has never harmed us. Japan is not threatening us. Japan has treated us better than any other world power in the matter of paying debts, courtesy to our visitors and residents, and never attempting to meddle in our affairs. Japan is the only world power that has paid back all sums borrowed without delay or default on a single penny. If we are going to answer this fair treatment

of us by enmity, no incentive is left for any country to treat us well in the future." Quoted in Neumann, "American Policy," 231.

9. Sherk, *Pacific Trade Basin*, 42. It is difficult to estimate China's share precisely because of Japan's control of Manchuria and the port of Kwantung. The United States sold $289 million worth of goods to Japan in 1937 but less than $90 million to China; even the Philippines offered a greater market than China. Furthermore the United States had a trade surplus of about $84 million with Japan but a deficit of almost $54 million with China proper. See U.S. Department of Commerce, *Foreign Commerce*.

10. U.S. investment in China amounted to only $132 million in 1935, compared to $387 million in Japan, according to Department of Commerce figures from William Lockwood, Jr., "America's Stake in the Far East—II: Investments," *Far Eastern Survey* (August 12, 1936), 182. Total U.S. investments in China had never surpassed $250 million. See C. F. Remer, *Foreign Investments in China* (New York: Macmillan, 1933), 332–333. For more figures on U.S. investments in China and Japan, and for a discussion of Japan's superior record of repayment on U.S. loans, see Royal Institute of International Affairs, *China and Japan*, Information Department Papers No. 21 (New York: Royal Institute of International Affairs, 1938), 114, 121. On investment in the Philippines, see Helmut Callis, *Foreign Capital in Southeast Asia* (New York: Institute of Pacific Relations, 1942), 11, and Catherine Parker, "The Philippines as an American Investment," *Far Eastern Survey* (September 25, 1940), 222.

11. America First Committee Speakers Bureau, "To what extent does our economic life depend on foreign trade?" 1941, in Doenecke, *In Danger Undaunted*, 152.

12. Griswold, *Far Eastern Policy*, 469. Admittedly, government officials have often have gone to great lengths to protect modest investments by influential corporations; consider the State Department's strenuous exertions on behalf of U.S. oil companies in Indonesia in the 1920s. As Harold Quigley argued, "While it would seem that an approximate total investment of $160,000,000 in these enterprises [U.S. businesses in China] would exert a negligible leverage upon American policy it must be presumed that our insistent reaffirmation of the 'Open Door' doctrine is directly related to these interests. In themselves and in their importance to trade they compose a considerable stake requiring protection from local and outside infringement." At the same time, however, these investments did not convince Washington to rethink its cautious, almost timid policy toward Japan in the 1930s. See Harold Quigley, *The Far Eastern War 1937–1941* (Boston: World Peace Foundation, 1942), 40–41.

13. Useful studies include: John Masland, "American Attitudes Toward Japan," *The Annals of the American Academy of Political and Social Science* (May 1941), 160–165 [hereafter *Annals*]; Masland, "Commercial Influences Upon Far Eastern Policy, 1931–1941," *Pacific Historical Review* 11 (September 1942), 281–299; Peter Hoffer, "American Businessmen and the Japan Trade," *Pacific Historical Review* 41 (May 1972), 189–206; Roland Stromberg, "American Business and the Approach of War," *Journal of Economic History* (Winter 1953), 58–78; Mira Wilkins, "The Role of U.S. Business," in Borg and Okamoto, *Pearl Harbor as History*, 341–376. It is interesting to note that Masland, a critic of economic explanations of U.S. policy in the Far East, hints at the significance of imports from Southeast Asia when he admits, "The Netherlands East Indies assumed considerable importance as a source of tin, rubber, and other strategic materials" (Masland, "Commercial Influences," 284). Southern cotton interests, which were particularly dependent on the large market Japan provided, formed an especially unified lobby opposing retaliation against Japan. Will Clayton, the nation's greatest cotton industrialist and an important political figure, wrote Sen. Alben Barkley on February 23, 1940, protesting moves to limit U.S. trade with Japan—despite his voluntary refusal to trade with the European Axis powers. "I am sure it is unnecessary to point out to you," he wrote, "that American cotton would be the greatest sufferer from any serious interruption of trade between this country and Japan." See Dobney, *Papers of Will Clayton*, 47. See also *Amerasia* II (November 1938), 458–461 for a discussion of the pro-Japan bias of certain southern cotton journals.

14. William Johnstone, *The United States and Japan's New Order* (New York: Oxford University Press, 1941), 216–217.

15. Tyler Dennett, "Alternative American Policies in the Far East," *Foreign Affairs* 16 (April 1938), 392. In this article, Dennett expressed serious concern that the Japanese threat to Southeast Asia could mean direct material losses to the United State. For a counterargument about Japanese-occupied China, predicting serious consequences to the U.S. economy if trade with it dried up, see Nathaniel Peffer, "Would Japan Shut the Open Door in China?" *Foreign Affairs* 17 (October 1938), 37–50.

16. Hoffer, "American Businessmen," 194–195; Masland, "Commercial Influences," 289, 293–294.

17. *Fortune* 22 (September 1940), 114. See also the statement of Nelson Johnson in Gardner, *New Deal Diplomacy*, 141–142.

18. Hoffer, "American Businessmen," 202, 204.

19. Larry W. Moses, "Soviet-Japanese Confrontation in Outer Mongolia: The Battle of Nomonhan-Khalkin Gol," *Journal of Asian*

History 1 (1967), 64–85; Hata Ikuhiko, "The Japanese-Soviet Confrontation, 1935–1939," in Morley, *Deterrent Diplomacy*, 115–178; Ienaga, *The Pacific War*, 82.

20. Adolf Berle, Jr., recorded in his diary for September 14, 1937, that although Roosevelt and Hull wanted very much to keep the United States out of war, Roosevelt showed great concern that "the Japanese were getting ready to seize the Island of Hainan which lies half way on the road to Singapore and which accordingly would threaten both French Indo-China and also the British trade route." Thus, when a year and a half later Japan did move into Hainan, the Administration's concern was quite understandable. See Berle and Jacobs, *Navigating the Rapids*, 135–136.

21. Hull, *Memoirs*, I, 628. For further evidence of the administration's strategic anxieties about Hainan, see Grew to Hull, March 31, 1939, in box 329, Hornbeck papers.

22. Ch'ao-Ting Chi, "Far Eastern Notes," *Amerasia* 1 (July 1937), 236. He noted, "Recent events indicate that control of Hainan Island is definitely an immediate objective of Japan's policy of southern expansion." See also "Growing Interest in Hainan Mainly Strategic," *Far Eastern Survey* 7 (August 24, 1938), 203–204. As early as 1936, Japan's navy began drawing up contingency plans to seize Borneo's oil fields. See Tsunoda Jun, "The Navy's Role in the Southern Strategy," in James William Morley, ed., *The Fateful Choice: Japan's Advance into Southeast Asia, 1939–1941* (New York: Columbia University Press, 1980), 241.

23. Andrew Roth, *Japan Strikes South* (New York: Institute of Pacific Relations, 1941), 16.

24. Ibid., 16–17. When Hamilton, chief of the Division of Far Eastern Affairs, was informed of Japan's move by the counselor of the Japanese embassy, his first reaction was to remark that "the Sinnan Island Group appeared to be very near to the Philippine Islands" (*FR, Japan, 1931–1941*, II, 277).

25. Hull, *Memoirs*, I, 628.

26. *FR, Japan, 1931–1941*, II, 4–5, 280–281.

27. Hull, *Memoirs*, I, 630. See also Tracy Kittredge, "Joint Strategic Planning, 1937–40," 41–43, in box 30, Kittredge papers.

28. *New York Herald Tribune*, January 26, 1939.

29. *New York Herald Tribune*, January 19, 1939.

30. *Washington Evening Star*, March 6, 1939.

31. Erle Dickover (Batavia) dispatch no. 274, June 27, 1939, 811.24 Raw Materials/221, RG 59, National Archives.

32. Berle and Jacobs, *Navigating the Rapids*, 230 (June 27, 1939 diary entry).

33. Henry Stimson, *The Far Eastern Crisis* (New York: Council on Foreign Relations, 1936), 138.

34. Stark to Richardson, March 15, 1940, in PHA Exhibits, XIV, 932. See also Neumann, "American Policy," 255–256. Quick action was taken in the autumn, probably as a result of the signing of the Nazi-Soviet pact, which relieved pressure on the Soviet Union's western front and effectively stymied any plans by Japan to invade Siberia. In fact, the State Department worried that the pact would force Japan to "limit its ambitions to the south. But the more its ambitions there were realized, the greater would be the menace to the Philippines and to the legitimate strategic and commercial interests of the United States in the southern reaches of the Pacific." Sumner Welles, "Roosevelt and the Far East," *Harper's* 202 (February 1951), 32.

35. Stark to Richardson, March 15, 1940, in PHA Exhibits, XIV, 932. Note also the Navy's viewpoint expressed in Stark to Richardson, January 18, 1940: "I have a letter from Tommy Hart [Commander in chief of the Asiatic Fleet], just received, in which he thinks the situation in the Far East is very serious and that this year may prove to be a crucial and critical one. As I have written Bloch [former Commander in chief of the United States Fleet], and as you undoubtedly know, I have continually asked him to bear in mind what is going on to the Westward which in this particular period in this old world's history may be far more important to us than the troubles in Europe, especially if something should break and break quickly and without warning" (PHA Exhibits, XIV, 923).

36. Minutes of February 21, 1940 JB Meeting, cited in Kittredge, "United States Neutrality Policies . . . " in box 29, Kittredge papers.

37. Richardson testimony, PHA Hearings, I, 255; Stark to Richardson, April 8, 1940, PHA Exhibits, XIV, 933.

38. Jun, "Southern Strategy," 243–246.

39. *New York Times*, April 14, 1940, and April 15, 1940.

40. *FR, Japan, 1931–1941*, II, 281; *New York Times*, April 16, 1940.

41. *New York Times*, April 17, 1940.

42. Israel, *War Diary of Breckinridge Long*, 81.

43. Feis, *Seen From E. A.*, 55.

44. *FR, Japan, 1931–1941*, II, 282.

45. For instance, in a public response to a later Japanese expression of "increased concern" for the fate of the Indies, Hull declared that in view of his April 17 statement, "commitments and expressions of intention to respect the status quo of the Netherlands East Indies cannot be too often reiterated" (*FR, Japan, 1931–1941*, II, 285). Undersecretary of State Welles stressed Hull's April 17 message and other affirmations of the status quo principle in an address before the Cleveland

Foreign Affairs Council in September ("Our Foreign Policy and National Defense," *Department of State Bulletin*, September 28, 1940, 243).

46. On April 19, the *San Francisco Chronicle* ran a front-page column on the problem by Royce Briar and an editorial inside praising Hull's statement: "This is to the good. The Dutch are admirable people. Also, their East Indies are the source of rubber and tin we must have for industry or national defense. Without them some of our factories would shut down and daddy would not get any more pay checks. Also there would be no tires on the car to take mother to the peace meetings."

47. *Washington Star*, April 18, 1940; *New York Times*, April 18, 1940, and April 19, 1940. The French complained that Japan would soon be in a position to "menace French positions in New Caledonia, which has one of the richest nickel deposits in the world, it was pointed out" (*New York Times*, April 18, 1940).

48. *Iron Age*, May 16, 1940. The department's release said, "Richly endowed climatically and geologically, the Netherlands Indies ranks among the world's most important sources of rubber, tin, petroleum, sugar, coconut products, vegetable oils, tobacco, spices, and fibers, and one noted for a variety of minor tropical products which have become increasingly important in the markets of industrial countries. Practically a world monopoly is held in the production of quinine, while the special trade significance of many other products enhances the importance of the Netherlands Indies as a source of articles of present-day commerce; kapok for upholstering and other fibers for cordage manufacture, tanning and dyeing materials, palm oil for the preparation of soaps and margarine, cassava products for food and sizing purposes, flavoring extracts and raw materials for the manufacture of medicines" See Department of Commerce, Bureau of Foreign and Domestic Commerce, press release, "The Netherlands Indies," April 19, 1940, in box 311, Hornbeck papers; also reprinted in *Amerasia* 4 (May 1940), 121-122.

49. *Iron Age*, May 16, 1940; minutes of May 24, 1940, Business Advisory Council meeting in box 110, Hopkins papers.

50. Feis, *Seen from E. A.*, 56. For more on the administration's concern for raw materials, see William Langer and S. Gleason, *Challenge to Isolation, 1937-1940* (New York: Harper & Bros., 1952), 587-588. In a memo to the Interdepartmental Committee on Strategic Materials, May 15, 1940, Feis wrote, "Recent events have convinced virtually everybody of the urgent necessity of trying to augment our stocks of these materials. The necessity rests not only on the needs of our fighting forces in the event of a war emergency, but on the needs of indus-

try. Shortage of supplies would greatly upset our whole economic situation" (box 302, Hopkins papers).

51. Roosevelt press conference, 645-A, May 23, 1940. A copy of his speech to the Business Advisory Council and transcript of the meeting are in PSF: Harry L. Hopkins, Roosevelt papers. The council was not persuaded; it passed a resolution calling "in the strongest terms at its command" for a hugely expanded stockpiling program. "The international situation," they insisted, "will not permit continued delay and obstruction to this permanent strategic reserve without prejudicial and possibly very dangerous effect upon our national security." Two years later, with the country at war, Stanley Hornbeck expressed doubts as to whether the lessons of German raw material conservation could be applied at home: "It is believed that any . . . assumption that this country could within a few months or even within a few years readjust its economy along such lines [as] . . . that achieved by the Germans would lead to highly disappointing and very unfortunate consequences. . . . None but Germans, in Germany and under the Nazi system, can do what the Germans are doing. None but Japanese, in Japan and under the prevailing militant militaristic system of Japan can do what the Japanese are doing. . . . [O]ur national economy and our private economy are and long have been different from those of the Germans or the Japanese . . . " See Hornbeck to Colonel Cortier, April 7, 1942, box 263, Hornbeck papers.

52. T. A. Bisson, "America's Dilemma in the Far East," *Foreign Policy Reports* (July 1, 1940), 105–106.

53. "Japanese Comment on US Naval Maneuvers," US Naval Attache (Tokyo) report, April 26, 1940, Naval Attache Tokyo file, II, PSF:Documents N, Roosevelt Library.

54. Langer and Gleason, *Challenge to Isolation*, 588.

55. Richardson testimony, PHA Hearings, I, 260.

56. PHA Exhibits, XIV, 933–934.

57. PHA Exhibits, XIV, 938.

58. PHA Exhibits XIV, 940–942, 943–950. For the debate within the administration, see Berle and Jacobs, *Navigating the Rapids*, 316 (May 21, 1940 entry).

59. *FR, 1940*, IV, 19. But on May 13 Frederick Moore, a U.S. journalist hired by the Japanese "in an advisory capacity by the Japanese Embassy" and long associated with Japanese officials, reported to a U.S. official that the Japanese were "prepared to go" in the direction of the Netherlands East Indies and seemed "unwilling to believe that we would act in event of their moving on the Netherlands East Indies" (*FR, 1940*, IV, 16). Nor did Hornbeck agree with Grew that the Japa-

nese leaders recognized the United States' willingness to fight rather than lose the Indies. See ibid., fn 35.

60. *FR, Japan, 1931–1941*, II, 288; Hull, *Memoirs*, I, 893.

61. Roth, *Japan Strikes South*, 46.

62. *FR, Japan, 1931–1941*, II, 66. Arita made his speech just as the Japanese were undertaking a major military buildup on Hainan involving thousands of troops and many aircraft. Chinese officials felt Japan was capable of launching an attack from Hainan toward Indochina or the Netherlands East Indies. See Johnson to Hull, July 4, 1940, *FR, 1940*, IV, 23.

63. *FR, Japan, 1931–1941*, II, 68.

64. See June file, box 461, Hornbeck papers. Hornbeck also prepared a similar memorandum on June 24 consisting of a summary of Rupert Emerson's article, "Dutch East Indies Adrift."

65. June 15, 1940 memorandum in box 414, Hornbeck papers. Emphasis in original.

66. June 15, 1940 memorandum in boxes 414 and 461, Hornbeck papers.

67. Congressman John McCormack inserted it into the *Congressional Record* 88 (August 13, 1941), A3913, and the article was quoted in C. F. Remer, "American Interest in the Economic Future of the Pacific," in Mayling Soon Foundation, *America's Future in the Pacific* (New Jersey: Rutgers University Press, 1947), 49. The Hornbeck quote and reprint are in his June 14, 1940 memorandum, in boxes 414 and 461, Hornbeck papers.

68. Historian James Thompson notes that "it was the Hornbeck memorandum, usually addressed to the secretary and undersecretary, that was the chief internal carrier of policy continuity toward the Far East" (Thompson, "The Role of the State Department," in Borg and Okamoto, *Pearl Harbor as History*, 88). Stimson called Hornbeck "the foremost expert in the State Department" on Far Eastern affairs (Stimson diary, September 11, 1940). Sumner Welles called him "one of the ablest men with whom I have ever been associated in the State Department" (letter to Colonel Langhorne, September 12, 1950, in Hornbeck papers). Joseph Ballantine, another State Department official involved in policy toward Japan, said, "Hornbeck, with his disciplined mind, his clarity of thought, his fertility in useful ideas for dealing with questions presented, and his ripe experience, was invaluable in our deliberations" (Ballantine autobiography, chapter 10, "Prelude to Pearl Harbor," in box 1, Ballantine papers, Hoover Library). On Hornbeck's great influence throughout the administration, see also Kenneth McCarty, Jr., "Stanley K. Hornbeck and the Far East, 1931–1941" (unpublished Ph.D dissertation, Duke University, 1970); Jonathan Utley,

"The Department of State and the Far East, 1937–1941," (Ph.D dissertation, University of Illinois, 1970), 9; Spotswood, "Japan's Southward Advance," 86–88. For opposing evidence, see Breckinridge Long's diary for October 9, 1940, in Israel, *War Diary of Breckinridge Long,* 139. Long told Hull that Hornbeck's influence extended too far outside the department and should be curbed, especially given "the lengths to which his rather violent mentality will lead him." Hull apparently agreed and noted that he would seek more advice from Hamilton, chief of the Division of Far Eastern Affairs. However, on key matters such as the importance of Southeast Asia to the national interest and tactical issues such as the need to aid China to keep Japan's troops bogged down, there was widespread consensus.

69. The Japanese also demanded that the French hand over all Chinese silver on deposit in French banks in Tientsin. The French authorities agreed, and Japan assumed de facto control of the city on June 20. Roth, *Japan Strikes South,* 50–52; Hull, *Memoirs,* I, 896. Note that aid to Chungking via Indochina was ended completely by July 11 (*FR, Japan, 1931–1941,* II, 94–95; *FR, 1940,* 30–31).

70. *FR, Japan, 1931–1941,* II, 86.

71. Memorandum by Grew, June 24, 1940, in *FR, Japan, 1931–1941,* II, 88–89.

72. The influential *Asahi* daily announced a similar line, with particular reference to Southeast Asia (Roth, *Japan Strikes South,* 53).

73. *FR, Japan, 1931–1941,* II, 92, 94.

74. Hornbeck to Wells, June 25, 1940, box 493, Hornbeck papers.

75. Hull, *Memoirs,* I, 896–899.

76. Barnhart, *Japan Prepares,* 159–175; Jun, "Southern Strategy," 247; Hosoya Chihiro, "The Tripartite Pact, 1939–1940," in Morley, *Deterrent Diplomacy,* 207–211.

77. Israel, *War Diary of Breckinridge Long,* 107.

78. PHA Exhibits, XIV, 946. For other samples of Navy opinion, see memo prepared for Stark, Marshall, and directors of the War Plans Divisions of the Navy and Army, "Decisions as to National Action," in box 30, Kittredge papers.

79. Memorandum of conversation by Grew, June 10, 1940, in *FR, Japan, 1931–1941,* II, 69–70.

80. Richardson testimony, PHA Hearings, I, 282.

81. Richardson testimony, PHA Hearings, I, 297.

82. PHA Exhibits, XVI, 1989–1996; also in box 461, Hornbeck papers. On July 24, Stimson sent Morgenthau a copy of this memo. See Stimson diary, July 24, 1940. For more on Hornbeck's views, see Berle and Jacobs, *Navigating the Rapids,* 316 (May 21, 1940 entry); Hornbeck memo to Welles, July 24, 1940, box 155, Hornbeck papers. See

also Hornbeck memo, "Reflections on the Situation in Europe, the Situation in the Far East . . . " June 17, 1940, box 309, Hornbeck papers.

83. *FR, Japan, 1931-1941*, II, 289.

84. *FR, 1940*, IV, 381-383.

85. *FR, Japan, 1931-1941*, II, 95-100.

86. Ibid., 101; Hull, *Memoirs*, I, 900-901. When the Yunnan-Indochina railroad was closed, all tungsten shipped out of China came over the Burma Road. See Harry Holmes, *Strategic Materials and National Defense* (New York: Macmillan, 1942), 39. On December 3, 1941, Roosevelt wrote Hull and Welles a memorandum showing that keeping the Burma Road open was as much in the United States' interest as in China's, as two-thirds of U.S. tungsten came out through that route. He told them: "I think it is well worthwhile that this aspect of closing the Burma Road should be brought out. The Burma Road is China's life-line for goods going in but it is also a very important life-line for our very much needed tungsten and tung oil." Elliott Roosevelt, (ed.,) *FDR, His Personal Letters, 1928-1945*, Volume II (New York: Duell, Sloan and Pearce, 1950), 1249.

87. Chihiro, "The Tripartite Pact, 1939-1940," 285.

88. Hull, *Memoirs*, I, 894.

89. Press release issued by the White House on July 2, 1940, *Department of State Bulletin*, July 6, 1940, 11.

90. Morgenthau diary (unpublished), v. 284, 122; v. 286, 86ff; v. 287, 151ff, 163-164; v. 173, 287, Roosevelt Library; Stimson diary, July 18, 19, 24, 26, 1940; Julius Pratt, *Cordell Hull*, Volume II (New York: Cooper Square Publishers, 1964), 469-470; Wells, "Roosevelt and the Far East," 33; and Harold Ickes, *The Secret Diary of Harold L. Ickes: The Lowering Clouds, 1939-1941* (New York: Simon and Schuster, 1954), 299. For an excellent account of the bureaucratic maneuvering over licensing, see Utley, "Department of State," 97-100.

91. *FR, Japan, 1931-1941*, II, 218-219; Roth, *Japan Strikes South*, 58.

92. *FR, 1940*, IV, 59.

93. Ibid. 60, 63.

94. Ibid., 63-64; Hull, *Memoirs*, I, 903.

95. *FR, Japan, 1931-1941*, II, 289-291.

96. *FR, 1940*, IV, 65.

97. Ibid.; see also Welles to Murphy (at Vichy), August 7, 1940, 66, etc.; Consul at Hanoi (Reed) to Hull, August 7, 1940, *FR, 1940*, IV, 67; see also Grew to Hull, August 9, 1940, ibid., 69-70.

98. Matthews to Hull, August 27, 1940, ibid., 86-87.

99. Reed to Hull, September 3, 1940, ibid., 92-93; Hull, *Memoirs*, I, 903; Johnson to Hull, September 3, 1940, *FR, 1940*, IV, 93; Johnson to Hull, September 3, 1940, ibid., 93-94.

100. *FR, Japan, 1931-1941*, II, 291-293.

101. The British government actually encouraged Washington to make this decision, figuring that the U.S. naval presence in the Pacific would relieve pressure on Singapore and allow the British to focus all their resources in Europe and the Middle East. See Miner, "United States Policy," 36-37.

102. Roth, *Japan Strikes South*, 64; *Washington Post*, September 5, 1940.

103. Hull, *Memoirs*, I, 903-904; Roth, *Japan Strikes South*, 65.

104. *FR, 1940*, IV, 106-107.

105. *Washington Post*, September 11, 1940.

106. Joseph Grew, *Turbulent Era*, Volume II (Boston: Houghton Mifflin, 1952), 1228; Department of State, *Peace and War*, 571-572.

107. *FR, Japan, 1931-1941*, II, 221-222.

108. Pratt, *Cordell Hull*, 470-471. At this point, Hornbeck once again fought off all attempts to shift part of the fleet away from Hawaii. See memos in PHA Exhibits, XVI, 2001-2013. Advocates of a cautious response had to weigh the possibility, raised by one Japanese admiral, that Japan could survive an embargo better than the United States could survive the ensuing loss of Southeast Asia, "when she will no longer be able to obtain rubber and tin" (Rear Adm. Gumpei Sekine [sic], quoted in U.S. Naval Attache [Tokyo] report no. 131-140, September 5, 1940, in PSF: Documents N. Naval Attache Tokyo, v. II, Roosevelt papers.

109. Chihiro, "The Tripartite Pact," 238-240.

110. *FR, 1940*, IV, 131; *FR, Japan 1931-1941*,, II, 294-296.

111. *Department of State Bulletin*, September 28, 1940, 253.

112. Furthermore, the French already had about ninety unused U.S. planes stationed in Martinique, which the Vichy Government refused to release to Indochina. Hull, *Memoirs*, I, 907; *FR, 1940*, IV, 146-147.

113. *FR, Japan, 1931-1941*, II, 222-223; *New York Times*, September 26 and 27, 1940. Utley notes that the China loan had been approved in July 1940 but was slow to be disbursed owing to bureaucratic infighting over where the money should come from (105).

114. Breckinridge Long noted in his diary on September 28, 1940, after the signing of the Tripartite Pact, "And so we go—more and more—farther and farther along the road to war. But we are not ready to fight any war now—to say nothing of a war on two oceans at once—and that is what the Berlin-Rome-Tokyo agreement means. Nor will we be ready to fight any war for eighteen months in the future" (Israel, *War Diary of Breckinridge Long*, 132).

115. The wording of the pact is from Herbert Feis, *The Road to Pearl Harbor* (Princeton: Princeton University Press, 1950), 111; the

Asahi quote is from David Bergamini, *Japan's Imperial Conspiracy* (New York: William Morrow & Co., 1971), 728–729.

116. *Department of State Bulletin*, September 28, 1940, 251.
117. Stimson diary, September 27, 1940.
118. Feis, *Road to Pearl Harbor*, 122n.
119. *Los Angeles Times*, September 28, 1940.
120. Langer and Gleason, *Undeclared War*, 34.
121. *FR, 1940*, I, 658. See also Grew, *Ten Years in Japan* (New York: Simon and Schuster, 1944), 340–342.
122. *Washington Post*, September 28, 1940.
123. *San Francisco Chronicle* September 28, 1940.
124. October 1, 1940 memorandum, box 4, Hornbeck papers; Stimson diary, October 1–2, 1940.
125. The *New York Times*, in an editorial on September 26, argued for more aid to China instead: "There is only one real check upon Japan's freedom of action and that is the stubborn opposition of the people and the Government of China. So long as this opposition continues, Japan cannot use her full power elsewhere. But the moment Japan has crushed China's resistance, that moment Japan is wholly free to embark upon aggressive action in any other part of the Pacific area; against Indo-China; against the Philippines; against the Dutch East Indies, source of raw materials of the utmost importance to us; against Singapore, the eastern outpost of the British Empire."
126. Nancy Hooker, ed., *The Moffat Papers* (Cambridge: Harvard University Press, 1956), 330–331.
127. Ibid., 331–332.
128. Ibid., 333.
129. Ibid., 334.
130. Israel, *War Diary of Breckinridge Long*, October 7, 1940, 136.
131. Ibid., 912; *FR, 1940*, IV, passim (October).
132. Miner, "United States Policy," 52.
133. Stimson to FDR, October 12, 1940; quoted in Leonard Baker, *Roosevelt and Pearl Harbor* (New York: Macmillan Co., 1970) 115; cf. Stimson diary, October 12, 1940.
134. PHA Hearings (Richardson testimony), I, 265–266. Richardson claimed that Roosevelt told him, "if the Japanese attack Thailand, or the Kra Peninsula, or the Dutch East Indies, we would not enter the war; that even if they attacked the Philippines he doubted whether we would enter the war, but that they could not always avoid making mistakes, and that as the war continued and the area of operations expanded, sooner or later they would make a mistake and we could enter the war" (PHA Hearings, I, 266). Admiral Leahy, who participated

in the onversation, could not remember Roosevelt uttering such a statemet but concluded that it was possible and that the president was desondent over the public's disinclination to fight. Roosevelt himself Leahy insisted, would have gone to war to protect the Philippines if given the chance. See Leahy testimony, PHA Hearings, I, 356–357.

135. *FR, 1940*, IV, 180; 185–186.
136. Israel, *War Diary of Breckinridge Long*, November 7, 1940, 150–151.
137. Stimson diary, November 6 and 12, 1940.
138. *FR, 1940*, IV, 211.
139. December 1940 file, box 461, Hornbeck papers.
140. On its wide distribution, see accompanying papers in ibid. The Stae Department sent it to Roosevelt (see PSF:State Deptarment, June-Dcember 1940, Roosevelt Library; also Gardner, *New Deal Diplomcy*, 145, and Langer and Gleason, *Undeclared War*, 309n). Lauchli Currie's favorable comments appear in box 389, Hornbeck papers; Grew, *Ten Years in Japan*, 370; and Grew to Hull, February 7, 1941, in PHA Hearings, VI, 2917–2919. Wells liked it enough to send it off t< Westmore Wilcox, Jr., who was convinced. See Wilcox to Welles, April 2, 1941, 740.0011 PW/241, RG 59, National Archives. Hornbek also showed the memorandum to a number of appreciative busines leaders in the Council on Foreign Relations, including Allen Dulles nd T. W. Lamont (see boxes 151 and 272, Hornbeck papers). The on negative comments Hornbeck received came from General Marshd, who sent a short note to Stimson complaining that the memo lid not sufficiently emphasize the Atlantic. Hornbeck responde in typical fashion with a twenty-page rebuttal, sent to Stimson on une 9, 1941. Copies of both can be found in boxes 389 and 462, Hornbek papers.
141. Grew, *Turbulent Era*, II, 1255–1257.
142. *FR, 1941*, IV, 6–8; also in PHA Hearings, II, 632–633. An almost icntical letter, again drafted by Hornbeck, was sent by Roosevelt t Francis Sayre, U.S. High Commissioner to the Philippine Islands, α December 31, after Sayre had written expressing his fear that "any da Japan may start moving southwards." See E. Roosevelt, *Personal Lters*, II, 1093–1095, and miscellaneous folders, box 525, Hornbeck poers.
143. December 19, 1940 instructions, cited in Miner, "United States blicy," 78.
144. Joseph Ballantine, "Far Eastern Affairs," November 22, 1940 lecture o Naval War College, in box 127, Hornbeck papers.
145. Hull, *Memoirs*, I, 905.

4. War of Nerves

1. Hull, *Memoirs*, II, 982.
2. Roth, *Japan Strikes South*, 89–91.
3. *FR, 1941*, V, 1. Various export restrictions and other commercial obstacles forced Japan to turn to Thailand for rubber, tin, and even some rice.
4. Ibid., 5.
5. Roth, *Japan Strikes South*, 91–92; *FR, 1941*, V, 12..
6. Ibid., 10, 15.
7. Roth, *Japan Strikes South*, 92.
8. *FR, 1941*, V, 14.
9. Ibid., 16–17, 20.
10. Roth, *Japan Strikes South*, 93. See also "Announcement of the Board of Information Concerning the Acceptance by the Governments of Thailand and France of the Proposal by the Japanese Government For Mediation in the Border Dispute Between Thailand and French Indo-China, January 24 1941"; "Announcement of the Board of Information Concerning Japanese Delegation for the Armistice Conference Between Thailand and French Indo-China, January 29 1941"; and "Announcement of the Board of Information Concerning the Armistice Agreement Between Thailand and French Indo-China, January 31, 1941" in [Japan] Board of Information, *Official Announcements Concerning Foreign Relations* (Tokyo, 1941), 3–5.
11. *FR, 1941* V, 29.
12. *FR, Japan, 1931–1941*, II, 133; Hull, *Memoirs*, II, 984.
13. *FR, 1941*, V, 55.
14. *FR, Japan, 1931–1941*, II, 303–305.
15. Grew cable, February 7, 1941, in Grew, *Ten Years in Japan*, 371.
16. February 1 diary entry, in Grew, *Ten Years in Japan*, 369.
17. This discussion of the private diplomacy of Drought and Walsh is based largely from the following sources: R.J.C. Butow, *The John Doe Associates* (Stanford: Stanford University Press, 1974); John Boyle, "The Drought-Walsh Mission to Japan," *Pacific Historical Review* 34, 141–161; Ladislas Farago, *The Broken Seal* (New York: Random House, 1967), ch. 14; Lewis Strauss, *Men and Decisions* (Garden City, N.Y.: Doubleday, 1962), 123–126; *FR, 1941*, IV, 14; Hull, *Memoirs*, II, 984–985.
18. *FR, 1941*, IV, 14; Farago, *Broken Seal*, 175.
19. Hull, *Memoirs*, II, 984–985.
20. *FR, 1941*, IV, 21–22. The exchange on this subject between Roosevelt and the State Department may also be found in PHA Exhibits, XX, 4284ff.
21. Farago, *Broken Seal*, 176.

22. *FR, 1941*, IV, 21-22.
23. February 5 memorandum in *FR, 1941*, IV, 22-27; also found in PHA Exhibits, XX, 4289-4291.
24. *FR, 1941*, V, 61-62.
25. Roth, *Japan Strikes South*, 95-96.
26. Israel, *War Diary of Breckinridge Long*, 176.
27. Roth, *Japan Strikes South*, 95-96.
28. *FR, 1941*, V, 77. The French authorities also denied U.S. requests to purchase raw materials in Indochina but gave Japan (and Germany) free access to its resources. This action aggravated the crisis facing U.S. leaders. Ibid., 66-68.
29. Israel, *War Diary of Breckinridge Long* (February 11 and 17), 177, 182. Hull, *Memoirs*, II, 985-986, cited these chances as his low estimate.
30. Stimson diary, February 10, 1941.
31. *FR, Japan, 1931-1941*, II, 387-388.
32. Grew, *Turbulent Era*, II, 1307; *FR, Japan, 1931-1941*, II, 139ff.
33. On his approval (and instigation) of the meeting, see Grew, *Turbulent Era*, II, 1307. Grew informed the department of the conversation on February 14—see *FR, 1941*, IV, 37-39. No reprimand was ever sent back. Furthermore, on February 26, Grew told Matsuoka of his approval of Dooman's message and handed him a copy of the conversation record. He must have had approval from the State Department to do this. See Langer and Gleason, *The Undeclared War*, 326.
34. Hull, *Memoirs*, II, 988; *FR, 1941*, IV, 39-40.
35. Roth, *Japan Strikes South*, 96; *New York Times*, February 20, 1941. See also *Washington Star* editorial, February 13, 1941, on Japan's threat to the "incalculable wealth" of the region.
36. Roth, *Japan Strikes South*, 96-97. See also "Statement of the Spokesman of the Board of Information Concerning Alarming Reports With Reference to the East Asiatic Situation, February 18, 1941" in [Japan] Board of Information, *Official Announcements*, 8-9.
37. *Department of State Bulletin*, February 22, 1941, 211.
38. *FR, 1941*, V, 103-105.
39. *FR, 1941*, V, 102.
40. Roth, *Japan Strikes South*, 99-102. See also, "Joint Communique of Japan, France and Thailand Concerning the Conclusion of the Mediation, March 11, 1941" and "Statement of the Foreign Office Concerning the Conclusion of the Mediation, March 11, 1941," in Board of Information, *Official Announcements*, 15-19.
41. These conversations, aimed at finding a feasible settlement for the Pacific area, continued with a short break in July until late November.
42. Hull, *Memoirs*, II, 989.

43. *FR, Japan, 1931-1949*, II, 397.

44. *FR, 1941*, V, 115-118. Lauchlin Currie, Roosevelt's adviser, reported after visiting China that "all of the people I talked to who had been trained in Japan or who claimed to know the Japanese thought that, being so methodical, they would consolidate their positions in Indochina and Thailand, construct air and supply bases before moving on Singapore, and would move on Singapore before venturing to take the Dutch East Indies." See his "Report on Some Aspects of the Current Political, Economic and Military Situation in China," March 15, 1941, in *FR, 1941*, IV, 91.

45. *FR, 1941*, V, 121.

46. Testimony of Admiral Ingersoll, PHA Hearings, IX, 4272-4278. Ingersoll was sent to London as director of the Navy's War Plans Division. All understandings reached with the British during these conversations were superseded by ABC-1. See also Samuel Eliot Morison, *The Rising Sun in the Pacific* (Boston: Little Brown, 1948), 49.

47. PHA Exhibits, XV, 1487; Morison, *Rising Sun*, 49-50. The quotation (reprinted in Morison) is taken from the minutes of the conference.

48. For the whole text of the agreement, see Exhibit 49, PHA Exhibits, XV, 1485-1542. Quote is from ibid., 1491-1492. The same passage noted, "Even if Japan were not initially to enter the war on the side of the Axis Powers, it would still be necessary for the Associated Powers to deploy their forces in a manner to guard against eventual Japanese intervention" (ibid., 1491). For the relevant text from "Rainbow 5," see Proceedings of the Navy Court of Inquiry, PHA Exhibits, XXXII, 70-71.

49. Testimony of Admiral Turner, Hart Inquiry, PHA Exhibits, XXVI, 265. The admiral explained, "While the Navy Department believed that our major military effort considered as a whole, should initially be against Germany—that view, I may add, was also held by the War Department—we were all in agreement that the principal naval effort should be in the Pacific. . . . The United States believed that our strongest naval concentration and naval effort ought to be in the Central Pacific" (ibid., 266).

50. PHA Exhibits, XV, 1511-1512.

51. On the administration's approval of ABC-l, see Feis, *The Road to Pearl Harbor*, 168; also, testimony of Admiral Stark, PHA Hearings, V, 2391. The Singapore agreements, known as ADB (for American-Dutch-British conversations), are reprinted in PHA Exhibits, XV, 1551-1584; see also Morison, *Rising Sun*, 53-56. On the importance of these later conversations, Herbert Feis writes that "this Singapore report left one lasting mark on American official thinking and planning.

The conferees defined the geographical limits on land and sea beyond which Japanese forces could not be permitted to go. . . . They drew the line at which, in their judgment, military resistance against Japan was dictated. When in December next, Japanese warships and troop transports were reported on their way south to an unknown destination, Stark and Marshall advised the President to declare these limits, and to warn Japan that we would join the fight if they were passed. Had not the Japanese struck at Pearl Harbor, this line would have become the boundary between war and peace" (Feis, *The Road to Pearl Harbor*, 170.

52. Farago, *Broken Seal*, 182.

53. Ibid., 183; see also *FR, 1941*, IV, 123.

54. *FR, Japan, 1931-1941*, II, 398-402. Many specific terms were cited, but those mentioned here were salient.

55. Hull, *Memoirs*, II 993.

56. *FR, 1941*, IV, 136. Hornbeck wrote his analysis on April 7 based on his knowledge of the April 5 draft.

57. Ibid., 124-125.

58. *FR, 1941*, IV, 150-152.

59. Ibid., 944; "Statement of the Prime Minister, Prince Fumimaro Konoye, April 13, 1941," in Board of Information, *Official Announcements*, 29-30; Hull, *Memoirs*, II, 993.

60. Grew, *Ten Years in Japan*, 382 (April 22 diary entry).

61. Knox address, in box 268, Hornbeck papers. See also T. W. Lamont's address, "China and the Dictators," to Economic Club of Detroit, April 28, 1941, Hornbeck papers, and *New York Herald Tribune*, April 29, 1941.

62. Hull, *Memoirs*, II, 994-995; *FR, Japan, 1931-1941*, II, 407-408.

63. *FR, Japan, 1931-1941*, II, 407-409.

64. Nomura to Tokyo, April 17, 1941, in Department of Defense, *The "MAGIC" Background of Pearl Harbor*, Volume I (Washington: Department of Defense, 1978), 41.

65. Robert J.C. Butow, "The Hull-Nomura Conversations: A Fundamental Misconception," *American Historical Review* 65 (July 1960), 822-836.

66. Hull, *Memoirs*, II, 996-997; *FR, 1941*, V, 132-136.

67. Hull, *Memoirs*, II, 997.

68. *FR, 1941*, V, 138-139.

69. *FR, 1941*, IV, 168.

70. *FR, 1941*, IV, 191. Hornbeck believed Japan's pledges would be worthless in any case.

71. Department of State, *United States Relations with China, with Special Reference to the Period 1944-1949* [China White Paper] (Washington: U.S. Government Printing Office, 1949), 26-27. In early 1941,

the United States was sending about 4,000 tons of supplies to China each month. By November, this figure had risen to 15,000 tons.

72. Hull, *Memoirs*, II, 997. Hull was aware of increasing Japanese pressure on Indochina. See *FR, 1941*, V, 144-146.

73. "Contents of the Convention and the Agreement, May 6, 1941," Board of Information, *Official Announcements*; for an analysis of the agreement, see U.S. Office of Strategic Services, Research and Analysis Branch, "Survey of Indo-China" (R&A No. 719), second edition, September 24, 1943, 38.

74. *FR, Japan, 1931-1941*, II, 419, 422; Hull, *Memoirs*, II, 1000. As to Japan's "peaceful nature," Hull knew from Grant that the Japanese were planning a coup d'etat in Thailand to install a friendly government there (*FR, 1941*, V, 150).

75. Hull, *Memoirs*, II, 1002.

76. Welles's covering letter to Roosevelt can be found in *FR, 1941*, IV, 208; the actual excerpt from Grew's diary (along with the Welles letter) is in box 188, Hornbeck papers. It was first distributed throughout the State Department on May 19. The original diary entry is on pages 4904-4909, Grew papers.

77. Memorandum, May 14, 1941 (revised May 22), boxes 188 and 425, Hornbeck papers. Grew read the memo "with keen interest" (Grew letter to Hornbeck, June 17, 1941, Grew papers).

78. Marshall to Stimson, May 20, 1941, cited in Miner, "United States Policy," 210-211.

79. Stimson and Bundy, *On Active Service*, 386. "In these opinions the Navy under Admiral Stark concurred . . . ; the Pacific Ocean had for years been the Navy's assumed area of combat."

80. Stimson diary, April 24, May 5 and 6, 1941.

81. Miner, "United States Policy," 199, 231.

82. Stimson and Bundy, *On Active Service*, 387; Morison, *Rising Sun*, 57.

83. Israel, *War Diary of Breckinridge Long* (June 4, 1941), 202-203.

84. Hull, *Memoirs*, II, 1007; *FR, Japan, 1931-1941*, II, 454-455.

85. Most of these later discussions centered around China, but the fate of Southeast Asia remained an unresolved issue (see *FR, Japan, 1931-1941*, II, 482). Hull realized well that Japan's Co-Prosperity Sphere program "envisage[s] the placing of areas in the southern Pacific, including the Philippine Commonwealth, under Japanese economic and political hegemony" (*FR, 1941*, V, 177). Hull's suspicions of Japanese intentions, and particularly his anxiety over China, were not new, as indicated by his February 5 letter to Roosevelt. Nonetheless, they owed much to the constant barrage of Hornbeck's memoranda; see, for example, his May 15 memo to Welles in *FR, 1941*, IV, 192-193, and another written May 26, 1941, box 52, Hornbeck papers.

Secretary Hull heard similar arguments from the Chinese ambassador, Hu Shih. The old Chinese scholar understood that Americans were aiding his country less from sympathy than self-interest. In a letter to Hull on May 26, Hu Shih argued, like Hornbeck: "So far two things—and two things only—have prevented Japan from going to the aid of her European partners: First, the war in China has bogged down her millions of troops and service men and has tied up hundreds of ships for the transport of troops and for keeping these troops supplies. And, secondly, the presence of the American fleet in the Pacific has made Japan hesitate either to carry out her 'southward advance', or to raid the commerce and cut the supply lines for the British Commonwealths as well as for China. I am reasonably sure that, as long as China fights on and a sufficiently strong portion of the American fleet is maintained in the Pacific, there will not be active and effective Japanese assistance to the Axis powers in the Pacific. But, if Japan is freed from her war in China or from the danger of being effectively flanked by the American fleet, then no amount of appeasement, nor any Japanese pledge can stop Japan from playing the role of an active partner of the Axis powers and completely cutting off Australia and New Zealand from participation in the war in Africa and Asia, as well as effectively intercepting all material supplies from the United States and Canada"(*FR, 1941*, IV, 225–227).

86. *FR, 1941*, V, 141–142. U.S. leaders worried that the Dutch might accede to Japanese demands (*FR, Japan, 1931–1941*, II, 233, 250).

87. *FR, 1941*, V, 174.

88. Ibid., 178.

89. *FR, 1941*, V, 178, 169–170.

90. Ibid., 206.

91. Ibid., 180–181, 186–188, 188–189, 192, 235.

92. *FR, 1941*, IV, 276–277.

93. Ibid., 279.

94. Nobutaka Ike, ed., *Japan's Decision for War: Records of the 1941 Policy Conferences* (Stanford: Stanford University Press, 1967), 78; see also Nagaoka Shinjirō, "The Drive into Southern Indochina and Thailand," in Morley, *The Fateful Choice*, 236.

95. Ike, *Japan's Decision*, 80.

96. Ibid., 81–82.

97. Memorandum by Joseph Ballantine to George Renchard, of the Secretary's Office, July 5, 1941 in *FR, 1941*, IV, 291.

5. Japan Moves South

1. Hornbeck reported on July 5 that the best intelligence reports agreed that although Germany was pressuring Japan to enter the war

against the Soviet Union, Japan intended instead to consolidate and expand its position in Indochina (*FR, 1941*, IV, 290).

2. Captain Schuirmann to Welles, July 9, 1941 in *FR, 1941*, IV, 298-299.

3. Hull, *Memoirs*, II.

4. *FR, 1941*, IV, 299. Chinese intelligence, which Chiang sent to FDR on July 8, confirmed these estimates (*FR, 1941*, IV, 1004).

5. Foreign Office minutes, July 7, 1941, F8054/8054/61, Public Records Office, London.

6. *FR, 1941*, IV, 288. Sumner Welles argued along similar lines to Harry Hopkins on July 7. See Robert Sherwood, *Roosevelt and Hopkins, an Intimate History* (New York: Harper, 1950), 403.

7. PHA Exhibits, XII, 1.

8. Matsuoka (Tokyo) to Washington, July 2, 1941, ibid., 2; also in Department of Defense, "*MAGIC*," Appendix II, 56-57. This cable was not decoded until August 8, however.

9. Barnhart, *Japan Prepares*, 264-266, notes that some naval officers were willing to give diplomacy more time and that some in the Imperial Army still hoped to shift the direction of Japan's expansion against the Soviet Union.

10. Feis, *The Road to Pearl Harbor*, 228-229.

11. PHA Exhibits, XX, 4363; *FR, 1941*, V, 213-214, 220. Darlan informed Ambassador Leahy on July 15, 1941, that Japan would soon occupy bases in southern Indochina, preparatory to moving south. When he met Darlan and Petain again on July 19th, Leahy delivered a message from Washington to the effect that "if Japan was the winner, the Japanese would take over French Indo-China; and if the Allies won, we would take it." See William Leahy, *I Was There* (New York: Whittlesey House, 1950), 44.

12. *FR, 1941*, IV, 329.

13. PHA Exhibits, XII, 2. The State Department also knew that Ambassador Nomura himself was utterly frustrated with his government's bad faith. The uncompromising Japanese foreign minister, in fact, considered the embassy to be shot through with "fellow travelers" who "willingly allowed the United States to mold your opinions." See Nomura cable to Tokyo, July 14, 1941, and Matsuoka cable to Washington, July 14, 1941, in Department of Defense, "*MAGIC*," Appendix II, 73, 77.

14. *New York Times*, July 17, 1941, and July 18, 1941; *Wall Street Journal*, July 18, 1941.

15. *FR, Japan, 1931-1941*, II, 522; *FR, 1941*, IV, 334-335.

16. Hull, *Memoirs*, II, 1013.

17. Department of Defense, "*MAGIC*," Appendix II, 450-451. This cable was translated July 24.

18. Ibid., 1013–1014; *FR, Japan, 1931–1941*, II, 525.
19. Department of State, *Peace and War*, 127; *FR, Japan, 1931–1941*, II, 342.
20. Notter, *Postwar Foreign Policy*, 48.
21. Department of State, *Peace and War*, 127; *FR, Japan, 1931–1941*, II, 342. 503.
22. *Wall Street Journal*, July 24, 1941.
23. *FR, 1941*, IV, 340–341.
24. *Department of State Bulletin*, July 26, 1941, 71–72.
25. Barnet Nover, a columnist for the *Washington Post*, wrote on July 25 that if Japan seized the Netherlands East Indies, it "would make this Nation dependent, in turn, on Japan's good will for certain indispensable supplies such as rubber and tin. That is why action against Japan is called for at once." Royce Briar of the *San Francisco Chronicle* explained the same day that the U.S. stake in opposing Japan's southward expansion was "a rational self-interest in our supplies of rubber and tin." The *New York Times* editorialized on July 24: "The Japanese Government must be made to understand clearly that aggressive action on its part in any one of three possible areas— Siberia, the Netherlands Indies or Indo-China—will be met by prompt retaliation on the part of the United States. In Siberia this interest is geographical: only a few miles of open water separate Siberia from American territory in Alaska. . . . In the Netherlands Indies our interest is economic: most of our tin and rubber, commodities indispensable to us in times either of war or peace, come from these islands and the surrounding area; with the Netherlands Indies in unfriendly hands, both our national defense and our peacetime commerce would be jeopardized. In Indo-China our interest is strategic." The editorial concluded: "Any action by Japan that threatens a legitimate American interest in the Far East should be met at once by efforts on our part to deal Japanese finance and industry and trade a deadly blow."
26. *FR, Japan, 1931–1941*, II, 528–529. Roosevelt cabled Hopkins in London on July 26, 1941 to relay news of the proposal to Churchill. The president wrote that Japan's response would probably be unfavorable, but he offered the deal anyway in order to make "one more effort to avoid Japanese expansion to South Pacific." See E. Roosevelt, *Personal Letters*, II, 1189–1190.
27. On his own, Grew had decided to speak with the Japanese foreign minister, Admiral Toyoda, "not only [to] make sure that Admiral Toyoda had clearly understood the full purport of the proposal but that I should also exert every ounce of my own influence to secure it acceptance." The ambassador was shocked to find that the foreign minister knew nothing of the plan, which Nomura had hardly men-

tioned in his reports back to Tokyo. Nomura was immediately instructed to send a complete report, but by then the embargo and freeze were in effect. See Grew diary entry for July 27, 1941, in *Ten Years in Japan*, 411-412. Even so, Japan probably would not have accepted the proposal, as it granted them nothing they did not already have and would have prevented them from pursuing their course of expansion. Roosevelt's chief intent, probably, was to expose the false pretenses behind Japan's foreign policy.

28. *FR, Japan, 1931-1941*, II, 317-318.

29. *New York Times*, July 26, 1941; *FR, Japan, 1931-1941*, II, 266-267. The embargo actually overcame resistance by the Japanese Navy to pursuing its southward advance, which now saw the Indies as a vital source of its own raw material needs (Chihiro Hosoya, "Miscalculations in Deterrent Policy: Japanese-US Relations, 1938-1941," *Journal of Peace Research* (1968), 97-115). Within the United States itself, the freeze order also seemed to portend war. Roosevelt put the Philippines on a war footing on July 26 (*Washington Post*, July 27, 1941). News of the Japanese seizure of Indochina and the resultant freeze caused sharp advances on the commodity markets—a sign of expected trouble. *Wall Street Journal*, July 26, 1941; see also National City Bank of New York, *Economic Conditions, Governmental Finance, United States Securities*, August 1941; and "Threat to Far Eastern Supplies," *Barron's* 21 (August 4, 1941), 6.

30. Feis, *The Road to Pearl Harbor*, 245, 246-247; *Washington Post*, July 29, 1941.

31. *New York Times*, August 2, 1941; Feis, *The Road to Pearl Harbor*, 248. Much of the responsibility for making the embargo total, possibly without Roosevelt or Hull intending it so, rests with Dean Acheson. See Irvine Anderson, Jr., *The Standard Vacuum Oil Company and United States East Asian Policy, 1933-1941* (Princeton: Princeton University Press, 1975), 178; Barnhart, *Japan Prepares*, 232; Utley, *Going to War*, 153-156.

32. Department of State, *Peace and War*, 88.

33. "Gallup and Fortune Polls," *Public Opinion Quarterly* 4 (March 1940), 114. On the administration's cautious attitude, see Berle and Jacobs, *Navigating the Rapids*, 233 (August 4, 1939 entry) and Ickes, *Secret Diary*, 96.

34. Israel, *War Diary of Breckinridge Long*, 81. A few days earlier, Long noted that it would be a mistake to provoke Japan, because the Navy's inability to mobilize far from the United States' shores "lays bear the route to the Dutch East Indies" (Long diary, April 5, 1940, in Long papers, Library of Congress).

35. This episode has been described above, but see Welles, "Roosevelt and the Far East," 33. See also Dooman's statement to Ohashi,

supra. Feis, *The Road to Pearl Harbor*, 92-93; Blum, *Morgenthau Diaries*, 350-353; State Judiciary Committee, *Morgenthau Diary (China)*, I, 351-352.

36. Israel, *War Diary of Breckinridge Long*, October 10.
37. Ibid., 150.
38. E. Roosevelt, *Personal Letters*, II, 1077.
39. Ickes admitted the possibility that Japan would attack the Netherlands East Indies if cut off from U.S. petroleum products. See Ickes, *Secret Diary*, III, 132, 299, for his views in 1940 and pages 537, 543-548, 552-560 for his correspondence with Roosevelt in June. Roosevelt's reply is printed in the Ickes diary, 567-568, and in E. Roosevelt, *Personal Letters*,II, 1174. T. A. Bisson commented on the discrepancy between the great hostility shown by the administration to Tokyo and its refusal to embargo oil to Japan: "[T]he Administration firmly resisted considerable popular pressure for an embargo on oil shipments, which remained high despite the reduction in exports of other war materials. In June an oil shortage threatened to develop on the east coast of the United States.... To meet this situation, exports of petroleum products were placed under the license system on June 20 and an embargo was imposed on shipments from east coast ports except to the British Empire, Egypt and the western hemisphere. No restriction was placed on shipments from the west coast. These regulations did not, therefore, seriously interfere with the Japanese trade, except in the case of Pennsylvania lubricating oil. Further evidence that the United States was handling Japan with gloves was seen in the omission of any reference to Japan in the President's speech of May 27 proclaiming a national emergency, and in the failure to include Japan in the general order of June 14 freezing the assets of Axis nations in this country" (Bisson, *America's Far Eastern Policy*, 121-122).
40. Welles, "Roosevelt and the Far East," 202; see also Feis, *The Road to Pearl Harbor*, 227.
41. Hornbeck memorandum, July 16, 1941 in box 145, Hornbeck papers.
42. PHA Hearings, V, 2384.
43. Ibid., 326.
44. *FR, 1941*, IV, 325.
45. *FR, Japan, 1931-1941*, II, 527-528.
46. Ibid., 531.
47. *Department of State Bulletin*, July 26, 1941, 72. The Volunteer Participation Committee was a civilian defense organization. Roosevelt's statement is reprinted in most collections of official foreign policy documents from this period. Its official quality may also be gleaned from Acheson, *Present at the Creation*, 25, and Feis, *The Road to Pearl Harbor*, 23.

48. Looking back on the debate, Joseph Grew noted that he had opposed sterner measures against Japan in 1940. "In those years we were certainly not in such a position [to go to war], either morally or physically, for it might have meant fighting a two-ocean war with a one-ocean navy. I felt through those years that the term of 'appeasement' to characterize our policy was inadequate. It seemed to me to be a policy of plain common sense. Later, when Japan began to surround the Philippines and to threaten our own and Great Britain's life-lines in the east, and when we were at least getting ready in our country for what might come, I took the position that embargoes should then be applied, as our own national security was being menaced." Grew letter to Richard Gurley, October 5, 1943, Grew papers, Houghton Library.

49. Telegram translated August 4; PHA Exhibits, XII, 9.

50. Grew, *Turbulent Era*, II, 1284.

51. Hull, *Memoirs*, I, 270.

52. See *FR, 1941* V, passim, for information on Japanese troop movements threatening Thailand; Exhibit 33, PHA Exhibits, XIV, 1346-1384.

53. Stimson diary, August 8 and 12, 1941; Stimson and Bundy, *On Active Service*, 387-388.

54. Memorandum by Cecil Gray, assistant to the secretary of state, August 2, 1941, in *FR, 1941*, IV, 358-359.

55. On the various "routes" used by the China lobbyists, see *FR, 1941*, V, "The Undeclared War," passim. For more on the lobbying effort, see J. M. Burns, *Roosevelt: The Soldier of Freedom* (New York: Harcourt Brace Jovanovich, 1970), 145. For a typical cable from Lattimore, see *FR, 1941*, IV, 361-362.

56. Hornbeck memorandum to Welles, July 31, 1941, in box 463, Hornbeck papers.

57. *FR, 1941*, IV, 358-359. See also Blum, *Morgenthau Diaries*, 380.

58. *FR, 1941*, V, 260.

59. *FR, Japan, 1931-1941*, 549-50; Hull, *Memoirs*, II, 1016.

60. Hull, *Memoirs*, II, 1016.

61. *FR, 1941*, I, 347-348. The U.S. military was in full agreement with the civilians on this course. General Miles argued on September 23 that "forceful diplomacy vis-a-vis Japan, including the application of ever increasing military and economic pressure on our part offers the best chance of gaining time, the best possibility of preventing the spread of hostilities in the Pacific area, and also the hope of the eventual disruption of the Tripartite Pact." See Hornbeck memorandum, September 30, 1941, in box 463, Hornbeck papers.

62. *FR, Japan, 1931-1941*, 552-553.

63. Ibid., 553.

64. Hull testimony, PHA Hearings, II, 423; Winston Churchill, *The Grand Alliance* (Boston: Houghton Mifflin, 1950), 439.
65. *FR, Japan, 1931-1941*, II, 556-559.
66. Hull, *Memoirs*, II, 1022.
67. Hornbeck memorandum, August 21, 1941, box 188, Hornbeck papers.
68. Stimson diary, August 9, 1941. He reported this directly to Hull.
69. Hull, *Memoirs*, II, 1022. On Grew's reaction to the proposal, see Waldo Heinrichs, *American Ambassador: Joseph C. Grew and the Development of the United States Diplomatic Tradition* (Boston: Little Brown, 1966), 339-350.
70. Hull, *Memoirs*, II, 1022.
71. Hull, *Memoirs*, II, 1024; Hull testimony, PHA Hearings, II, 425. Hornbeck argued along somewhat similar lines in a memorandum written on September 5, "The chief danger attendant upon the holding of a meeting between the President and the Japanese Prime Minister is that if such a meeting is held there must emanate from it an agreement. The only kind of an agreement that could possibly be arrived at would be an agreement in most general terms. Such an agreement would not (in the light of what we know of this country's attitude and policy and of what we are now given regarding Japan's attitude and policy) represent any real meeting of the minds of the people of the two countries thus committed by it" (*FR, 1941*, IV, 425-428).
72. Hull testimony, PHA Hearings, II, 425; Stimson diary, October 6, 1941.
73. *FR, 1941*, IV, 426; Hull, *Memoirs*, II, 1024. A number of memoranda by Hornbeck specifically emphasized this point.
74. Hornbeck memorandum, September 5, 1941, "Reasons which make disadvantageous any personal meeting between the President and Prince Konoye," in box 145, Hornbeck papers.
75. Hull, *Memoirs*, II, 1024. Or, as the secretary put it during the Pearl Harbor investigation, such a meeting "would have a critically discouraging effect upon the Chinese" PHA Hearings, II, 425.
76. Hornbeck memorandum, September 5, 1941, "Reasons why it is contrary to the interests of the United States to enter at this time into any agreement of a general political nature with Japan," in box 145, Hornbeck papers; Langer and Gleason, *Undeclared War*, 718.
77. PHA Hearings, V, 2092. The estimate was prepared by Hayes Kroner, and entitled "Japanese-American Relations." See PHA Exhibits, XIV, 1357-1359. Cf. Stimson diary, October 6, 1941.
78. Hull, *Memoirs*, II, 1026-1027.

79. Ike, *Japan's Decision*, 129-133. This decision was reaffirmed at the September 6 conference (ibid., 133-163). The policy of southward advance was reaffirmed at this meeting.

80. *FR, Japan, 1931-1941*, II, 608-609; Hull, *Memoirs*, II, 1028-1029.

81. Ike, *Japan's Decision*, 135-136 ("The Minimum Demands of Our Empire to Be Attained Through Diplomatic Negotiations with the United States [and Great Britain], and the Maximum Concessions to Be Made by Our Empire").

82. Hull, *Memoirs*, II, 1028.

83. Ibid., 1029.

84. *FR, 1941*, IV, 497-499.

85. Examples may be found in box 463, Hornbeck papers.

86. *FR, 1941*, IV, 436-441.

87. Quoted in Langer and Gleason, *Undeclared War*, 710.

88. *FR, 1941*, IV, 459-461.

89. See for example Hornbeck's memorandum of October 22, citing portions of this Gauss dispatch, in box 463, Hornbeck papers.

90. *FR, 1941*, IV, 478-480.

91. These points are confirmed by Langer and Gleason, *Undeclared War*, 721. See also the following memoranda and communications: Grew to Hull, August 14, 740.0011 PW/448; Reed to Hull, September 11, 740.0011 PW/518; Reed to Hull, October 3, 740.0011 PW/551; Grew to Hull, October 10, 1941, 740.0011 PW /560, RG 59; Leahy to Hull, September 29, *FR, 1941*, V, 298-299; Leahy to Hull, October 2, ibid., 302-303; Reed (Consul at Hanoi) to Hull, October 3, ibid., 305-306; Grew to Hull, October 8, ibid., 315; Leahy to Hull, October 8, ibid., 313-314; Leahy to Hull, October 11, ibid., 317; Reed to Hull, October 14, ibid., 319; Peck to Hull, October 15, ibid., 320-322; Reed to Hull, October 17, ibid., 329-330; Browne (Consul at Saigon) to Hull, October 29, ibid. Browne pointed out that in the preceding two weeks Japan had put into Indochina more than 30,000 new troops (mostly into the south), as well as all kinds of new military equipment. The building of airfields, barracks, and other structures was moving ahead rapidly, as if in preparation for an invasion to the south. Also see Browne to Hull, November 3, ibid., 332. Hornbeck contrasted Japan's continuing encroachments on Indochina with the administration's position that it should withdraw as a precondition for better relations with the United States. "While Japanese 'moderates' . . . are still carrying on conversations with the United States envisaging the possibility of some significant settlement between Japan and the United States, while these representatives declare that the Japanese Government is in accord with the principles to which the United States is

committed," he wrote, "a new Japanese move of aggression is now ordered by the Japanese Government" (*FR, 1941*, IV, 493-494). Hornbeck went so far as to argue that Japan's hedging of its obligations toward its Axis partners proved that Japan could never be trusted to live up to its commitments. See Hornbeck memorandum, September 27, 1941, box 463, Hornbeck papers. Hull felt the same way. "This Government finds it especially difficult at this time to reconcile the reported Japanese actions in Indochina with recent declarations of high Japanese officials that Japan's fundamental policy is based upon the maintenance of peace and pursuit of courses of peace," he wired Grew on October 2. Hull to Grew, October 2, *FR, 1941*, V, 304-305.

92. *FR, Japan, 1931-1941*, II, 660.

93. Washington (Nomura) to Tokyo, October 3, 1941. PHA Exhibits, XII, 51. The ambassador did believe, however, that it should not "be considered as an absolutely hopeless situation."

94. See text of the 57th Liaison Conference, October 4, 1941, in Ike, *Japan's Decision*, 179-181. Bishop Walsh described the Japanese reaction when news of Hull's October 2 reply came in: "With some difficulty, the protagonists of peace in the Japanese government . . . had held Cabinet, army, navy and all the other elements in line, or at least in quiescence, pending the conclusion of the negotiations. . . . Many, both in the civil government and the army, now think that the deception goes back to the beginning, that is to say, that the American government wanted only to draw them out in order to gain time, and to get a statement of their policy in order to condemn it. . . . After the receipt of the message it was very difficult to make any one in the Japanese government believe in the sincerity of the American government" (*FR, 1941*, IV, 527-539).

95. Hornbeck as usual took a vanguard position, declaring even that an apparent diplomatic victory with regard to China would really produce a defeat in Southeast Asia: "If the Japanese troops were withdrawn from China now in consequence of a diplomatic arrangements distinguished from a physical and material failure to make good their effort of conquest, the withdrawal would be made only for the purpose of preparing for a bigger and better assault a) upon some other region now and b) upon China at a later date." See Hornbeck memorandum, October 14, box 145, Hornbeck papers.

96. United Press news flash from Tokyo, October 17, 1941, quoted in Hornbeck memorandum, October 18, in box 463, Hornbeck papers.

97. Memorandum of R. E. Schuirmann, quoted in Sherwood, *Roosevelt and Hopkins*, 419.

98. Stimson diary, October 16, 1941.

99. Tokyo to Washington, #698, in PHA Exhibits, XII, 81.

100. Washington (Nomura) to Tokyo, October 22, 1941, ibid.
101. Tokyo to Washington (unnumbered), ibid., 82.
102. Foreign Minister Tōgō Shigenori complained to Sir Robert Craigie in late October that the United States was deliberately foot-dragging to draw out the negotiations, which Japan could not continue for long. E. L. Woodward, *British Foreign Policy in the Second World War*, 178–179.
103. PHA Exhibits, XII, 90.
104. Ibid., 92–93.
105. *FR, Japan, 1931–1941*, II, 704.
106. Ike, *Japan's Decision*, 208–239.
107. PHA Exhibits, XII, 100; Tokyo to Washington, November 11 (#762) and November 15 (#775), ibid., 116, 130; Hull, *Memoirs*, II, 1057.
108. Tokyo to Washington, November 4, 1941 (#726), PHA Exhibits, XII, 94–96.
109. "Instances Since the Outbreak of the Present Hostilities in China in which Japanese Statements of Policy Have Proved Unreliable," October 11, 1940. Prepared with Alger Hiss. Leo Pasvolsky office files, box 1, National Archives.
110. The Japanese plan did not explicitly bar U.S. aid to China; it provided only for no U.S. interference in the peace negotiations between Japan and China. But Hull knew that Japan really meant "no aid" in place of "no interference." In one telegram to Nomura, for instance, the Japanese government explained: "[I]t goes without saying . . . that the United States would not interfere with the peace to be established between Japan and China (This promise includes cessation of activies for aiding CHIANG)" (Tokyo to Washington, November 10 (#755), pt. 1, PHA Exhibits, 107–108). In part 2 of the message cited above, Japan's leaders reaffirmed that if the United States was of the intention "of continuing aid to CHIANG, we shall not be able to accept the proposal" (Ibid., 108).
111. The correspondence on the "imminent" Japanese attack on Kunming began on October 28 and is reprinted in PHA Exhibits, XIV, 1078ff. The letter quoted here is in ibid., 1476–1478. Cf. Stimson diary, November 4, 1941.
112. On November 5, after a conference with Hull, Marshall, and Stark, Stanley Hornbeck drafted a memorandum with these considerations in mind: "Suppose that . . . by virtue of a break-down in Chinese morale . . . Chinese resistance to Japan were to cease. Japan would then be relieved of the entanglement of her 'China Incident' and would be in a position to turn her fleet and whatever else she still possesses of capacity for military adventuring into new moves either southward or northward or eastward. Should it not be a constant object of British

and American political, economic and military strategy to keep China's moral and material capacity to resist Japan at a high enough point to ensure against a termination of Chinese resistance?" (PHA Hearings, III, 1395). The Japanese minister of embassy, Wakasugi Kaname, summed up the U.S. position on China in a cable to Tokyo on October 29, 1941: "The United States wants to tackle the China problem as merely one phase of the aforementioned 'peace on the Pacific' issue. On the other hand, it should be recalled that Hull once said to the late Ambassador Saito that it was exceedingly doubtful that there should be war between Japan and the United States over merely the China problem. There are indications that the United States is still not anxious to fight Japan over only the China problem. However, it must be borne in mind that China is now relying solely on the United States. It is said that T. V. Soong and others in the United States are working on the Treasury Department in particular and the United States is doing everything in its power to prevent the bringing about of a truce between Japan and the United States. Since China is entirely dependent on the United States, the United States cannot turn a cold shoulder to her pleas. It is impossible for the United States to cruelly impose terms on China which would be almost impossible for the United States herself to endure." See Washington (Nomura) to Tokyo, October 29, 1941 (#1008), in PHA Exhibits, XII, 86–87.

113. *FR, Japan, 1931–1941*, II, 708–710. Perhaps to gain more time, Hull also suggested bringing an influential representative of the Chinese government into the talks, to help promote friendly relations with Japan and speed a peace settlement. The effect would also have been to reduce Chinese suspicion of U.S. motives.

114. Ibid., 717–718.

115. Quote from Feis, *The Road to Pearl Harbor*, 304.

116. Tokyo to Washington, November 16, 1941, PHA Exhibits, XII, 138.

117. Hull, *Memoirs*, II, 1062–1063; Israel, *War Diary of Breckinridge Long*, 233.

118. *FR, Japan, 1931–1941*, II, 755–756.

119. Washington to Tokyo, November 20, 1941, #1147, pts. 1&2, PHA Exhibits, XII, 161–62.

120. Tokyo to Washington, November 24, 1941, #821, ibid., 172. An official Japanese analysis of this final plan reaffirms the contention that Japan required a cessation of U.S. aid to China: "Regarding the above proposal, the Secretary of State contended that it was impossible for the American Government to accept the item 4 of our proposal and cease aiding the Chiang Kai-shek regime unless Japan clarified her relations with the Tripartite Pact and gave assurances regarding

her adoption of a peaceful policy, and that the President's offer to act as 'introducer' of Sino-Japanese peace was predicated upon Japan's adoption of a peaceful policy. Thereupon, the Japanese Government instructed the two Ambassadors to request reconsideration by the American Government, pointing out to the Secretary of State that, in case direct negotiations were opened between Japan and Chungking through 'introduction' by the President, the continuation of aid to the Chiang Kai-shek regime by the United States, the peace introducer, would constitute an interference with the realization of peace, and that the American contention was therefore inconsistent"("Summary of the Japanese-American Negotiations, December 7, 1941," in [Japan] Board of Information, *Official Announcements*, 95).

121. On November 18, 1941, Nomura actually cabled his government suggesting that it agree to return to the pre-July status quo; the reply came back the next day: "[T]he internal situation in our country is such that it would be difficult for us to handle it if we withdraw from southern French Indo-China, merely on assurances that conditions prior to this freezing act will be restored." A MAGIC translation of this cable was available on November 20 (Tokyo to Washington, November 19, #798, PHA Exhibits, XII, 155–156).

122. Hull testimony, PHA Hearings, XI, 5370–5371; see also Hull, *Memoirs*, II, 1070. Herbert Feis's insight into the collapse of Japanese-American negotiations should also be kept in mind: "Even if Japan was genuinely ready for reform, the repentence had come too late. The situation had grown too entangled by then for minor measures, its momentum too great. Germany-Italy-Japan had forced the creation of a defensive coalition more vast than the empire of the Pacific for which Japan plotted. This was not now to be quieted or endangered by a temporary halt along the fringe of the Japanese advance" (Herbert Feis, "War Came at Pearl Harbor: Suspicions Considered," *Yale Review* 45 (Spring 1956).

123. Department of State, *Peace and War*, 802–807; *FR, Japan, 1931–1941*, II, 757ff. The British government approved of Hull's negotiating position: "The Foreign Office agreed with Mr. Hull's firmness in insisting that nothing should be conceded to Japan except in return for definite Japanese action. They doubted whether the Japanese would withdraw from Indo-China on the terms put forward by Mr. Kurusu, but the offer would be worth considering if it were not accompanied by unacceptable conditions. We should have to take care to avoid any suggestion of abandoning China; it therefore seemed better not to make even limited economic concessions until an understanding had been reached about an ultimate settlement in China." E. L. Woodward, *British Foreign Policy in the Second World War* (London: His Majesty's Stationery Office, 1962), 179.

124. For further evidence, see memo of conversation, December 5, 1941, *FR, Japan, 1931–1941*, II, 774.

125. Stimson diary, September 12, October 6, 7, 28, 1941; also Stark to Kimmes, PHA Exhibits, XIV, 1064–1065.

126. The timing on this draft is still unclear. The State Department claims Roosevelt prepared it after November 20; however, Langer and Gleason (*Undeclared War*, 872) suggest that it was ready by November 17.

127. *FR, 1941*, IV, 626; PHA Exhibits, XIV, 1109. Earlier that month Roosevelt had toyed with a different formulation. Stimson shot it down: "He was trying to think of something which would give us further time. He suggested he might propose a truce in which there would be no movement or armament for 6 months and then if the Japanese and Chinese had not settled their arrangement in that meanwhile, we could go on on the same basis. I told him I frankly saw two great objections to that: first, that it tied up our hands just at a time when it was vitally important that we should go on completing our reenforcement of the Philippines; and second, that the Chinese would feel that any such arrangement was a desertion of them. I reminded him that it has always been our historic policy since the Washington Conference not to leave the Chinese and Japanese alone together, because the Japanese were always able to overslaugh the Chinese and the Chinese know it. I told him that I thought the Chinese would refuse to go into such an arrangement." See Stimson diary, November 6, 1941.

128. Secretary Morgenthau began work on a draft on November 17 (see *FR, 1941*, IV, 606–613). His proposals were long and unwieldy. The Division of Far Eastern Affairs took up the idea on November 19th (ibid., 621–625; Hull, *Memoirs*, II, 1072).

129. For the various drafts of the *modus vivendi*, see *FR, 1941*, IV, 627–630, 635–637, 637–640, 642–644, 645–646; final draft, 661–665.

130. Ibid., 645–646.

131. Admiral Stark and an assistant to General Marshall saw the draft on November 21 (PHA Exhibits, XIV, 1106).

132. *FR, 1941*, IV, 640.

133. PHA Exhibits, XIV, 1170.

134. *FR, 1941*, IV, 652–653.

135. Senate Judiciary Committee, *Morgenthau Diary (China)*, I, 530; *FR, 1941*, IV, 660–661. Treasury Secretary Morgenthau received a copy of this communication, passing it along to Hull and Roosevelt on November 26. Stimson also passed it along. On that morning, Stimson recorded in his diary, "Hull told me over the telephone this morning that he had about made up his mind not to give (make) the proposition that Knox and I passed on the other day to the Japanese but to kick the whole thing over—to tell them that he has no other proposi-

tion at all. The Chinese have objected to that proposition—when he showed it to them; that is, to the proposition which he showed to Knox and me, because it involves giving to the Japanese the small modicum of oil for civilian use during the interval of the truce of the 3 months. Chiang Kai-shek had sent a special message to the effect that that would make a terrifically bad impression in China; that it would destroy all their courage and that they (it) would play into the hands of his, Chiang's, enemies and that the Japanese would use it. T. V. Soong had sent me this letter and has asked to see me and I called Hull up this morning to tell him so and ask him what he wanted me to do about it. He replied as I have just said above—that he had about made up his mind to give up the whole thing in respect to a truce and to simply tell the Japanese that he had no further action to propose"(Stimson diary, November 26, 1941). A similar message reached the White House via the Lattimore-Curre route; see PHA Exhibits, XIV, 1160.

136. PHA Exhibits, XIV, 1300; Winant to Hull, *FR, 1941*, IV, 665.

137. Hornbeck autobiography, box 497, Hornbeck papers. Actually the State Department knew of Churchill's views before the final telegram came in at 12:55 A.M. on November 26. The actual decision to dump the *modus vivendi* was made by Hull and Hornbeck on November 25.

138. Hull, *Memoirs*, II, 1081.

139. *FR, 1941*, IV, 665–666.

140. Stimson diary, November 26, 1941.

141. Hull offered the ten-point plan merely as a final summary of the U.S. position, as a record for posterity and not in the hopes of peace. Roosevelt told Stimson that although the State Department had closed up the negotiations, "they had ended up with a magnificent statement prepared by Hull." Stimson "found out afterward that this was not a reopening of the thing but a statement of our constant and regular position." (Stimson diary, November 27, 1941).

142. Ibid. Actually, Hull may have hoped to further delay Japan by some relaxation of economic pressure, but hardliners such as Hornbeck won out. Hull to Hornbeck, November 28, 1941, box 49, Hull papers.

6. Roosevelt Plans for War

1. Sherwood, *Roosevelt and Hopkins*, 259.

2. Testimony of Admiral Turner, Hart Inquiry, PHA Exhibits, XVI, 263–264, 267. See also testimony of Admiral Newton, ibid., 340–341; also Morison, *Rising Sun*, 56.

3. *FR, 1941*, V, 254–256.

4. Churchill to General Smuts, November 9, 1941, reprinted in Churchill, *The Grand Alliance*, 593.

5. Exhibit 22-C, PHA Exhibits, XIV, 1275–1291; quote from 1279–1280.

6. See p. 188 herein; *FR, Japan, 1931–1941*, II, 556–559.

7. Stimson diary, August 19, 1941.

8. Cited in Raymond Esthus, "President Roosevelt's Commitment to Britain to Intervene in a Pacific War," *Mississippi Valley Historical Review* 50 (June 1963), 32.

9. Gerow to Marshall, November 3, 1941, in PHA Exhibits, XIV, 1066–1067.

10. "Minutes of Meeting (Joint Board)," November 3, 1941, ibid., 1062–1065.

11. PHA Exhibits, XIV, 1061–62; Hull, *Memoirs*, II, 1057; Feis, *Road to Pearl Harbor*, 302. Note that any advance south of the 10th parallel was explicitly viewed as a threat to Singapore. See Stark memo to Roosevelt, November 27, 1941, in PHA Exhibits, XIV, 1083.

12. Stimson diary, November 7, 1941; Stimson testimony, PHA Exhibits, XI, 5420.

13. Hull, *Memoirs*, II, 1058.

14. Ibid. Secretary of the Navy Frank Knox gave the first of these speeches on November 11, when he described the nature of Japan's threat in the Pacific and the chance that "at any moment war may be forced upon us" (Department of State, *Peace and War*, 785).

15. On efforts to strengthen the defenses of the Philippines, see Stimson testimony, PHA Hearings, XI, 5420–5421; Stimson diary, November 10, 1941. The poison gas episode is from Stimson diary, November 21.

16. Tokyo to Washington, November 22, 1941, #812, in PHA Exhibits, XII, 165.

17. PHA Exhibits, XIV, 1083. Hull's hopelessness has already been described by his comment to Stimson on November 27 that he had "washed his hands of it." Note also his statement to the British ambassador on November 29 to the effect that "the diplomatic part of our relations with Japan was virtually over and . . . the matter will now go to the officials of the Army and Navy" (Department of State, *Peace and War*, 816–817).

18. Stimson diary, November 27, 1941; also, Stimson testimony, PHA Hearings, XI, 5423.

19. Stimson diary, November 27.

20. Memorandum of conversation between Welles and Halifax, November 27, 1941, *FR, 1941*, IV, 667.

21. PHA Exhibits, XIV, 1406; also Department of Defense, "*MAGIC*," IV Appendix, 117. On Roosevelt's decision to send out the theater warnings, see Stimson testimony, PHA Hearings, XI, 5423.

22. PHA Exhibits, XIV, 1328; also quoted in dispatch by Stark, November 28, 1941, in ibid., 1407; PHA Hearings, XI, 5424; PHA Hearings, III, 1032–1033; and Department of Defense, "*MAGIC*," IV Appendix, 119. The final line clearly undermines conspiracy theories that the administration was prepared to lose the fleet at Pearl Harbor in order to get the country into war.

23. Stimson testimony, PHA Hearings, XI, 5426; Stimson diary, November 28, 1941.

24. Stimson diary, November 28, 1941.

25. See recollections of Harry Hopkins, quoted in Sherwood, *Roosevelt and Hopkins*, 428.

26. Stimson diary, November 28, 29, 30, 1941.

27. *FR, 1941*, IV, 675–678.

28. Ibid., 678–680.

29. A copy of the editorial, with a note of Hull's request for a check of its many figures by his Far Eastern Affairs branch, is in Leo Pasvolsky office file, box 2, RG 59, National Archives.

30. Berle and Jacobs, *Navigating the Rapids*, 380 (December 1, 1941 entry). Hornbeck seems to have first prepared an intermediate draft based almost entirely on those submitted by Knox and Stimson; see PHA Exhibits, Exhibit 161A, XIX, 3520–3533. The style of the State Department draft is that of Hornbeck; see also, *FR, 1941*, IV, 689 fn.

31. *FR, 1941*, IV, 689–697.

32. Stimson diary, December 2, 1941.

33. Influential media, however, continued to frame the growing conflict in terms of "tin and rubber." See for example, the editorial "Spotlight on Singapore," *New York Times*, December 3, 1941, and "If War Reaches the Pacific," *Barron's* 21 (November 17, 1941), 6.

34. Roberta Wohlstetter, *Pearl Harbor: Warning and Decision* (Stanford: Stanford University Press), 386.

35. Washington embassy to Foreign Office, December 1, 1941, PREM3 156/5, Public Record Office; Anthony Eden memo to War Department, December 2, 1941, ibid.; Woodward, *British Foreign Policy*, 186–187.

36. Woodward, *British Foreign Policy*, 187. See also S. W. Kirby, *Singapore: the Chain of Disaster* (London: Cassell, 1971), 109–111, 122–123.

37. S. Woodburn Kirby, *The War Against Japan*, Volume I (London: His Majesty's Stationery Office, 1957), 175; G. Herman Gill, *Royal Australian Navy, 1939–1942* (Adelaide: The Griffen Press, 1957), 462–463.

Brooke-Popham was "the most important military figure in Malaya." See Creighton testimony, PHA Hearings, X, 5086.

38. PHA Hearings, X, 5082-5083.

39. PHA Exhibits, Exhibit 40, XIV, 1412; Husband Kimmel, *Admiral Kimmel's Story* (Chicago: Henry Regnery Company, 1955), 113.

40. Stimson diary, November 25, 1941; Stimson testimony, PHA Hearings, XI, 5421-5422.

41. PHA Exhibits, XIV, 1407.

42. Rear Admiral Kemp Tolley (Rtd.), "The Strange Assignment of USS Lanikai," *United States Naval Institute Proceedings* 83 (September 1962), 71-84. Tolley was captain of the *Lanikai*, the only vessel actually sent out under this order from Roosevelt. Tolley believes the president ordered this mission to create a casus belli, as do all of the early revisionists who base their contention on the reasoning of Frank Keefe in the *Report of the Joint Committee on the Investigation of the Pearl Harbor Attack* (Washington: U.S. Government Printing Office, 1946), 266-P. See also the exchange in *United States Naval Institute Proceedings* 89 (October 1963), 125-129, and Kemp Tolley, *Cruise of the Lanikai* (Annapolis: U.S. Naval Institute, 1974).

43. Ingersoll testimony, PHA Hearings, IX, 4251-4254. For other discussion on this incident, see Ibid., II, 955ff; III, 1248; V, 2190; VI, 2670, 2873; X, 4807. The *Lanikai* had a dead radio—making it of no use at all for "reconnaissance." See *United States Naval Institute Proceedings* 89 (October 1963), 125-129.

44. Tolley, *Lanikai*, 73-74.

45. Toland, *Infamy*, 291-292.

46. *FR, Japan, 1931-1941*, II, 785-786. The message was delivered 10:30 P.M. December 7 (Tokyo time). See Grew, *Ten Years in Japan*, 497.

47. Testimony of Commander Schultz, PHA Hearings, X, 4662.

48. Sherwood, *Roosevelt and Hopkins*, 428; c.f. Frances Perkins, *The Roosevelt I Knew* (New York: Viking Press, 1946), 379f. Stimson felt much the same way. He recorded in his diary for December 7: "When the news first came that Japan had attacked us, my first feeling was of relief that the indecision was over and that a crisis had come in a way which would unite all our people. This continued to be my dominant feeling in spite of the news of catastrophes which quickly developed. For I feel that this country united has practically nothing to fear; while the apathy and divisions stirred up by unpatriotic men have been hitherto very discouraging" (Stimson diary, December 7, 1941).

7. Defining the National Interest

1. A. J. Muste, "Where Are We Going," in Nat Hentoff, (ed.), *The Essays of A. J. Muste* (New York: Simon and Schuster, 1967), 236. (I

am indebted to Noam Chomsky for pointing out that passage.) Muste put things baldly, but he was not alone. In 1942, *Newsweek* business editor Milton Van Slyck called the conflict "essentially one of minerals," between "haves" and "have-nots" (cited in Eckes, Jr., *Global Struggle*, 84.) In 1940, the National Policy Committee, which was one of several propaganda arms for the Council on Foreign Relations and which included such State Department officials as Stanley Hornbeck and Leo Pasvolsky, convened a postwar planning committee that concluded that only an Anglo-American condominium could enforce peace, much as Rome had centuries earlier. "They own half the earth; they carry on two-thirds of the world's trade; they have control of more than fifty percent of every essential material and practically all of the world's gold; their armed strength as well as their economic strength is such as to give them a clear-cut preponderance," the committee observed. One central aim of this Pax America would be to overthrow the autarkic economic system of the 1930s. "To function, modern industry requires supplies and markets over wide areas. If we are not to undergo a revolutionary recasting of economic life, we must recognize the failure of the autarchic experiment and the need for a reinterpretation of the idea of sovereignty as a condition of peace." See memorandum no. 9 of the Special Committee on Steps Toward a Durable Peace, 1940.

2. Robert Keohane, *After Hegemony: Cooperation and Discord in the World Political Economy* (Princeton: Princeton University Press, 1984), 32. Keohane does not endorse simplistic theories that assume a hegemonic state can ensure either economic or military order.

3. Emeny, *Strategy of Raw Materials*, 174.

4. Raymond Vernon, *Two Hungry Giants: The United States and Japan in the Quest for Oil and Ores* (Cambridge: Harvard University Press, 1983), 1-2.

5. A. W. Griswold, "The United States and the Far East," paper presented to the Conference for Instructors on "The Bases of American Foreign Policy," April 28-30, 1939, pamphlet edition (New York: Council on Foreign Relations, 1938).

6. Owen Lattimore, "American Responsibilities in the Far East," *Virginia Quarterly Review* 16 (Spring 1940), 162. Probably hundreds of articles were written in magazines and newspapers from 1939 to 1941 protesting the administration's failure to embargo trade with Japan.

7. Charles Yost memo, April 9, 1941, *FR, 1941*, IV, 805-806.

8. "Policy in Regard to the Far East," March 15, 1935, box 196, Hornbeck papers.

9. Laurence Salisbury memo, January 30, 1939, 793.94/14667 1/2, RG 59, National Archives.

10. Grew diary, November 1940, in Grew, *Turbulent Era*, II, 1232–1233.

11. Stimson to Roosevelt, December 20, 1941, in PSF Box 1, Roosevelt papers; also in Stimson diary, December 20, 1941.

12. *FR, 1935*, III, 855–857.

13. Israel, *War Diary of Breckinridge Long* (September 9, 1940), 129.

14. Stimson diary, November 29, 1940. See also Berle to Hull, December 15, 1941, box 49, Hull papers; Joseph Ballantine autobiography, 210, box 1, Ballantine papers.

15. Stimson diary, July 18, 1940. Roosevelt himself told the White House Correspondents' Association on March 15, 1941, that aid to China was geared to keeping Japan's army "busy and more or less tied up" so it could not "move southward in full force" (text of Roosevelt's address in box 52, Hornbeck papers). Even without access to all the documents, early analysts were able to discern this strategy clearly enough. See, for example, Bisson, *Far Eastern Policy*, 123.

The strategy was mapped out at the 1939 conference of the Institute of Pacific Relations, where it was "emphasized that if economic sanctions are effective, they will inevitably force the nation affected to adopt some form of retaliatory measures in self-defense. In the case of Japan, they might take the form of . . . an attack on Netherlands India, Malaya or Indo-China in an effort to secure at least a partial replacement of American supplies, especially oil. It was suggested by some that in such an event, the United States might feel compelled . . . to go to the defense of the Philippines and the colonial areas of Southeastern Asia. In view of this possibility, certain members expressed the view that Japan would be unlikely to undertake new and costly military adventures so long as China continued to put up effective resistance. If, therefore, the United States wished to avoid the risk of provoking a Japanese attack on the countries of Southeastern Asia, the surest method was to accompany economic measures against Japan with really substantial aid to China"(Mitchell and Holland, *Problems of the Pacific, 1939*, 103).

Dean Acheson voiced similar views that year. In a speech at Yale on "An American Attitude Toward Foreign Affairs," he said: "In the Far East the prophylactic measures take the form of hindering and creating deterrent hazards to the Japanese domination of Asia and the elimination of the white populations from the South Seas. To state the means by which this can be done requires technical knowledge to which I cannot pretend. One obvious objective is to strengthen resistance to the Japanese and weaken their striking power. Whether it is practicable to get necessary material to the Chinese through cooperation with powers upon their borders and to cut off supplies from the

Japanese, I do not know. Neither do I know the risks involved. But practicality and risk are the factors which should govern. Another objective is to create a menace to imperialistic adventure in the South Seas. Naval men can enlighten us as to whether strong bases in the Philippines and Guam are practicable means to this end." See Dean Acheson, *Morning and Noon* (Boston: Houghton Mifflin, Co., 1965), 272–273.

16. "In Greater East Asia," *Fortune* 23 (April 1941), 89.

17. Grew, *Turbulent Era*, II, 1368.

18. "There are evidences of a growing feeling among the Chinese," Ambassador Gauss reported to Hull, "that the American-British policy of aid to China is designed for the purpose of maintaining Chinese resistance to Japan in order that America and Great Britain may not have to engage in hostilities in the Far East" (*FR, 1941*, IV, 396). By making little pretense to the contrary, one U.S. intelligence analysis argued, the aid program did not accomplish its full objective: "American aid to China has been based on self-interest, not sentiment. The first two loans, for instance, were purely commercial deals. Later assistance has seemed to be directed chiefly at keeping China in the war to check Japan. This has been well-calculated realism. It would be a mistake to assume that it has seemed otherwise to the Chinese. In short, the American program has lacked a certain higher realism; little has been done to hearten Chinese morale or to bolster the democratic cause within China." See "American Aid to China," Far Eastern Study No. 21, U.S. Office of Coordinator of Information, Research and Analysis Branch, Far Eastern Section, n. d.

19. Hiss memorandum, box 462, Hornbeck papers.

20. Sumner Welles, *The Time for Decision* (New York: Harper & Bros., 1944), 288–289.

21. The participants were Henry Wallace and Senators Alven Barkley, Charles McNary, Tom Connolly, Warren Austin, Hiram Johnson; Speaker Sam Rayburn; and congressmen Sol Bloom and Charles Easton (Sherwood, *Roosevelt and Hopkins*, 432–433). The text of Roosevelt's statement is in PHA Exhibits, XIX, 3503.

22. Schroeder, *Axis Alliance*, 100–101.

23. David Lawrence, in the *San Francisco Chronicle*, September 30, 1940.

24. John Stewart, "U.S. Exports to Manchukuo Reach New High," *Far Eastern Survey* (March 29, 1939), 82–83. For another optimistic analysis, see Roy Akagi, "Future of American Trade with Manchukuo," *The Annals* 211 (September 1940), 138–143.

25. Gen. Robert E. Wood, "Our Foreign Policy," address before the Chicago Council on Foreign Relations, October 4, 1940 (reprint in

pamphlet form). The same point was made tellingly in an editorial, "The South China Sea and Our Raw Materials," *Commercial and Financial Chronicle* 151 (November 30, 1940), 3138–3141. For a general overview of isolationist responses to the economic threat of the Axis powers, see Justus Doenecke, "Power, Markets, and Ideology: The Isolationist Response to Roosevelt Policy, 1940–1941," in Leonard Liggio and James Martin, eds., *Watershed of Empire: Essays on New Deal Foreign Policy* (Colorado Springs: Ralph Myles, 1976), 132–161.

26. Miner, "United States Policy," 132–134. Miner acknowledges that civilian planners did not share this view (292). The U.S. Staff Committee consisted of Gen. Stanley D. Embick, Gen. L. T. Gerow (chief of the War Plans Division of the U.S. Army), Col. Joseph T. McNarney, Brig. Gen. Sherman Miles, Adm. Robert Ghormley, Capt. Alan G. Kirk, Adm. Kelly Turner, Capt. DeWitt C. Ramsey, and Lt. Col. Omar T. Pfeiffer.

27. Miner, "United States Policy," 337, 343. See also discussion of ABC-1 accords above.

28. Nathan Rosenberg, "Innovative Responses to Materials Shortages," *American Economic Review* 63 (May 1973), 111–118; Julian Simon, *Population Matters: People, Resources, Environment and Immigration* (New Brunswick: Transaction Publishers, 1990), 67–77; Stephen Moore, "So Much for 'Scarce Resources,'" *Public Interest* (Winter 1992), 97–107; Jerry Taylor, "The Growing Abundance of Natural Resources," in David Boaz and Edward Crane, eds., *Market Liberalism: A Paradigm for the 21st Century* (Washington: CATO Institute, 1993), 363–378.

29. Many of their critics in the isolationist camp, moreover, argued that the United States could cope with supply disruptions not by letting prices freely adjust supply and demand but by imposing even tighter regimentation over the economy—an outcome neither the administration nor the business community was prepared to accept except in a wartime emergency. See Doenecke, *In Danger Undaunted*, 22.

30. In the spring of 1942, the chief economist at the Bureau of Mines, Elmer Pearson, said Japan's attacks had been devastating. "The shutting off of supplies of tungsten and antimony from China, and of tin, manganese, and chromite, as well as rubber, manila fiber, and other non-mineral commodities from Southeastern Asia, already constitutes a serious loss to the United Nations, and if the anticipated pincer movement on the Indian Ocean isolates the Asiatic Continent, we face the loss of more important sources of manganese and chromite, strategic mica and flake graphite" (Eckes, Jr., *Global Struggle*, 83–84).

31. "Far Eastern Shipments Curtailed by War in Pacific," *Oil, Paint and Drug Reporter* 140 (December 15, 1941), 3, 51.

32. Assistant Attorney General Wendell Berge said, "Pearl Harbor shocked us into the recognition of widespread shortages resulting from cartel restrictions. Plant capacity in many industries which could have been built and operating in this country were not in existence, because cartels had prevented its construction. Strategic products, materials and processes which were absolute necessities to our defense were under cartel restrictions. These shortages and deficiencies had to be made good; new processes and techniques which cartels had pigeonholed had to be freed and applied under the severe pressure of war needs" (Office of War Information release, March 17, 1945, box 440, Hornbeck papers). For other postmortems stressing the impact of Far Eastern supply losses, see Harry Holmes, *Strategic Materials and National Defense* (New York: Macmillan, 1942) and M. S. Hessel, et al., *Strategic Materials in Hemisphere Defense* (New York: Hastings House, 1942).

33. Radio appeal on the scrap rubber campaign, June 12, 1942, in *Public Papers of the President*, 1942, 270–271; Presidential Press Conference no. 832, June 12, 1942, in *Complete Presidential Press Conferences of Franklin D. Roosevelt* (New York: Da Capo Press, 1972, v. 19, 384–386.

34. Leo Crowly, administrator of Foreign Economic Administration, to Roosevelt, February 7, 1944, in OF 510, Roosevelt papers. The need for natural rubber in addition to the synthetic substitute was also emphasized by Isador Lubin, the White House statistician, in a memorandum to Harry Hopkins, April 23, 1942, in box 327, Hopkins papers.

35. Joseph Grew speech to Overseas Writers Organization, March 1, 1945, box 183, Hornbeck papers.

36. Associates in International Relations, *Raw Materials*, 51–52.

37. Secretary of State to embassy in the Netherlands, May 16, 1947, in *FR, 1947*, VI, 924. A 1948 CIA assessment took the same line: "The growth of nationalism in colonial areas . . . has major implications for US security, particularly in terms of possible world conflict with the USSR. This shift of the dependent areas from the orbit of the colonial powers not only weakens the probable European allies of the US but deprives the US itself of assured access to vital bases and raw materials in these areas in the event of war." Cited in Lipschutz, *When Nations Clash*, 121.

38. Quote from Eckes, Jr., *Global Struggle*, 152. For further discussion of strategic materials as a guiding interest in U.S. policy toward Southeast Asia, see National Security Council NSC 48/1, "The Position of the United States With Respect to Asia," December 23, 1949, in Department of Defense, *United States: Vietnam Relations, 1945–1967* (Washington: U.S. Government Printing Office, 1971), book 8, xvi, 248–249, 261–262; NSC 124/2, June 25, 1952, in ibid., 470–471, 523, 526.

39. Department of State, *Indochina: The War in Southeast Asia*, October 1951, 2.

40. Letter from J. D. Small, chairman of the Munitions Board, to Jess Larson, administrator of the General Services Administration, January 5, 1951, in House Government Operations Committee, hearings, *Investigation of United States Government Contracts for the Purchase of Tungsten in Thailand* (Washington: U.S. Government Printing Office, 1954), 32.

41. President's Materials Policy Commission, *Resources for Freedom* (Washington: U.S. Government Printing Office, 1952), I, iv.

Bibliography

Unpublished Papers

Franklin D. Roosevelt Library, Hyde Park, NY
   Henry Hopkins papers
   Henry Morgenthau diary
   Franklin Roosevelt papers
   Rubber Survey Committee papers
   Whitney Shepardson papers
Library of Congress, Washington, D.C.
   Herbert Feis papers
   Cordell Hull papers
   Jesse Jones papers
   Breckinridge Long papers
   Arthur Sweetser papers
Hoover Institute, Stanford, California
   Joseph Ballantine papers
   Bay Region Institute of Pacific Relations papers
   Charles Cooke papers
   Henry Francis Grady papers
   Stanley Hornbeck papers
   Tracy Kittredge papers
Houghton Library, Harvard University
   Joseph Grew papers
National Archives, Washington, D.C.
   Record Group 59, Records of the Department of State
   Record Group 179, Records of the War Production Board
Navy Yard, Washington, D.C.
   Operational Navy archives
Public Records Office, London
   Foreign Office papers

258   *Bibliography*

   War Cabinet minutes
Yale University
   Henry Stimson diary (microfilm)

Unpublished Council on Foreign Relations Papers

CFR Study Group Discussion minutes

A-A8, February 14, 1941.
A-A11, June 4, 1941.
E-A11, November 23, 1940.
E-A12, December 14, 1940.
E-A13, February 15, 1941.
E-A15, April 12, 1941.
E-A16, May 17, 1941.
P-A5, February 19, 1941.
P-A10, May 22, 1941.
P-A12, June 25, 1941.
T-A14, June 17, 1941.

CFR War and Peace memoranda

A-B19, "The Far Eastern Crisis," March 15, 1941.
E-B12, "A Pan-American Trade Bloc," June 7, 1940.
E-B15, "Geographical Directions of United States Foreign Trade: A Study in National Interests," June 28, 1940.
E-B16, "Alternative Outcomes of the War: American Interests and Re-Orientation," June 28, 1940.
E-B17, "The Resources of Germany and the United States," June 28, 1940.
E-B18, Supplement II: "The Future Position of Germany and the United States in World Trade: A Western Hemisphere-Pacific Area Economic Bloc," September 6, 1940.
E-B19, "The War and the United States Foreign Policy," October 19, 1940.
E-B19, Supplement I: "A Comparison of the Trade Position of a German-Dominated Europe and a Western Hemisphere-British Empire-Far East Trade Bloc," October 19, 1940.
E-B26, "American Far Eastern Policy," January 15, 1941.
E-B27, "Economic Trading Blocs and Their Importance for the United States," February 15, 1941.
E-B31, "Problems of Bloc Trading Areas for the United States: Intra-Bloc Preferential Tariff and Other Devices for Encouraging Economic Integration," March 7, 1941.

E-B33, "The Economic Organization of Peace in the Far East," June 20, 1941.
E-B34, "Methods of Economic Collaboration: Introductory. The Role of the Grand Area in American Economic Policy," July 24, 1941.
T-B8, "Political Regions of Eastern Asia," May 20, 1940.
T-B17, "Alternatives of United States Policy in the Western Pacific," October 5, 1940.
T-B20, "Aid to China," October 11, 1940.
T-B22, "Alternatives of American Policy Toward Russia," December 9, 1940.

Other CFR documents

Council on Foreign Relations, "Proceedings at the Opening of the Harold Pratt House," April 6, 1945.
Whitney Shepardson, "The Early History of the Council on Foreign Relations," privately printed.
Dr. George Smith, director of U.S. Geological Survey, at January 6, 1922 conference of Council on Foreign Relations, "Mineral Resources and Their Distribution as Affecting International Relations."
Wood, Gen. Robert E. "Our Foreign Policy." Address before the Chicago Council on Foreign Relations, October 4, 1940.

Unpublished Ph.D. Theses

McCarty, Kenneth Jr. "Stanley K. Hornbeck and the Far East, 1931–1941." Duke University, 1970.
Miner, Deborah. "United States Policy Toward Japan 1941: The Assumption that Southeast Asia was Vital to the British War Effort." Columbia University, 1976.
Spotswood, Rogers D. "Japan's Southward Advance as an Issue in Japanese-American Relations, 1940–1941." University of Washington, 1974.
Utley, Jonathan. "The Department of State and the Far East, 1937–1941." University of Illinois, 1970.

U.S. Government Publications

Army and Navy Munitions Board. *The Strategic and Critical Materials.* Washington: Army and Navy Munitions Board, 1940.
Baruch Committee. *The Rubber Situation.* House Document No. 836. Washington: Government Printing Office, 1942.
Congress, House of Representatives, Government Operations Committee. *Investigation of United States Government Contracts for the*

Purchase of Tungsten in Thailand. Hearings. Washington: U.S. Government Printing Office, 1954.

———, House Committee on Foreign Affairs. *The Tin Investigation.* Hearings and Report. Washington: U.S. Government Printing Office, 1935.

———, House Committee on Military Affairs. *Strategic and Critical Raw Materials.* Hearings. Washington: U.S. Government Printing Office, 1939.

———, Joint Committee on the Investigation of the Pearl Harbor Attack. *Hearings and Exhibits.* 39 volumes. Washington: U.S. Government Printing Office, 1946.

———, Joint Committee on the Investigation of the Pearl Harbor Attack. *Report.* Washington: U.S. Government Printing Office, 1946.

———, Senate Committee on Naval Affairs. *Naval Expansion Program.* Hearings. Washington: U.S. Government Printing Office, 1938.

———, Senate Naval Affairs Committee. *Nomination of William Franklin Knox.* Hearings. Washington: U.S. Government Printing Office, 1940.

———, Senate, Committee on Naval Affairs. *Construction of Certain Naval Vessels.* Hearings. Washington: U.S. Government Printing Office, 1940.

———, Senate Committee on the Judiciary. *Morgenthau Diary (China).* 2 volumes. Washington: U.S. Government Printing Office, 1965.

———, Senate report 1611, *Naval Expansion Program.* 75th Congress, 3rd session, April 18, 1938.

———, Special Committee Investigating the Munitions Industry. *Munitions Industry.* Hearings. Washington: U.S. Government Printing Office, 1936.

Department of Commerce. *Foreign Commerce and Navigation of the United States, 1940.* Washington: U.S. Government Printing Office, 1941.

Department of Defense. *The "MAGIC" Background of Pearl Harbor.* 5 volumes. Washington: Department of Defense, 1978.

———. *United States–Vietnam Relations, 1945–1967.* 12 volumes. Washington: U.S. Government Printing Office, 1971.

Department of State. *Foreign Relations of the United States: The Far East, 1939.* Volumes I & II. Washington: U.S. Government Printing Office, 1956.

Department of State. *Foreign Relations of the United States: The Far East, 1940.* Volume IV. Washington: U.S. Government Printing Office, 1955.

Department of State. *Foreign Relations of the United States: The Far East, 1941*. Volumes IV and V. Washington: U.S. Government Printing Office, 1956.
Department of State. *Foreign Relations of the United States: The Far East, 1947*. Volume VI. Washington: U.S. Government Printing Office, 1972.
Department of State. *Foreign Relations of the United States, Japan, 1931-1941*. 2 volumes. Washington: U.S. Government Printing Office, 1943.
Department of State. *Indochina: The War in Southeast Asia*. October 1951. Washington: Government Printing Office, 1951.
Department of State. *Peace and War*. Washington: U.S. Government Printing Office, 1943.
Department of State. *United States Relations with China, with Special Reference to the Period 1944-1949*. Washington: U.S. Government Printing Office, 1949.
Notter, Harley. *Postwar Foreign Policy Preparation, 1939-1945*. Washington: Department of State, 1949.
Office of Emergency Management. *Materials for Defense*. Washington: Government Printing Office, 1941.
Office of Strategic Services, Research and Analysis Branch. *Survey of Indo-China*. R&A No. 719, second edition, September 24, 1943.
Office of War Mobilization. *Rubber, First and Second Reports of the Inter-Agency Committee on Rubber*. Washington, 1946.
President's Materials Policy Commission. *Resources for Freedom*. Washington: U.S. Government Printing Office, 1952.
Rubber Reserve Company. *Report on the Rubber Program 1940-1945*. Washington: U.S. Government Printing Office, 1945).
U.S. Army. *Strategic and Critical Raw Materials*. Washington: U.S. Government Printing Office, 1944.
U.S. Tariff Commission. *United States-Philippine Trade*. Report no. 118, 2nd series. Washington: U.S. Government Printing Office, 1937.

Books and pamphlets

Acheson, Dean. *Morning and Noon*. Boston: Houghton Mifflin, 1965.
———. *Present at the Creation*. New York: Norton & Co., 1969.
Anderson, Irvine Jr. *The Standard Vacuum Oil Company and United States East Asian Policy, 1933-1941*. Princeton: Princeton University Press, 1975.
Armstrong, Hamilton Fish. *Peace and Counterpeace: From Wilson to Hitler*. New York: Harper & Row, 1971.

Bibliography

Ashley, Richard. *The Political Economy of War and Peace*. New York: Nichols Publishing Co., 1980.
Associates in International Relations, Department of Social Sciences. *Raw Materials in War and Peace*. West Point: U.S. Military Academy, 1947.
Baker, Leonard. *Roosevelt and Pearl Harbor*. New York: Macmillan, 1970.
Baldwin, Hanson W. *United We Stand*. New York: Whittlesey House, 1941.
Barnes, Harry Elmer, ed. *Perpetual War for Perpetual Peace*. Caldwell, Idaho: The Caxton Printers, Ltd., 1953.
Barnet, Richard. *The Lean Years: Politics in the Age of Scarcity*. New York: Simon and Schuster, 1980.
Barnett, Robert. *America Holds the Balance in the Far East*. New York: Institute of Pacific Relations, American Council, 1940.
Barnhart, Michael. *Japan Prepares for War*. Ithaca: Cornell University Press, 1981.
Baruch, Bernard. *Baruch: The Public Years*. New York: Holt, Rinehart & Winston, 1960.
Ben-Zvi, Abraham. *The Illusion of Deterrence: The Roosevelt Presidency and the Origins of the Pacific War*. Boulder: Westview Press, 1987.
Bergamini, David. *Japan's Imperial Conspiracy*. New York: William Morrow & Co., 1971.
Berle, Beatrice, and Travis Jacobs, eds. *Navigating the Rapids 1918–1971: From the Papers of Adolf A. Berle*. New York: Harcourt Brace Jovanovich, 1973.
Bernstein, Barton, ed. *Towards a New Past*. New York: Random House, 1968.
Bidwell, Percy. *Raw Materials: A Study of American Policy*. New York: Council on Foreign Relations, 1958.
Bisson, T. A. *America's Far Eastern Policy*. New York: Institute of Pacific Relations, 1945.
Blum, John. *From the Morgenthau Diaries: Years of Urgency, 1938–1941*. Boston: Houghton Mifflin, 1965.
Boaz, David, and Edward Crane, eds. *Market Liberalization: A Paradigm for the 21st Century*. Washington: CATO Institute, 1993.
Borg, Dorothy, and Shumpei Okamoto, eds. *Pearl Harbor as History*. New York: Columbia University Press, 1973.
Borg, Dorothy, et al. *Proceedings of the Lake Kawaguchi Conference on Japanese-American Relations, 1931–1941*. July 1969 mimeo.
Brandes, Joseph. *Herbert Hoover and Economic Diplomacy*. Pittsburgh: University of Pittsburgh Press, 1962.
Burns, J. M. *Roosevelt: The Soldier of Freedom*. New York: Harcourt Brace Jovanovich, 1970.

Bibliography   263

Buss, Claude. *War and Diplomacy in Eastern Asia*. New York: Macmillan, 1941.
Butow, R. J. C. *The John Doe Associates*. Stanford: Stanford University Press, 1974.
Callis, Helmut. *Foreign Capital in Southeast Asia*. New York: Institute of Pacific Relations, 1942.
Choucri, Nazli, and Robert North. *Nations in Conflict: National Growth and International Violence*. San Francisco: W. H. Freeman, 1975.
Choucri, Nazli, Michael Laird, and Dennis Meadows. *Resource Scarcity and Foreign Policy: A Simulation Model of International Conflict*. Cambridge: Massachusetts Institute of Technology, 1972.
Churchill, Winston. *The Grand Alliance*. Boston: Houghton Mifflin, 1950.
Conroy, Hilary, and Harry Wray, eds. *Pearl Harbor Reexamined*. Honolulu: University of Hawaii Press, 1990.
Crowley, James. *Japan's Quest for Autonomy*. Princeton: Princeton University Press, 1966.
Council on Foreign Relations. *Mineral Resources and Their Distribution as Affecting International Relations*. New York: Council on Foreign Relations, 1922.
———. *Some Regional Views on our Foreign Policy, 1941*. New York: Council on Foreign Relations, 1941.
———. *The War and Peace Studies of the Council on Foreign Relations, 1939–1945*. New York: Council on Foreign Relations, 1946.
Dallek, Robert. *Franklin D. Roosevelt and American Foreign Policy, 1932–1945*. New York: Oxford University Press, 1979.
Dietrich, Ethel. *Far Eastern Trade of the United States*. New York: Institute of Pacific Relations, 1940.
Dobney, Frederick, ed.. *Selected Papers of Will Clayton*. Baltimore: Johns Hopkins Press, 1971.
Doenecke, Justus, ed. *In Danger Undaunted: The Anti-Interventionist Movement of 1940–1941 as Revealed in the Papers of the America First Committee*. Stanford: Hoover Institution Press, 1990.
Eckes, Alfred E., Jr. *The United States and the Global Struggle for Minerals*. Austin: University of Texas Press, 1979.
Emeny, Brooks. *The Strategy of Raw Materials*. New York: Macmillan, 1934.
Farago, Ladislas. *The Broken Seal*. New York: Random House, 1967.
Farley, Miriam. *America's Stake in the Far East*. New York: American Council, Institute of Pacific Relations, 1936.
Feis, Herbert. *The Road to Pearl Harbor*. Princeton: Princeton University Press, 1950.
———. *Seen from E. A.* New York: Alfred A. Knopf, 1947.
Foster Bain, H. *Ores and Industry in the Far East*. New York: Council on Foreign Relations, 1927.

Fox, William. *Tin: The Working of a Commodity Agreement*. London: Mining Journal Books Ltd., 1974.
Gall, Norman. *Bolivia: The Price of Tin. Part I: Patino Mines and Enterprises*. New York: American University Field Staff, 1974.
Gardner, Lloyd. *Economic Aspects of New Deal Diplomacy*. Boston: Beacon Press, 1971.
Gayn, Mark. *The Fight for the Pacific*. New York: William Morrow & Co, 1941.
Gill, G. Herman. *Royal Australian Navy, 1939–1942*. Adelaide: The Griffen Press, 1957.
Gilpin, Robert. *War and Change in World Politics*. Cambridge University Press, 1981.
Gould, James. *Americans in Sumatra*. The Hague: Martinus Nijhoff, 1961.
Grew, Joseph. *Ten Years in Japan*. New York: Simon and Schuster, 1944.
———. *Turbulent Era*. 2 volumes. Boston: Houghton Mifflin, 1952.
Griswold, A. Whitney. *The Far Eastern Policy of the United States*. New York: Harcourt, Brace, 1938.
———. "The United States and the Far East." Paper presented to the Conference for Instructors on "The Bases of American Foreign Policy," April 28–30, 1939. Pamphlet edition. New York: Council on Foreign Relations, 1938.
Heinrichs, Waldo H. *American Ambassador: Joseph C. Grew and the Development of the United States Diplomatic Tradition*. Boston: Little Brown, 1966.
———. *Threshhold of War: Franklin D. Roosevelt and American Entry into World War II*. New York: Oxford University Press, 1988.
Hentoff, Nat, ed. *The Essays of A. J. Muste*. New York: Simon and Schuster, 1967.
Herzog, James. *Closing the Open Door*. Annapolis: Naval Institute Press, 1973.
Hessel, M. S., et al. *Strategic Materials in Hemisphere Defense*. New York: Hastings House, 1942.
Hexter, Ervin. *International Cartels*. Chapel Hill: University of North Carolina, 1945.
Holland, W. L., ed. *Commodity Control in the Pacific Area*. Stanford: Stanford University Press, 1935.
Holmes, Harry. *Strategic Materials and National Defense*. New York: Macmillan, 1942.
Hooker, Nancy, ed. *The Moffat Papers*. Cambridge: Harvard University Press, 1956.
Horowitz, David, ed. *Corporations and the Cold War*. New York: Monthly Review Press, 1969.

Hudson, G. F., and Marthe Rajchman. *An Atlas of Far Eastern Politics.* New York: John Day Co., 1942.
Hull, Cordell. *The Memoirs of Cordell Hull.* 2 volumes. New York: Macmillan, 1948.
Ickes, Harold. *The Secret Diary of Harold L. Ickes: The Lowering Clouds, 1939-1941.* New York: Simon and Schuster, 1954.
Ienaga, Saburo. *The Pacific War: World War II and the Japanese, 1931-1945.* New York: Pantheon Books, 1978.
Ike, Nobutaka, ed. *Japan's Decision for War: Records of the 1941 Policy Conferences.* Stanford: Stanford University Press, 1967.
Iriye, Akira. *Power and Culture: The Japanese-American War, 1941-1945.* Cambridge: Harvard University Press, 1981.
Israel, Fred, ed. *The War Diary of Breckinridge Long.* Lincoln: University of Nebraska Press, 1966.
Janeway, Eliot. *Struggle for Survival.* New York: Weybright and Talley, 1968.
Japan Board of Information. *Official Announcements Concerning Foreign Relations.* Tokyo: Japan Board of Information, 1941.
Johnson, Walter. *The Battle Against Isolation.* Chicago: Chicago University Press, 1944.
Johnstone, William. *The United States and Japan's New Order.* New York: Oxford University Press, 1941.
Jones, Jesse. *Fifty Billion Dollars.* New York: Macmillan, 1951.
Keohane, Robert. *After Hegemony: Cooperation and Discord in the World Political Economy.* Princeton: Princeton University Press, 1984.
Kimmel, Husband. *Admiral Kimmel's Story.* Chicago: Henry Regnery Company, 1955.
Kirby, S. W. *Singapore: The Chain of Disaster.* London: Cassell, 1971.
Kirby, Woodburn. *The War Against Japan, I.* London: His Majesty's Stationery Office, 1957.
Knorr, K. E. *Tin Under Control.* Stanford: Food Research Institute, 1945.
———. *World Rubber and its Regulation.* Stanford: Stanford University Press, 1945.
Kolko, Gabriel. *The Roots of American Foreign Policy.* Boston: Beacon Press, 1969.
Krasner, Stephen. *Defending the National Interest: Raw Materials Investments and US Foreign Policy.* Princeton: Princeton University Press, 1978.
Langer, William, and S. Gleason. *Challenge to Isolation, 1937-1940.* New York: Harper & Bros., 1952.
———. *The Undeclared War 1940-1941.* New York: Harper & Bros., 1952.
League of Nations. *The Network of World Trade.* Geneva: League of Nations, 1942.

Leahy, William. *I Was There*. New York: Whittlesey House, 1950.
Leith, C. K. *World Minerals and World Politics*. New York: McGraw Hill, 1931.
Liggio, Leonard, and James Martin, eds. *Watershed of Empire: Essays on New Deal Foreign Policy*. Colorado Springs: Ralph Myles, 1976.
Lipschutz, Ronnie. *When Nations Clash: Raw Materials, Ideology and Foreign Policy*. Cambridge: Ballinger, 1989.
Magdoff, Harry. *The Age of Imperialism*. New York: Monthly Review Press, 1969.
Marks, Frederick III. *Wind Over Sand: The Diplomacy of Franklin Roosevelt*. Athens: University of Georgia Press, 1988.
Meadows, Donella, et al. *The Limits to Growth*. New York: University Books, 1974.
Mineral Inquiry. *Elements of a National Mineral Policy*. New York: Council on Foreign Relations, 1933.
Mitchell, Kate, and W. L. Holland, eds. *Problems of the Pacific, 1939*. New York: Institute of Pacific Relations, 1940.
Morison, Samuel Eliot. *The Rising Sun in the Pacific*. Boston: Little Brown, 1948.
Morley, James William, ed. *Deterrent Diplomacy: Japan, Germany and the USSR, 1935-1940*. New York: Columbia University Press, 1976.
———, ed. *The Fateful Choice: Japan's Advance into Southeast Asia, 1939-1941*. New York: Columbia University Press, 1980.
National City Bank of New York. *Economic Conditions, Governmental Finance, United States Securities, August 1941*. New York: National City Bank, 1941.
National Foreign Trade Council. *Report of the Twenty-Seventh National Foreign Trade Convention*. New York: NFTC, 1940.
Perkins, Frances. *The Roosevelt I Knew*. New York: Viking Press, 1946.
Pratt, Julius. *Cordell Hull*. 2 volumes. New York: Cooper Square Publishers, 1964.
Quigley, Harold. *The Far Eastern War 1937-1941*. Boston: World Peace Foundation, 1942.
Redfield, William C. *Dependent America*. New York: Houghton Mifflin, 1926.
Remer, C. F. *Foreign Investments in China*. New York: Macmillan, 1933.
Reynolds, David. *The Creation of the Anglo-American Alliance, 1937-1941*. Chapel Hill: University of North Carolina Press, 1982.
Robertson, Esmonde, ed. *The Origins of the Second World War*. London: Macmillan, 1971.
Roosevelt, Elliott, ed. *FDR, His Personal Letters, 1928-1945*. 2 volumes. New York: Duell, Sloan and Pearce, 1950.

Roosevelt, Franklin D. *Complete Presidential Press Conferences of Franklin D. Roosevelt.* New York: Da Capo Press, 1972.

———. *Public Papers and Addresses of Franklin D. Roosevelt, 1940-1942.* New York: Macmillan Co., 1941 (Volume I); New York: Harper & Brothers, 1950 (Volumes II and III).

Rosenau, James, ed. *Domestic Sources of Foreign Policy.* New York: The Free Press, 1967.

Roth, Andrew. *Japan Strikes South.* New York: Institute of Pacific Relations, 1941.

Roush, G. A. *Strategic Mineral Supplies.* New York: McGraw Hill, 1939.

Royal Institute of International Affairs. *China and Japan.* Information Department Papers No. 21. New York: Royal Institute of International Affairs, 1938.

———. *Notes on Raw Materials in the Far East and Pacific Dependencies.* London: Royal Institute of International Affairs, 1933.

Schlesinger, Arthur, Jr. *The Bitter Heritage* New York: Fawcett World Library, 1967.

Schroeder, Paul. *The Axis Alliance and Japanese-American Relations, 1941.* Ithaca: Cornell University Press, 1958.

Sherk, Donald. *The United States and the Pacific Trade Basin.* San Francisco: The Federal Reserve Bank of San Francisco, 1972.

Sherwood, Robert. *Roosevelt and Hopkins, an Intimate History.* Revised edition. New York: Harper, 1950.

Shoup, Laurence, and William Minter. *Imperial Brain Trust: The Council on Foreign Relations & United States Foreign Policy.* New York: Monthly Review Press, 1977.

Simon, Julian. *Population Matters: People, Resources, Environment and Immigration.* New Brunswick: Transaction Publishers, 1990.

Smith, Robert Aura. *Our Future in Asia.* New York: Viking Press, 1940.

Soong (Mayling) Foundation. *America's Future in the Pacific.* New Jersey: Rutgers University Press, 1947.

Staley, Eugene. *Raw Materials in Peace and War.* New York: Council on Foreign Relations, 1937.

Stimson, Henry, and William Bundy. *On Active Service in Peace and War.* New York: Harpers, 1948.

Stimson, Henry. *The Far Eastern Crisis.* New York: Council on Foreign Relations, 1936.

Stone, I. F. *Business as Usual.* New York: Modern Age, 1941.

Strauss, Lewis. *Men and Decisions.* Garden City, N.Y.: Doubleday, 1962.

Taylor, George. *America in the New Pacific.* New York: Macmillan, 1942.

Timmons, Bascom. *Jesse Jones: The Man and the Statesman.* New York: Henry Holt and Co., 1956.

Toland, John. *Infamy: Pearl Harbor and Its Aftermath*. Garden City, N.Y.: Doubleday, 1982.
Tolley, Kemp. *Cruise of the Lanikai*. Annapolis: U.S. Naval Institute, 1973.
Utley, Jonathan. *Going to War with Japan, 1937–1941*. Knoxville: University of Tennessee Press, 1985.
Vernon, Raymond. *Two Hungry Giants: The United States and Japan in the Quest for Oil and Ores*. Cambridge: Harvard University Press, 1983.
Walker, William O. III, ed. *Drug Control Policy: Essays in Historical Perspective*. University Park: Pennsylvania State University Press, 1992.
Wallace, B., and L. Edminster. *International Control of Raw Materials*. Washington: Brookings Institution, 1930.
Weaver, Denis. *The Battle of Supplies*. London: Hodder & Stoughton Ltd., n.d.
Welles, Sumner. *The Time for Decision*. New York: Harper & Bros., 1944.
Williams, Benjamin. *Economic Foreign Policy of the United States*. New York: McGraw Hill, 1929.
Williams, William Appleman. *The Tragedy of American Diplomacy*. New York: Dell Publishing, 1962.
Wohlstetter, Roberta. *Pearl Harbor: Warning and Decision*. Stanford: Stanford University Press, 1962.
Woodward, E. L. *British Foreign Policy in the Second World War*. London: His Majesty's Stationery Office, 1962.

Articles

Akagi, Roy. "Future of American Trade with Manchukuo." *Annals of the American Academy of Political and Social Science* 211 (September 1940): 138–146.
Barber, Alvin. "Philippine Chromite Now a Factor in World Market." *Far Eastern Survey* 8 (March 1, 1939): 58–59.
Barnett, Robert. "Opening El Dorado With a Loan." *Amerasia* 4 (April 1940): 72–75.
Beukema, Herman, and Arnold Sommer. "Dependence of U. S. Economy on Raw Materials from the Far East." *Amerasia* 3 (May 1939): 108.
Bisson, T. A. "America's Dilemma in the Far East." *Foreign Policy Reports* (July 1, 1940): 105–106.
Boyle, John. "The Drought-Walsh Mission to Japan." *Pacific Historical Review* 34 (1975): 141–161.
Bregman, Adolph. "Non-Ferrous Materials and Strategic Position." *Iron Age* 145 (January 4, 1940): 98–100.
———. "Tin." *Iron Age* 146 (July 4, 1940): 29–31.
Burton, Wilbur. "The Dutch East Indies: Vital Resources." *The Living Age* 359 (November 1940): 263–267.

Butow, Robert J.C. "The Hull-Nomura Conversations: A Fundamental Misconception." *American Historical Review* 65 (July 1960): 822–836.
Chi, Ch'ao-Ting. "Far Eastern Notes." *Amerasia* 1 (July 1937): 236.
Christians, William, and Otis Starkey. "The Far East as a Source of Vital Raw Materials." *Annals of the American Academy of Political and Social Science* 215 (May 1941): 84–85.
Cole, Charles Woolsey. "International Economic Dependence." *International Conciliation* 369 (April 1941).
Condliffe, John. "We Must Keep China and the Indies Within the World's Free Trade Area." *San Francisco Chronicle*, June 30, 1941.
Dennett, Tyler. "Alternative American Policies in the Far East." *Foreign Affairs* 16 (April 1938): 392.
Douglas, Henry. "Japan's Expansion." *China Today* (March 1940).
Emerson, Rupert. "Dutch East Indies Adrift." *Foreign Affairs* 18 (July 1940): 736–737.
———. "The Outlook in Southeast Asia." *Foreign Policy Reports* 15 (November 15, 1939).
Esthus, Raymond. "President Roosevelt's Commitment to Britain to Intervene in a Pacific War." *Mississippi Valley Historical Review* 50 (June 1963).
Ethridge, Mark. "The Economic Consequences of a Hitler Victory." Address before the Retail Merchants Association of Louisville, January 21, 1941. *International Conciliation* 370 (May 1941).
Farley, Miriam. "America's Stake in the Far East: Trade." *Far Eastern Survey* 5 (July 29, 1936): 161–170.
Feis, Herbert. "War Came at Pearl Harbor: Suspicions Considered." *Yale Review* 45 (Spring 1956): 378–390.
Fermer, Lewis. "Burma's Mineral Resources and the War." *Far Eastern Review* 36 (April 1941): 124–127.
Gallup, George. "American Institute of Public Opinion Surveys, 1935–38." *Public Opinion Quarterly* 2 (July 1938): 389.
———. "American Institute of Public Opinion—Surveys, 1938–1939." *Public Opinion Quarterly* 3 (October 1939): 599.
Greenberg, Michael. "Malaya—Britain's Dollar Arsenal." *Amerasia* 5 (June 1941): 144–151.
Hall, Robert Burnett. "American Raw Material Deficiencies, and Regional Dependence." *The Geographical Review* 30 (April 1940): 177–186.
Hauser, Ernest. "Britain's Economic Stake in Southeast Asia." *Far Eastern Survey* 6 (December 22, 1937): 283–288.
Hoffer, Peter. "American Businessmen and the Japan Trade." *Pacific Historical Review* 41 (May 1972): 189–206.

Holt, E. G., and Warren S. Lockwood. "How International Rubber Restrictions Came About." *Asia* 35 (June 1935): 327–331.
Hoover, Herbert. "America Solemnly Warns Foreign Monopolists of Raw Materials." *Current History* 23 (December 1925): 307–311.
Hosoya, Chihiro. "Miscalculations in Deterrent Policy: Japanese-US Relations, 1938–1941." *Journal of Peace Research* 5 (1968): 97–115.
Janeway, Eliot. "The Americans and the New Pacific." *Asia* 39 (February 1939): 109–113.
Kerbosh, M. "Some Notes on Cinchona Culture and World Consumption of Quinine." *Far Eastern Review* 36 (April 1940): 156–160.
Kiralfy, Alexander. "American Pacific Strategy." *Asia* 39 (November 1940): 567–569.
Kraft, Joseph. "School for Statesmen." *Harper's*, July 1958.
Lattimore, Owen. "American Responsibilities in the Far East." *Virginia Quarterly Review* 16 (Spring 1940).
Leith, C. K. "Mineral Resources and Peace." *Foreign Affairs* 26 (April 1938), 522–523.
———. "Mineral Resources of the Far East." *Foreign Affairs* 4 (April 1926): 433–442.
———. "Role of Minerals in the Present War." *Mining Congress Journal* 26 (November 1940): 34–38.
———. "Strategic Minerals in War and Peace." *Science* 93 (March 14, 1941): 244–246.
———. "The Political Control of Mineral Resources." *Foreign Affairs* 3 (July 1925): 541–555.
Lockwood, William Jr. "America's Stake in the Far East—II: Investments." *Far Eastern Survey* 5 (August 12, 1936): 175–185.
Maffry, August. "Strategic Materials in United States Import Trade." *Survey of Current Business* 20 (December 1940): 10–15.
Marshall, Jonathan. "Opium, Tungsten and the Search for National Security, 1940–1952." *Journal of Policy History* 3 (Fall 1991).
Masland, John. "American Attitudes Toward Japan." *Annals of the American Academy of Political and Social Science* 215 (May 1941): 160–165.
———. "Commercial Influences Upon Far Eastern Policy, 1931–1941." *Pacific Historical Review* 11 (September 1942): 281–299.
McBride, Russell. "Strategic Buying Planned" *Engineering & Mining Journal* 141 (July 1940): 33–34.
Mitchell, Kate. "Japan's Southern Drive Faces Obstacles." *Amerasia* 5 (June 1941): 139–140.
Moore, Stephen. "So Much for 'Scarce Resources,'" *Public Interest* (Winter 1992): 97–107.
Moses, Larry W. "Soviet-Japanese Confrontation in Outer Mongolia: The Battle of Nomonhan-Khalkin Gol." *Journal of Asian History* 1 (1967): 64–85.

Newcomb, Robinson. "The United States and Southeast Asia's Strategic Products." *Far Eastern Survey* 8 (April 12, 1939): 88.
Oakie, John. "Today We Need Access to Eastern War Materials." *San Francisco Chronicle*, June 30, 1941.
Parker, Catherine. "The Philippines as an American Investment." *Far Eastern Survey* 9 (September 25, 1940).
Peffer, Nathaniel. "Would Japan Shut the Open Door in China?" *Foreign Affairs* 17 (October 1938): 37-50.
Rosenberg, Nathan. "Innovative Responses to Materials Shortages." *American Economic Review* 63 (May 1973): 111-118.
Roush, G. A. "Strategic Mineral Supplies." *Military Engineer* 30 (September-October 1938): 370-374.
Smith, Robert Aura. "Japan Forces America's Hand." *China Monthly* 1 (December 1940).
Spurr, Josiah. "Steel-Making Minerals." *Foreign Affairs* 4 (July 1926): 601-612.
Stewart, John. "U.S. Exports to Manchukuo Reach New High." *Far Eastern Survey* 8 (March 29, 1939): 82-83.
Stromberg, Roland. "American Business and the Approach of War." *Journal of Economic History* 13 (Winter 1953): 58-78.
Tolley, Kemp. "The Strange Assignment of USS *Lanikai*." *United States Naval Institute Proceedings* 83 (September 1962): 71-84.
Viner, Jacob. "National Monopolies of Raw Materials." *Foreign Affairs* 4 (July 1926): 595-600.
Wallace, Henry. "Science and the Military." *New Republic*, February 3, 1947.
Welles, Sumner. "Roosevelt and the Far East." *Harper's* 202 (February 1951): 29-38.
Whitford, Harry. "The Crude Rubber Supply." *Foreign Affairs* 1 (June 15, 1924): 613-621.
Wilde, J. C. de, and George Monson. "Defense Economy of the United States, An Inventory of Raw Materials." *Foreign Policy Reports* 16 (November 15, 1940): 202-212.
Woodward, Rear Admiral. "Philippines and U.S. Trade Routes Doomed if Japs Take Singapore." *New York Journal American*, February 23, 1941.
Yen, Po-shen. "The Economic Factor of American Far Eastern Policy." *China Monthly* 2 (April 1941).

Unsigned or Miscellaneous Periodicals

Asia
Baltimore Sun
Barron's

Business Week
China Weekly Review
Commercial and Financial Chronicle
Congressional Record
Department of State Bulletin
Engineering and Mining Journal
Far Eastern Review
Far Eastern Survey
Fortune
Houston Post
The Index
Iron Age
Los Angeles Times
Mining and Metallurgy
New York Herald Tribune
New York Times
Newsweek
Oil, Paint and Drug Reporter
Public Opinion Quarterly
Refrigerator Engineering
San Francisco Chronicle
Time
Vital Speeches
Wall Street Journal
Washington Evening Star
Washington Post

Index

ABC-1 Staff Agreement, 107–108, 158, 161
Acheson, Dean, 118, 251
Africa, ix
Allen, Rep. Leo, 44
Alsop, Joseph, 87
America First Committee, 27, 183
American Manganese Producers' Association, 45
American Society of Metallurgical Engineers, 7
Anti-Comintern Pact, 57
Arita, Hachirō, 60, 64–65, 67, 69, 73, 77, 78, 129
Armstrong, Hamilton Fish, 29, 204, 218
Army and Navy Munitions Board, 4, 10–13, 33
Atlantic Conference, 138, 159
Australia, 71, 78, 103, 104, 153, 158, 179, 214

Baldwin, Hanson, 27
Ballantine, Joseph, 93–94, 132, 222
Barkley, Sen. Alben, 43, 217
Barnett, Robert, 26
Barnhart, Michael, xiii
Baruch, Bernard, 4, 41, 209
Batt, William, 39

Bauxite, x
Beard, Charles, 3
Ben-Zvi, Abraham, xv
Berge, Wendell, 254
Berle, Adolf, 28, 70, 75, 166, 209
Bolivia, 23, 27, 38, 47, 52, 62, 67, 183
British Malaya, x, 12, 13, 15, 17, 20, 23, 24–25, 26, 37, 52, 62, 71, 78, 83, 93, 97, 104, 106, 108, 163, 166–167, 171, 181, 212, 214
Brooke-Popham, Robert, 168
Bryan, William Jennings, 4
Buaas, Lt. Marion, 170
Business Advisory Council, 67, 221
Business attitudes toward China and Japan, 58–60
Business Week, 25
Byas, Hugh, 65

Cadogan, Lord, 137
California Committee on Pacific Friendship, 215
Casey, Richard, 103
Chiang Kai-shek, 109, 135, 147, 153, 180, 243
China, 55, 61, 69, 98, 108, 153, 166, 171, 176; fear of American sell-out, 142–144, 148,

274 *Index*

China (*continued*)
  154–155; as limited American interest, 56–59, 161–162, 175–177, 216; as source of raw materials, 12, 25, 38–41, 52, 77, 85, 253; U.S. support for, as tactic for tying Japan down, 32, 99–100, 110, 113–114, 122–123, 131, 135, 161, 179–180, 206, 226, 233, 242, 251, 252
China lobby, 135–136
Chromium, 7, 8, 9, 10, 24, 33, 35, 43, 45, 46, 51, 52, 184, 210, 253
Churchill, Winston, 155, 159, 168
Clayton, Will, 19, 214, 217
Cobalt, ix
Coconut shell, 7, 10, 194
Cole, Wayne, xiii
Committee to Defend America by Aiding the Allies, 202
Commodity Credit Corporation, 36
Congress and raw materials, 22–23, 34, 35, 36, 38, 43–46
Copper, ix
Copra, x, 66, 70
Cotton, 36
Council of National Defense, 8
Council on Foreign Relations, 23, 26, 28–32, 88, 202, 204, 250
Creighton, John, 168
Currie, Lauchlin, 92, 113, 136, 230

Dallek, Robert, xv
Darr, F. M., 52
Davis, Norman, 28, 88, 205
Dennett, Tyler, 58
Dennis, Lawrence, 3
Dickover, Erle, 62–63

Dooman, Eugene, 102–103
Douglas, Henry, 26
Drought, Father James, 98–99, 109
Dulles, Allen, 205
Dunn, James, 81

Eden, Anthony, 158
Edminster, Lynn, 92
Elliott, William, 214
Emeny, Brooks, 174

Faddis, Rep. Charles, 44, 45
Far Eastern Survey, 26
Farley, Miriam, 26
Feis, Herbert, 29, 34, 38, 51, 53, 65, 67, 173
Finch, John, 9
Fish, Hamilton, 52
Foreign Affairs magazine, 3, 28, 29, 58
Fortune magazine, 24, 25, 59
French Indochina, x, 13, 16, 59, 66, 71, 77–78, 80–82, 84, 96–97, 105, 114, 121–127, 144, 171, 181, 218, 226, 229
Furness, James, 9

Gayn, Mark, 83
Geist, Raymond, 15, 19
General Motors, 19
Germany, Nazi, xv, 16, 50, 57, 63, 64, 74, 84, 85, 118, 200, 221, 229
Gerow, Brig. Gen. L. T., 153, 160, 163
Grady, Henry Francis, 54, 75
Graebner, Norman, xiii
Grand Area strategy, 30–31
Grant, Hugh, 105
Great Britain, x, 55, 66, 127, 131, 168, 171, 173; closure of the Burma Road, 77, 78, 81, 88; dependence on Southeast

Index 275

Asia, xiv, 16–18, 20–22, 71, 92, 93, 102, 106, 115–116, 178, 199–200, 202; fear of Japanese advance on Southeast Asia, 97, 101, 103–104, 126; fear of Japanese inroads in Thailand, 96–97; naval interests, 56; warning against allowing China to collapse, 155, 244
Greenbrier Mining Co., 45
Grew, Joseph, 29, 69–70, 73, 77, 81, 82, 83, 84, 98, 101, 103, 106, 110, 115, 133, 147, 180, 235; on proposal for Konoe summit, 139, 144; on Singapore and Southeast Asian raw materials, 70, 92, 115, 177–178, 185, 238; warning of Pearl Harbor attack, 97
Griswold, A. Whitney, 175
Guam, 61

Hainan, 16, 61, 62, 218, 222
Halifax, Lord, 103, 130, 159, 167, 168
Hamilton, Maxwell, 110, 131
Hansen, Alvin, 205
Hart, Adm. Thomas, 90, 164, 168, 170, 219
Hata Shunroku, 73, 77
Hay, John, 55
Heinrichs, Waldo, xiii
Henry-Haye, Gaston, 82
Hiss, Alger, 70–71, 180–181
Hoffer, Peter, 59
Hoover, Herbert, 5–6, 56
Hopkins, Harry, 67, 145, 158, 167, 171
Hornbeck, Stanley, xi, 29, 74, 166, 173, 233, 250; on China as quagmire for Japan, 76, 110, 113–114, 116, 136, 241, 242; on Far East as source of raw materials, xi, 70–73, 76, 91–92, 178; influence within Roosevelt administration, 72, 75, 222; on Konoe's proposal for a summit, 139, 141, 239; and location of U.S. Fleet, 75–76, 131; on need to oppose Japan's southward advance, 74, 87, 88, 100; on significance of Singapore, 91–93, 115–116
Hu Shih, 142, 153, 233
Hull, Cordell, xii, 1, 19, 31, 63, 78, 90, 92, 101, 109, 135, 160; and debate over export controls on Japan, 83, 128–133; discussions with Ambassador Nomura, 105, 111–112, 114, 117, 137–140, 144, 148–151, 242; distrust of Japan, 61, 74, 88–90, 95, 99, 103, 117, 134, 141, 149, 232; and fate of China, 99–100, 109, 117, 142, 151, 153, 155; and Japanese threat to Indochina, 73, 82, 84, 126; and Japanese threat to Netherlands East Indies and raw material supplies, 65–66, 69, 72, 77, 219; on Japanese threat to raw material trade routes, 126, 151, 154, 166; on Konoe's proposal for a summit, 140–141; and location of U.S. Fleet, 63, 75, 116; on need to defend Southeast Asia, 162, 163; on need to stockpile strategic materials, 34–36, 48, 51, 67, 208; strategy of delay in negotiations, 136, 137, 179; summary of policy in 1940, 94; and Ten Point note, 156; and Tripartite Pact, 85–86; withdrawal from negotiations, 156, 245–246, 247

276 *Index*

IBM, 25
Ickes, Harold, 79, 130, 237
India, 10, 11, 15, 52, 76, 91
Ingersoll, Adm. Stuart, 170
Institute of Pacific Relations, 23, 26
Interdepartmental Committee on Strategic Materials, 34, 35, 67
Iraq, ix
Iriye, Akira, xiii
Iron, ix, 15, 70
Isabel, 170
Isolationists, xii, 27, 44, 45, 52, 63, 211, 253
Italy, 84, 85
Iwakuro Hideo, 109, 111, 132

Japan: attack on Pearl Harbor, 171; commercial relations with United States, 58–59, 183, 215; demand for end to U.S. aid to China, 150; final negotiating period, 146; first probes toward Southeast Asia in 1939, 60, 218, 219; Imperial Conference, 119; invasion of Manchuria, 56–57, 176; interest in northward expansion, 60, 119, 234; navy's preparations for war, 84; Plan A, 147–149; Plan B, 149–151; plan for army's southward advance, 74; protest of Western "encirclement," 104; relations with U.S. in early 20th century, 55; setbacks against Red Army, 60; threat to U.S. multilateral trade in raw materials, 14–20; threats to French Indochina, 15, 59, 73, 80–84, 89, 101, 105, 106, 114, 121–127, 144, 234, 240; threats to Netherlands East Indies, 61, 63, 64, 68, 70–71, 77, 80, 83, 87, 89, 90, 106, 118, 125, 129, 219, 221, 230; threats to Thailand, 95–97, 113, 118, 135, 164, 167, 232; and Tripartite Pact, 85–87; troop buildup in summer and fall 1941, 136, 138, 156; yen bloc, 16–18, 114
Jones, Jesse, 38–40, 50, 52, 209

Keohane, Robert, 174
Kimmel, Adm. Husband, 164, 168
Kintner, Robert, 87
Knox, Frank, 78, 90, 101, 108, 116, 163–164, 247; favors embargoing Japan, 129; on need to defend U.S. raw material interests against Japan, 14, 111, 166
Koiso, General, 80
Koiso Kuniaki, 69
Kondō Nobutake, 84
Konoe Fumimaro, 56, 78, 83, 99, 120; fall from power, 145; proposal for a meeting with President Roosevelt, 138–142
Korean War, 187
Kraft, Joseph, 28
Kurusu Saburo, 149, 151
Kuwait, ix

Land, Adm. Emory Scott, 52, 209
Lanikai, 170, 249
Lattimore, Owen, 31, 32, 136, 176
Lawrence, David, 182
League of Nations, 17–18
Leahy, Adm. William, 61, 107
Leith, Charles K., 7–9, 29, 41, 121, 207
Lenin, 189
Liberia, 5

Index 277

Lindsay, Ronald, 34
Lippmann, Walter, 3, 62
London Economic Conference, 48
London Naval Disarmament Conference, 56
Long, Breckinridge, 41, 65, 75, 88–89, 117, 129, 205, 223
Lothian, Lord, 74, 78
Louden, A., 79

MacArthur, Gen. Douglas, 162, 164
MacLeish, Fleming, 27
MAGIC, 123, 125, 134, 145, 149, 163
Mallory, Walter, 29, 30
Manganese, 4, 7, 8, 9, 10–11, 14, 33, 35, 43, 44–45, 46, 51, 52, 184, 210, 212, 253
Manila fiber, 10, 11, 23, 35, 71, 186, 253
Marks, Frederick, III, xiii
Marshall, Gen. George, 79, 116, 160–161, 163, 186, 204, 227, 231
Maryknoll Society, 98
Matsuoka Yōsuke, 78, 84, 105, 115, 123
May, Rep. Andrew, 45
McCloy, John J., 29
Mercantilism, xii
Mercury, 7, 10
Messersmith, George, 29
Metals Reserve Company, 38, 40
Mica, 7, 10, 11, 91, 253
Milbraith, Lester, 28
Miner, Deborah, xiv
Mining and Metallurgical Society of America, 207
Mitchell, Kate, 21
Moffat, Jay Pierrepont, 29, 87–88
Moore, Frederick, 221

Morgenthau, Henry, 29, 39, 78–79, 83, 129
Muste, A. J., 173

Nagano Osami, 120
National Defense Advisory Council, 39
National Foreign Trade Convention, 19, 25
National Industrial Conference Board, 15
National Policy Committee, 250
National Security Council, 186
Netherlands, 153, 159
Netherlands East Indies, x, 11, 12, 13, 14, 15, 17, 20, 23, 26, 32, 37, 46, 47, 52, 62–66, 71, 77, 78, 79, 80, 83, 93, 97, 104, 106, 118, 125, 127, 154, 162, 166–167, 168, 181, 206, 214, 217, 220, 226, 235, 236
New Caledonia, 10, 38
New York Times, 65, 66, 104, 235
New York Trust Co., 25
Nickel, 7, 8, 10, 38
Nomura, Adm. Kichisaburō, 101, 111–112, 117, 120, 125, 131, 133, 136–139, 145–146, 148–149, 160, 171, 234, 235, 244
Nutmeg, x

Oil, ix, x, 14, 15, 117, 128, 131, 150, 177, 220
Open Door, xiv, xv, 55, 56, 135, 216

Paley, William, 187
Palm oil, x
Pasvolsky, Leo, 29, 31, 250
Pax Americana, 250
Pearl Harbor, 63, 64, 68, 88, 97, 117, 134, 167, 169, 172, 181, 231, 248

Pearson, Elmer, 253
Peck, Willys, 122
Philippines, x, 10, 11, 15, 23, 24, 25, 32, 52, 64, 71, 151, 152, 154, 162–163, 164, 167, 171, 181, 193, 214, 218, 226, 232, 238
Potash, 193

Quartz crystal, 10
Quinine, 10, 11, 15, 16, 24, 26, 66, 67, 83, 91, 203, 220
Quo Tai-chi, 143

Reconstruction Finance Corporation, 38, 49, 52
Redfield, William, 4, 5
Reynolds, Cushman, 27
Reynolds, David, xiii
Richardson, Adm. J. O., 64, 68, 75–76, 89
Rockefeller Foundation, 29
Roosevelt, Eleanor, 130
Roosevelt, Franklin, xv, 19, 21, 34, 53, 92, 107, 148, 155, 204, 246; and aid to China, 114, 251; and Ambassador Nomura, 101–102, 106, 127, 131, 136, 138–139, 160; and debate over export controls on Japan, 78–79, 83, 85, 127–133, 176–178, 181–182, 237; on disposition of U.S. fleet, 61, 63, 68, 89, 108, 117, 130; and Drought-Walsh mission, 99, 109; final alert to military commanders, 164; on Japanese threat to Southeast Asia and raw materials, 106, 127, 132, 181, 218; last plea to Japan, 171; national appeal to conserve rubber, 185; on need to defend Southeast Asia, 162, 163, 165; order for "defensive information patrol," 169–170; order for war speech, 165; proposed modus vivendi, 152, 156; reassurances to British, 157–160, 167–169; relief over U.S. entry into war, 171–172; and stockpiling, 34–39, 41–43, 51, 67–68, 209, 210, 211–212; on value of Chinese raw materials, 224
Roth, Andrew, 15
Rubber, x, xi, 1–53 passim, 61, 63, 65, 66, 67, 70, 80, 83, 87, 91, 94, 104, 106, 115, 116, 117, 118, 122, 154, 163, 166, 178, 183, 185, 186, 201, 202, 204, 213, 214, 217, 220, 225, 235, 248, 253
Rubber, synthetic, 27, 39, 42, 67, 185, 211, 254
Rubber cartel, 5–7, 49–50, 183, 194, 213
Rutherford, Col. H. K., 9

Saint-Quentin, Count de, 81
San Francisco Chronicle, 220, 235
Sayre, Francis, 29
Schroeder, Paul, xiii
Serugham, Rep. James, 45
Shellac, 4
Short, Lt. Gen. Walter, 164
Silk, 10, 22, 70, 201
Singapore, 20, 22, 32, 41, 46, 71, 76, 88, 89, 90, 91–92, 96, 101, 104, 106, 107, 108, 113, 115–116, 151, 154, 159, 168, 178, 179, 199, 206, 218, 225, 226
South Africa, 10, 24
Soviet Union, 11, 32, 60, 110–111, 118, 122, 131, 210
Spratley Islands, 61, 89

Stark, Adm. Harold, 21, 63, 64, 68–69, 79, 90, 158, 161, 169–170, 231; on importance of raw materials, 9, 14
Stettinius, Edward, 39
Stimson, Henry, 29, 56, 78–79, 86, 90, 101, 108, 116, 129, 135, 139–140, 160, 163–164; desire for Japan to fire the first shot, 89, 145, 165, 169, 249; on extending negotiations to buy time, 141–142; on importance of Southeast Asian raw materials, 166, 178; plan to defend Philippines, 151, 163, 245; on using China campaign to protect Southeast Asia, 179, 245
Stone, I. F., 27, 51
Swanson, Claude, 201

Thailand, x, 13, 71, 83, 95–97, 103, 105–106, 118, 164, 167, 168, 181
Thomas, Sen. Elbert, 46
Time magazine, 26
Tin, x, xi, 1–53 passim, 61, 63, 66, 67, 70, 80, 83, 87, 91, 94, 104, 106, 115, 116, 117, 118, 122, 154, 183, 184, 186, 196, 201, 202, 204, 212, 217, 220, 225, 235, 248, 253
Tin cartel, 47–48, 183, 207
Tōgō Shigenori, 146
Tōjō Hideki, 145–146, 147, 171
Tolley, Rear Adm. Kemp, 249
Tripartite Pact, 85–87, 129, 149, 182, 225, 238, 243
Truman, Harry, 187
Tung oil, 39, 184, 203, 224
Tungsten, x, 8, 9, 10, 11, 15, 16, 24, 33, 35, 38, 45, 62, 77, 91, 178, 181, 224, 253

Turner, Adm. Richard, 107, 108, 131, 158

United States Maritime Commission, 52
U.S. Navy: cooperation with foreign powers, 89, 105, 107–108, 158, 230–231; location of fleet, 63–64, 68, 75, 81, 88, 90, 116–117, 158, 230; and raw materials, 201; views on Japan's expansion plans, 98, 122
Universal Trading Corporation, 39
Uranium, ix
Utley, Jonathan, xiv

Van Slyck, Milton, 250
Vernon, Raymond, 174
Vietnam War, 187
Viles, A. L., 50

Wakasugi Kaname, 243
Walsh, Bishop James, 98–99, 109, 241
Walsh, Sen. David, 22
War Production Board, 4, 214
Washington Evening Star, 66
Washington Naval Disarmament Conference, 55
Washington Post, 66, 87, 235
Watson, Thomas, 25
Welles, Sumner, 29, 63, 70, 81, 88, 92, 125, 130, 137, 219; admiration for Stanley Hornbeck, 222; declaration of U.S. interest in Southeast Asian raw materials, 126–127; on need to defend Southeast Asia, 159, 181; resistance to embargo,

Welles, Sumner (*continued*)
  79, 83–84; on urgency of stockpiling raw materials, 35–36, 37, 51, 118
Wheat, ix
Williams, William Appleman, xiv
Wilsonian ideology, xiv

Wood, Robert, 183
Woodrow Wilson Foundation, 204

Yarnell, Retired Adm. Harry, 25, 201
Yonai Mitsumasa, 77

Compositor: BookMasters, Inc.
Text: 10/13 Aster
Display: Helvetica Condensed and Aster

www.ingramcontent.com/pod-product-compliance
Lightning Source LLC
Chambersburg PA
CBHW021654230426
43668CB00008B/616